Diana Eades is without doubt one of Australia's leading experts in understanding and explaining the many subtleties of meaning and intent of language as used by Aboriginal persons.

For more than 30 years Eades has written and lectured extensively on her lifelong passion — Aboriginal life practices and culture as reflected in a language peculiar to them, Aboriginal English. *Aboriginal ways of using English* is a compilation of a select nine of her many learned papers previously authored and published by her between 1982 and 2012.

Consequently, each chapter stands independent of others, yet the full collage reveals a rich lifetime of work in applying her linguistic skills to this relatively new field of expertise. In several chapters Eades refers to a number of court cases in which the clash of Aboriginal culture against the impenetrable wall of legal culture, practices and procedure point to instances of disadvantage, if not injustice for Aboriginal participants in the criminal justice legal system.

Aboriginal ways of using English is a 'must read' for health professionals, educators, lawyers, judges, and dare I add, sporting agents and administrators as well as all others, who, in the course of their professional livelihood, are interacting with Aborigines. Of course those interested in linguistics, communication or Aboriginal culture as reflected in speech, silence and communication would also be impressed by Eades' scholarly depth.

Despite any formidable, complex images and concepts that might be conjured up by a book on linguistics, Eades' writing style is a pleasure to read, her logic and arguments easy to follow and her insight brilliant.

Former District Court Judge, John Nicholson SC

Diana Eades has contributed extensively as an academic to the field of sociolinguistics in different ways, through her efforts to explain the intricacies of the pragmatics of Aboriginal English as spoken by the Aboriginal people of south-east Queensland, as compared to the more widely spoken Australian Standard English. Her work covers many areas such as contentious legal cases involving Aboriginal people where she has been called as an expert witness as well as publishing numerous articles on this topic, some of which will appear in this collection of her best work.

Jeanie Bell, linguist

Diana Eades has become established as one of the foremost experts in forensic linguistics (language and the law). Much of her work focuses on Australian Aboriginal English and the miscommunication that can arise not just in a legal context but more broadly. So an important part of her achievement has been her contribution to interactional sociolinguistics. Another is to raise awareness in the legal arena of the disadvantage that can be suffered by Indigenous people appearing before the courts. This has led to a commissioned report to the Queensland Law Society which has been used by legal practitioners there and in other jurisdictions. Aboriginal Studies Press is to be congratulated for bringing together this collection of her papers. Spanning some 30 years these papers have been scattered across quite a range of publication outlets so it is difficult for those already familiar with her work to get a sense of its development — let alone those coming to her output for the first time. Each contribution in the collection is prefaced by a brief statement by Diana which sets out its content and context. This collection will be valuable not just to legal practitioners and language and law experts, but to a wide audience interested in Aboriginal Studies.

Dr Michael Walsh, Australian Institute of Aboriginal and Torres Strait Islander Studies

Aboriginal Ways of Using English

Diana Eades

First published in 2013 by Aboriginal Studies Press
Reprinted in 2021 and 2026

Aboriginal Studies Press
is the publishing arm of the
Australian Institute of Aboriginal
and Torres Strait Islander Studies.
GPO Box 553, Canberra, ACT 2601
Phone: (61 2) 6246 1183
Fax: (61 2) 6261 4288
Email: asp@aiatsis.gov.au
Web: www.aiatsis.gov.au/asp

A Cataloguing-in-Publication entry is available from the National Library of Australia
www.trove.nla.gov.au
ISBN: 9781922059260 (pb)
ISBN: 9781922059277 (ebook PDF)
ISBN: 9781922059284 (ebook ePub)
ISBN: 9781922059291 (ebook Kindle)

Cover design by Upside Creative
Text design and typesetting by Upside Creative
Front cover artwork: Reimaged from 'Scythe Mystery' by Troy Anthony Bailis.

FOR RUTH AND JENNY AND BEN

Contents

Acknowledgments

Since the late 1970s, many people have influenced and encouraged my work on Aboriginal ways of speaking English. In particular I want to thank:

- the Aboriginal people who have taught me so much about using English. In the 1980s, many people graciously gave permission for me to listen to and record their conversations, and welcomed me into their homes and families, especially Michael Williams and his extended family (too many to name here) in Southeast Queensland. Michael also provided valuable bicultural insights and feedback on my early research. Barbara Bond helped with recording conversations in the New England region in the mid-1990s. Many other Aboriginal people, particularly in the north coast and New England regions of New South Wales, have supported my ongoing investigations into how they use English;
- two 1980s colleagues — Lilla Watson and Matt Foley — who first drew my attention to the legal relevance of my research into Aboriginal ways of speaking English;
- many Aboriginal people whose criminal cases I have been privileged to provide expert reports on, including Kelvin Condren, Robyn Kina, the witnesses in the Criminal Justice Commission investigation into the death of Daniel Yock, the boys in the Pinkenba case, and others who have requested anonymity;
- Australian colleagues in linguistics and anthropology who have supported, advised and enriched my work, especially Jeanie Bell, Michael Cooke, Ian Keen, Jeff Siegel, Ian Malcolm, Bruce Rigsby, and Michael Walsh;
- many participants — Aboriginal and non-Aboriginal — in workshops I have conducted over more than two decades, whose comments, stories and questions continually remind me of the thousands of reasons why Aboriginal ways of using English matter;
- lawyers who have understood the significance, for their clients and/or their broader work in the law, of sociolinguistic research into Aboriginal ways of using English, and have asked thought-provoking questions, and provided insights into the legal process, especially Andrew Boe, David Brereton, Dominic Brunello, Anne-Marie Donnelly, Ron Finney, Tony Keyes, Mark Lauchs, Brian Smith, and Lew Wyvill;

- Detective-Inspector Gary Jubelin whose enduring commitment to making the stories of Aboriginal people heard in the legal process provides inspiration and optimism;
- judges and magistrates who have openly shared with me their experiences and concerns at the "coalface" of the justice system, and their willingness to consider new ways of thinking about language use, including Kate Auty, Peter Gray, Annette Henderson, Wayne Martin, Dean Mildren, Helen Murrell, Jacqui Payne, and Stephanie Tonkinson;
- legal and judicial organisations which continue to provide opportunities for me to engage with lawyers, judges and magistrates on questions concerning Aboriginal participation in the legal process and to educate me about the legal process, including Aboriginal Legal Services in New South Wales and Western Australia, Aboriginal and Torres Strait Islander Legal Services in Queensland, Australian Institute of Judicial Administration, Federal Court of Australia, Legal Aid Queensland, Office of the Director of Public Prosecutions New South Wales, National Judicial College of Australia, Queensland Law Society, and state courts in New South Wales, Queensland, South Australia and Western Australia; and
- family and friends whose encouragement and friendship has always been so integral to my academic endeavours.

I am grateful to Kim Johnston and Rhonda Black from Aboriginal Studies Press (ASP) for suggesting this book, and for their supportive pursuit of it, despite my stalling efforts. ASP has been attentive and helpful at every stage, and Lisa Fuller has provided meticulous editing.

Finally, my greatest gratitude goes to my husband, Jeff Siegel, who has been by my side for the last twenty-six years, with emotional, intellectual, and material support, combined with wisdom and patience, and lots of good fun too.

Aboriginal Studies Press and the author kindly thank the following people and organisations for permission to reproduce previously published material. The publisher has used its best efforts to secure copyright clearance for this material. If anyone believes they have a claim to copyright in this material the publisher would be pleased to hear from them:

'"You gotta know how to talk...": ethnography of information seeking in Southeast Queensland Aboriginal society' first published in *Australian Journal of Linguistics*, courtesy of the publisher, vol. 2, no. 1, pp. 61–82, 1982, http://www.tandfonline.com/doi/abs/10.1080/07268608208599282.

'Misunderstanding Aboriginal English: the role of sociocultural context' first published in *Further applications of linguistics to Australian Aboriginal contexts*, Graham McKay & Bruce Sommer (eds), courtesy of the Applied Linguistics Association of Australia Occasional Papers, Melbourne, no. 8, pp. 24–33, 1984.

'They don't speak an Aboriginal language, or do they?' first published in *Being Black: Aboriginal cultures in settled Australia*, Ian Keen (ed.), courtesy of Aboriginal Studies Press, Canberra, pp. 97–117, 1998.

'Aboriginal English' first published in *Primary English Notes (PEN) 93*, courtesy of Primary English Teachers Association, 1993 (6 pages).

'Language and the law: white Australia vs Nancy' first published in *Language and culture in Aboriginal Australia*, Michael Walsh & Colin Yallop (eds), courtesy of Aboriginal Studies Press, Canberra, pp. 181–190, 1993.

'Aboriginal English in the criminal justice system' first published in *The habitat of Australia's Aboriginal languages: past, present and future*, Gerhard Leitner & Ian Malcolm (eds), courtesy Mouton de Gruyter, Berlin, pp. 299–326, 2007.

'Aboriginal English on trial: the case for Stuart and Condren' first published in *Language in Evidence: issues confronting Aboriginal and multicultural Australia*, Diana Eades (ed.), courtesy of University of New South Wales Press, Sydney, pp. 147–174, 1995.

'A case of mistaken assumptions' first published in *The Weekend Independent*, Indepth, March 10, p. 13, 1995.

'Telling and retelling your story in court: questions, assumptions, and intercultural implications' first published in *Current Issues in Criminal Justice*, courtesy of the publisher, vol. 20, no. 2, pp. 209–230, 2008.

'The social consequences of language ideologies in courtroom cross-examination' first published in *Language in Society*, courtesy of the publisher, vol. 41, no. 4, pp. 471–497, 2012.

Chapter 1

Introduction

1.1 Overview

The majority of Australian Aboriginal people speak some kind of English. But often this is not quite the same as English spoken by other Australians. This book presents results of sociolinguistic research about Aboriginal ways of using English in non-remote Australia, by bringing together a number of my publications over a thirty-year period. The focus is on language and communication of Aboriginal people who speak English as their first and main language, and who do not speak a traditional language fluently.

Continuing influences from traditional Aboriginal languages and cultures have helped to shape the way Aboriginal people speak English. Part I will show why understanding Aboriginal ways of speaking English is essential for recognising many contemporary Aboriginal societies and cultures. But there is more to it than Aboriginal identities: this understanding is also important for intercultural communication between Aboriginal and non-Aboriginal Australians. In Part II, the focus is on legal contexts, and we will see particularly how ways of speaking English introduced in Part I impact on the participation of Aboriginal people in the criminal justice system. Take for example the way that people use and interpret silences or pauses in conversation. No matter what language or dialect is being spoken, silence always sounds the same. But it doesn't always have the same meaning, as you will see in Chapter 5. In several chapters in Part II you will see the significance of this feature (and other features) of language use for Aboriginal participation in the legal process. The book will conclude in Chapters 10 and 11 with my latest research, which highlights problems with how the legal process hears and evaluates the evidence of Aboriginal witnesses who speak English as a first language. You will see how the courtroom linguistic trickery that causes difficulties for many witnesses can be compounded for Aboriginal witnesses, and a case study shows how this can be central to the perpetuation of inequality. (In the Further Reading section at the end of this chapter you will find references to research about language and communication issues in legal contexts for people who speak a traditional Aboriginal language as their first language.)

The approach used throughout the book is one which sees speaking and other forms of communication as central interactional activities in all social groups. In order to examine how language is being used (or language practices), we need to go beyond instances of language use — particular conversations, for example — to the investigation of how societies or social groups work, and how their members make sense of their world. Their beliefs, assumptions, values and expectations are integrally bound up with how and why they act and interact in certain ways, and how they interpret the actions of others. Social scientists use the term 'culture' to refer to these practices (or ways of doing things), together with the meanings that people create and share with others in their social group. Despite several decades of academic debate about the usefulness of the term 'culture', we can't do without it. For example, the latest major textbook in linguistic anthropology (Ahearn 2012) talks about knowing a language as being able to use the language 'in socially and culturally appropriate ways' (p. 12).

1.2 Aboriginal English or Aboriginal ways of speaking English

Aboriginal English is the name given to dialectal varieties of English spoken by the majority of Aboriginal people throughout Australia. The recognition since the 1960s of Aboriginal English as a valid, rule-governed dialect of English is one of the most valuable contributions that linguistics has made to Australian society. It provides strong evidence to debunk the popular myth that Aboriginal people who don't speak English like most other Australians are lazy, uneducated, bad-mannered or rude (see Chapter 5). Linguistic work on Aboriginal English, particularly by Ian Malcolm and his colleagues over more than three decades, is playing a significant role in educational equity for Aboriginal students (see Further Reading).

In my earliest Southeast Queensland work I did not use the term 'Aboriginal English', saying that the people I was researching were speakers of varieties of Standard English (see Section 2.1). Aboriginal English at that time was defined in terms of structural language features (such as grammar and sound system). My focus was instead on pragmatic features, that is, features of language use in specific social contexts. The particular features I examined were how people used language to achieve certain social functions: seeking and giving information, seeking and giving reasons for actions, and talking about the future (see Chapters 2, 3 and 4 respectively). I soon realised that there were indeed some structural features of Aboriginal English in the way that many Aboriginal people in Southeast Queensland were speaking English, but pointed out that 'the major language variety used by many Aboriginal people today is grammatically very close to Standard English' (see Section 3.1). As I continued the research, and also became aware of the applied relevance of my research — especially to education and the law — I realised the importance of including pragmatic features in the definition of Aboriginal English. In an overview chapter published in 1991, I wrote that

> definitions of Aboriginal English need to look beyond grammatical features and include aspects of communicative strategies. I therefore use the term 'Aboriginal English' to refer to Aboriginal varieties of English, which in some instances may differ from Standard Australian English primarily in features of pragmatics (and minimally in grammar) (Eades 1991a, p. 84, see also Eades 1993).

In his recent work, Sharifian (e.g. 2005, 2007) makes a similar argument about the role of cultural conceptualisations in the definition of Aboriginal English, that is, the way that meanings in Aboriginal English words are deeply rooted in Aboriginal cultures.

In the late 1980s, while giving courtroom evidence about the Aboriginal English of a defendant, I was asked a good question by a judge: 'How many dialects of Aboriginal English are there?' The short answer to this, as to so many other sensible questions that non-linguists ask linguists, is 'it depends ...'! It depends on how you define dialect and how much you take into consideration the overlaps between neighbouring ways of speaking the same language. A more specific answer is 'it's best to think of Aboriginal English as a cover term for overlapping varieties of the dialect(s) of English spoken by Aboriginal people'. (And you'd need a similar answer to the question 'How many dialects of American English are there?'.) Linguists sometimes use the terms 'light Aboriginal English' to refer to varieties closer to Standard English, and 'heavy Aboriginal English' to refer to varieties further from Standard English.

The judge's question highlights the difficulty, which has been pointed out by many scholars, of naming, separating and counting related language varieties. Thirty years ago (see Section 2.1), I referred to the problematic view of a language as 'a well-bounded static entity', a view termed the 'reification of languages'. That was part of my 1982 critique of the way that Australian linguists were conceptualising the relationships between traditional languages, only on the basis of structural features, to the exclusion of social dimensions of language use. But the issue of the reification of languages has continued to concern me in relation to Aboriginal English (see Eades, forthcoming). Language and dialect names are inventions — sometimes by speakers, sometimes by linguists. In attributing a language or dialect name to a person's speech, we are presenting a dynamic and fluid process (speaking) as a static thing — that is, we are reifying it. And this can be confusing and misleading, for example when trying to work out whether a particular person speaks a light variety of Aboriginal English or general Australian English with a few Aboriginal English features. But the decision about what label to give to this person's language variety might depend on the situation, particularly as people speak differently in different contexts, and distinctively Aboriginal features of 'English' may not occur at all in some conversations.

For this reason, I increasingly favour the use of expressions like 'Aboriginal ways of speaking English', coming back to my early 1980s approach. In highlighting that this is not the same as general Australian English, it can also be helpful to think in terms of how English can be an Aboriginal language, as in the title of my 1983 PhD thesis. (Of course, the label 'English' itself is also an invention.)

However, the label 'Aboriginal English' continues to work in constructive ways, particularly in the field of education. Indeed, the reification involved in this label can be particularly appropriate in applied areas, such as policy and provision of services, and for presenting the findings of linguistic research to non-linguists in practical and accessible ways. (This is an example of what Benor (2010) refers to as 'strategic reification', adopting the concept of 'strategic essentialism' which will be discussed in Section 1.5.2 below). For the reasons explained in this section, I now use both 'Aboriginal ways of speaking English' and 'Aboriginal English'.

While 'Aboriginal English' has mostly been defined in linguistic terms to refer to dialectal varieties of English, the term has also sometimes been extended to cover Aboriginal interlanguage varieties of English. Interlanguage English is the linguistic term for the language system of a person who speaks some English in addition to another or several other languages, but has not finished learning English. Aboriginal speakers of interlanguage English mostly live in the more remote and northern areas of Australia, where I have never conducted research. It appears that some of the sociolinguistic findings of the research reported in this book are also relevant to speakers of interlanguage varieties of English, but this is outside of the scope of this book. (See Cooke [2002, 2009], who refers to Aboriginal interlanguage varieties of English as 'Aboriginal Learners' English'.)

1.3 A few terminological notes

I rarely use the term 'Indigenous' in this book. It refers to both Aboriginal and Torres Strait Islander people. I have never done research with Torres Strait Islanders, and there are significant ways in which their cultures and ways of communicating differ from those of Aboriginal people, so my work is only about one of the two groups that make up the group 'Indigenous Australians'. I use the term 'Indigenous' only in those situations where referring to research, such as census analysis, which does not separate the two groups of Indigenous Australians.

The term 'traditional Aboriginal languages' refers to languages which were spoken before British invasion and colonisation, and had no connection to English before this time. Some of these languages continue to be spoken, and the term 'traditional' is not meant to imply that the languages have not changed: languages, societies and cultures are always in the process of change.

Over three decades I've been grappling with ways of characterising different kinds of Aboriginal societies and cultures, trying to balance the need in some situations for generalisations with the avoidance of overgeneralisations (see Section 1.5.2). I often use the terms 'traditionally oriented' and 'non-traditionally oriented' to refer to contemporary Aboriginal societies. 'Traditionally oriented' societies are found in remote Australia, where non-English related — or 'traditional' — languages often remain strong, as do a large number of social and cultural practices with strong continuities from pre-colonial times. This is not meant to imply that Aboriginal culture and language are dead in other parts of the country, but rather that they have undergone much more change, as captured in my use of the term 'non-traditionally oriented'. The terms 'traditional' and 'non-traditional', used in some of my early writing, were never intended to ignore the continuities between pre-invasion societies and languages on the one hand, and contemporary societies and their ways of using English, on the other.

Finding ways of talking about commonalities and shared cultural norms and ways of speaking in the broader Australian society is even more challenging. In my earliest work (see Chapter 2), I used the term 'middle class white Australians', with the acronym MCWA, in my comparisons between Aboriginal ways of speaking English and the norms and practices in which I was socialised, and which predominate in the institutions in which Aboriginal people participate, such as education and law. Walsh (1994) took a similar approach, using AWMC for 'Anglo white middle class'. Other terms I have used to contrast with Aboriginal people include 'whites' (e.g. Chapter 4), people in 'mainstream Australian society' (e.g. Chapter 4) and 'non-Aboriginal people' (e.g. Chapters 11 and 12). Reeders (2008) uses ADC for 'Australian Dominant Culture of mainstream Australian society'. None of these terms is meant to ignore the increasingly multicultural and complex nature of Australian society. Rather they are attempts to refer to the mainstream/dominant/majority society with its norms and expectations, which figure so prominently in much intercultural communication in education and law.

1.4 Introducing the chapters

The ten chapters which make up Parts I and II of this book have been selected from more than fifty of my chapters and articles, published over the last thirty years, about Aboriginal ways of speaking English as a first language. It has been impossible to represent all of my work over this time, although Chapter 9 provides summaries of several studies in legal contexts. In making the selection I have chosen some key works and a few hard-to-access publications, and the References section lists further material. I hope that the book will be useful for Year 11–12 high school students and undergraduate tertiary students in the fields of Aboriginal studies, linguistics, legal studies, criminology, education, communication and English. A glossary of technical terms is provided on p. 220.

While my academic training and employment have been in sociolinguistics and linguistic anthropology (which has also been called anthropological linguistics), for many years I have sought to make the findings of my research accessible to a wider readership than scholars and students in these disciplines. Thus Chapters 5, 6, 9 and 10 were originally written for readers without any linguistics background. While the remaining chapters were originally written for publications aimed at linguistically trained readers, I have mostly assumed this might include those who have not yet finished their training, or who are trained in a different sub-field of linguistics. Thus I hope that these chapters will also be accessible to students and scholars with little or no linguistics background. Some readers of this book might find Chapter 11 challenging reading. Although originally published in an international sociolinguistic journal, it was written to be as accessible as possible for any readers interested in an argument about how language is involved in a sociopolitical process — namely the perpetuation of neocolonial control — and wanting to see concrete evidence in support of this argument.

Spanning three decades of research and writing (1982–2012), the chapters in this book show some of the ways that sociolinguistic understandings have developed in this period and how my own work has matured. Sections 1.5.2 and 1.5.3 address issues which arise from using work written over this time span, and new introductions and textboxes — particularly in the earlier chapters — provide updates and contemporary reflections.

Where possible, I have avoided editing the original publications, with the exception of updating the spelling of language names and standardising punctuation conventions and organisational aspects such as section numbers and within text references. However, I have eliminated, replaced or edited some embarrassingly outdated expressions, gendered language and unhelpful overgeneralisations, mainly from chapters in Part I. Replacement or added words or sentences are indicated within square brackets [ ]. Where you see sentences with square brackets, you should read the whole sentence without omitting the words in brackets, with the understanding that the original version of the sentence did not contain those bracketed words. Where references in original publications are to theses or unpublished papers which have since been published, the original references to unpublished works have been replaced by references to published versions.

Readers will notice some recurring themes, as the ways of communicating introduced in the chapters in Part I are taken up in different ways in relation to specific legal contexts and cases examined in Part II. Part I begins with some of my earliest research on Aboriginal ways of using English, with a focus on seeking and giving information (in Chapter 2), talking about future actions (in Chapter 3), and seeking and giving reasons for actions (in Chapter 4). Chapter 5 is a short overview of Aboriginal English, originally written for primary school teachers of English. The focus on the criminal justice system in Part II begins with a fictionalised story of intercultural communication issues which arise during an Aboriginal woman's encounter with the police, lawyers and courts (Chapter 6). Chapter 7 draws on specific cases and research studies to present a recent overview of Aboriginal English in the criminal justice process. Two of the cases introduced in Chapter 7 are treated in more depth in Chapter 8, which shows how linguistic research has been presented to courts in relation to allegations of fabricated confessions, and how judicial officers in these two cases reacted to the idea that there are distinctively Aboriginal ways of speaking English.

At the heart of the legal process is not just what people say and how they say it, but how their talk is filtered, responded to and evaluated. Chapters 9–11 turn to a more subtle aspect of ways of speaking English that impacts on the participation of Aboriginal people in the criminal justice process, namely assumptions about how language works that are at the basis of the common law legal system. Chapter 9 was written originally as a newspaper column. This brief chapter points out that for Aboriginal people to be fairly heard in the legal process, we need to recognise that some fundamental notions often believed to be facts about language are instead culturally based assumptions, which are not shared with many Aboriginal people. In Chapter 10 some key assumptions about storytelling and retelling are explored, in relation to courtroom talk, and specifically the participation of Aboriginal people in the criminal justice process. Sociolinguistic research from these two chapters, as well as from earlier chapters, is drawn on in Chapter 11 to make an argument about the role of courtroom talk in continuing neocolonial control over Aboriginal people.

There is some inevitable overlap between chapters, as the book has been prepared to enable some readers to focus on individual chapters without necessarily reading the whole book. One specific case appears in several chapters, namely the 1995 Brisbane case known as the 'Pinkenba' case. This case is introduced in the overview in Chapter 7, and provides a telling example of one specific Aboriginal communication pattern (gratuitous concurrence) in Chapter 10. It was also the catalyst for the comment on facts and assumptions in Chapter 9. Chapter 11 focuses on a detailed analysis of one aspect of this case as it provides powerful evidence for the argument that assumptions about language in court have consequences beyond the courtroom and can contribute to ongoing social inequality. While Chapters 7, 10 and 11 all draw on the Pinkenba case, they use different examples in the analysis of different aspects of courtroom talk.

I hope that this book will show readers how and why understanding ways of speaking English provides insights into Aboriginality, and is central to intercultural communication, and that this understanding can reveal some of the actual linguistic mechanisms involved in the participation of Aboriginal people in the legal process.

1.5 Additional introductory material for scholars and advanced students

1.5.1 THEORETICAL APPROACHES

The theoretical approaches which have guided my research on Aboriginal ways of speaking English since the early 1980s are within the two overlapping scholarly sub-disciplines of sociolinguistics and linguistic anthropology. I use the term 'sociolinguistics' to refer to these overlapping approaches. At the core of these approaches is the axiom that language and interaction create society and culture, and at the same time they are created by society and culture.

My earliest sociolinguistic work in Southeast Queensland in the 1980s was within the frameworks of ethnography of speaking (also known as ethnography of communication), and interactional sociolinguistics. The ethnography of speaking/communication studies the ways of speaking (or more broadly ways of communicating) within a particular social group (sometimes referred to as a speech community, sometimes now referred to as a community of practice). It can be characterised as the study of who can talk to whom about what, where, when and how. It uses the anthropological approach of ethnography, in which researchers investigate how members of a social group live, and learn about their beliefs, values and practices from careful observation and participation in daily life (rather than, for example, from interviews).

Interactional sociolinguistics is a type of discourse analysis which examines the details of actual talk, typically from close analysis of audio- or video-recorded data. Like other kinds of linguistic discourse analysis, interactional sociolinguistics examines linguistic dimensions of interaction, including grammar, pronunciation, word choice, turn-taking, overlapping talk and interactional silence. This attention to specific instances of interactions between individuals helps to mitigate the problem of generalisation, to be discussed in Section 1.5.2. But unlike other kinds of linguistic discourse analysis (such as Conversation Analysis), interactional sociolinguistics highlights the contextual and cultural dimensions of language and interaction. This approach to the study of language in society, which began in the early 1980s and has had a strong influence on my work, takes a particular interest in diversity and intercultural communication in large-scale post-industrial, and now globalising, societies. One of its central concerns is with how taken-for-granted culturally specific knowledge works in interactions. This refers to the understandings or assumptions that people have learned (often indirectly) over time, from living and interacting with other people. If you're not sure what this means and how it works, turn to one or two of the shortest chapters in the book (3 or 9), or the longest chapter (11).

Like many other scholars, as my work has matured I have been driven more by research questions than by any need to remain loyal to a particular theoretical framework. However, in my ongoing exploration of Aboriginal ways of communicating in English, particularly in intercultural contexts in the legal process, I continue to find the most useful theoretical approach is one that is based in ethnography and interactional sociolinguistics, and is often referred to now as linguistic ethnography. But these two approaches are not enough to account for the way that communication works in the legal process in interactions between Aboriginal and non-Aboriginal people. Hence my most recent work (see Chapters 10 and 11) uses these approaches within a critical sociolinguistics framework. Like other critical approaches in the social sciences, this approach draws on social theoretical analysis, so that the analysis (here, of language use in interactions) is part of a broader study of power relationships (for more details see Eades 2008, pp. 47–52; Conley & O'Barr 2005).

1.5.2 THE PROBLEM WITH GENERALISATIONS

There are many different Aboriginal societies in Australia, many different ways of being Aboriginal and many different Aboriginal ways of speaking English. In my earliest work on Aboriginal communication using English, my concern to not overgeneralise my research findings led me to use the label 'SEQAB (Southeast Queensland Aboriginal) people' to refer to the large extended family group and their neighbours and friends that I worked with in Southeast Queensland (see Chapter 2). But I quickly dropped this invented label, because many people did not like it, especially as it sounded disastrously similar to the local electricity authority, which at the time was called SEQEB (South East Queensland Electricity Board). Thus, in Chapters 3 and 4 (first published in 1984 and 1988 respectively), I abandoned the uncomfortable term 'SEQAB people' for the longer expression 'Aboriginal people in Southeast Queensland'. As I continued to write about the findings of that Southeast Queensland research, I reflected on my previous interactions with and observations of Aboriginal people in northern and southern coastal New South Wales (whom I had done linguistic salvage work with on their traditional languages between 1973–1977). I also widened my understandings and reflections by talking with Aboriginal people, and with other scholars working in Aboriginal communities, and by reading about other Aboriginal communities. This led me to the view that my findings about patterns of in-group Aboriginal communication were applicable more widely than just the southeastern part of Queensland. Thus, in Chapter 3 (first published in 1984), while I focused on a specific example from my Southeast Queensland work, I said that it 'appears at this stage to typify language use in a wide range of southern Australian Aboriginal contexts' (note 4).

Unfortunately it seems that since my 1980s study (seen in Chapters 2–4), there has been no other detailed investigation of intra-group communication among Aboriginal people speaking English as their first language. Most linguistic work with Aboriginal English has been concerned with language and communication in education (see Further Reading). Since the mid-1980s, my research has moved beyond a focus on intra-group Aboriginal communication to intergroup communication between Aboriginal and non-Aboriginal people in the legal process, mostly in the criminal justice system.

I believe that there is much in the patterns of language use in English first described for Southeast Queensland Aboriginal people in the 1980s that remains current for Aboriginal speakers of English as a first language in many situations in many parts of Australia. I base this view on continuing feedback from Aboriginal and non-Aboriginal people, and continuing observation and participation with Aboriginal speakers of English around Australia, as well as research, primarily in legal contexts. This feedback, observation, participation, and research indicate that my accounts of Aboriginal ways of communicating and related issues in intercultural communication are relevant beyond the regions of my main research (Southeast Queensland and northern New South Wales).

Scholarly work in sociolinguistics and linguistic anthropology involves some generalisations. Indeed, many would argue that it is unavoidable. If my only interest in doing sociolinguistic research was to describe, analyse and interpret patterns of language use, I would only need to write about the groups of people being researched (although this still would involve some generalisations). But since my early 1980s work, Aboriginal and non-Aboriginal people, including professionals such as lawyers, teachers and health educators, have continued to tell me that my findings are helpful with everyday practical issues that arise in intercultural communication, and to ask me to write and speak about this work for a wide range of audiences. It is impossible to do this without some generalisations. Regrettably there were instances in my earlier work where I went beyond generalisation to overgeneralisation, and such instances have been edited in this book (as explained in Section 1.4).

In recent years, sociolinguists have become aware of the problem of 'essentialism'. This is the 'position that the attributes and behavior of socially defined groups can be determined and explained by reference to cultural and/or biological characteristics believed to be inherent to the group' (Bucholtz 2003, p. 400). An essentialist approach to language use might mistakenly hold that whether a person speaks Aboriginal English or not is dependent on biological characteristics, such as skin colour (see Section 8.7.2). However, sociolinguists and other social scientists have shown that it is not biology, but culture, particularly socialisation, that is at the heart of language acquisition and use. Another danger of essentialism is that it can lead to determinist thinking. For example, it can ignore individual differences and choices, and it can lead to views like 'she's Aboriginal, so she must speak or think in a certain way ...'

But scholars such as Bucholtz (2003) argue that we sometimes need to use 'strategic essentialism': this is when it is strategically helpful to talk or write with some generalisations about a particular social group, or by focusing on one aspect of a person's identity. For example, there are many differences between Aboriginal Australians, and there are many situations in which an individual's Aboriginal identity may not be as important as other aspects of their identity, such as their gender, age, sexual orientation, religious affiliation or professional identity. On the other hand, there are also many shared aspects of Aboriginal culture, including ways of speaking English. Further, Aboriginal people have suffered significant disadvantage and discrimination throughout the colonial and neocolonial past and present, precisely because of their Aboriginality. These realities mean that this aspect of their identity is often salient and cannot be ignored. Specifically in relation to my work in the legal process, it would be hard to argue that Aboriginality is irrelevant — or has ever been irrelevant — in interactions between Aboriginal people and the criminal justice process (see Chapter 11 and Eades 2008). Thus in my view, focusing on Aboriginal ways of using English is an example of what Bucholtz (2003, p. 403) is talking about when she says that 'strategic essentialism continues to be a necessary tool for both sociolinguists and the communities we study'.

But to mitigate the negative consequences of strategic essentialism in sociolinguistics, we have to always remember that no-one is a robot, and that language and culture are not static variables, but are constantly being created and shaped by interactions between people. There is nothing inherent about ways of communicating: like all social action this is dynamic, and is impacted by socialisation, group norms and individual experiences and choices. Further, there are often no clear boundaries between sociocultural groups. Indeed, many people participate in several different such groups, some of which may overlap. Thus, many people are bicultural, having the ability to participate in two or more sociocultural groups — just as bilingual people can speak two or more languages, and bidialectal people can speak two or more dialects. And as with bilingual and bidialectal ability, bicultural ability refers to a continuum. Many bicultural Aboriginal people can switch — consciously or unconsciously — between Aboriginal ways of interacting and non-Aboriginal ways, depending on the context, the people involved, and the goal to be accomplished. As a general rule, such bicultural Aboriginal people have had significant and successful long-term participation in non-Aboriginal education and/or employment and/or residential, family and leisure domains. Aboriginal people who have not had these kinds of participation in non-Aboriginal domains are less likely to be bicultural in this way (although they may have bicultural ability in two or more different Aboriginal ways of interacting). People develop bicultural ability from prolonged and extensive experiences in the particular sociocultural groups.

I have been addressing the problems of generalisation and overgeneralisation in my writing and speaking for some years now. But, unfortunately, I have noticed that overgeneralisation, and at times exaggeration, still characterises the ways that some people draw on my work for their own explanations about Aboriginal ways of speaking English and Aboriginal culture.

Generalisations have sometimes been made about the application of my findings with Aboriginal speakers of English as a first language to those in remote Australia who speak English as an additional language. Recent research by linguists in these areas suggests some ways in which my findings may be relevant, as well as some ways in which they may not be relevant. Linguists working on the Aboriginal Child Language Acquisition Project (see Simpson & Wigglesworth 2008) carried out detailed investigations on the ways that children and their caregivers communicate, and also investigated traditional and western teaching styles. The children all live in remote communities where people speak traditional languages and/or Kriol, and/or mixed languages which are influenced by both Kriol and traditional languages. While these studies are therefore outside of the scope of this book, their importance in raising issues about generalisations and common patterns and differences warrants brief mention here.

Most of these studies are focused on interactions between children and caregivers, often in dyadic (one-to-one) situations. Moses and Yallop (2008) and Reeders (2008) found that caregivers ask a high number of questions, and that children also seem confident asking questions. It seems that many of these questions correspond to what I have termed 'orientation questions' (see Chapters 2 and 4). Similar to my work in Southeast Queensland, Reeders found that Yolngu people in Arnhem Land often use indirect questions, including triggers, especially where more than a minimal response is required. She also found that in Yolngu conversations addressees do not have the same obligation to reply as in Anglo conversations. This is consistent with my observations on interactional privacy in Southeast Queensland (see Section 4.5.1), as well as Stephen Harris's (1984) work with Yolngu. Reeders' finding here is also similar to that of Mushin and Gardner (e.g. 2009) with people who mix a traditional language (Garrwa) with Kriol and Aboriginal English in a remote Gulf of Carpentaria community, and Walsh's work (e.g. 1994) with remote Aboriginal communities in the northwest of the Northern Territory. Using the micro-analytical tool of CA (Conversation Analysis), Mushin and Gardner uncover fine-grained support for Walsh's ethnographic finding that people spend a lot of time in 'continuing states of incipient talk', rather than in 'tightly focused and temporally bound conversation' (Gardner 2010, p. 423), and that they tolerate long periods of silence, which they treat as ordinary (Mushin & Gardner 2009, p. 2049). Thus, the work in remote communities by Walsh, Mushin and Gardner, and Moses and Yallop, as well as by Moses and Wigglesworth (2008), appears to suggest that there are similarities in the use and interpretation of conversational silence between Aboriginal people who speak English as a first language and those who speak traditional languages and/or Kriol and/or mixed languages which are influenced by both Kriol and traditional languages.

1.5.3 CHANGES OVER THREE DECADES

Societies, languages and patterns of language use do not remain static. In the thirty years since Chapter 2 was first published, much has changed in Australia, in Aboriginal societies, in intercultural communication, and in scholarly approaches to the study of these topics. In 1988 (Section 4.2) I wrote that few Aboriginal people in Southeast Queensland subscribe to a work ethic, meaning the stereotypical Protestant work ethic which predominated in much of Australian society at that time (and probably still does). While many sociopolitical factors have been involved in Aboriginal unemployment, in the twenty-first century there are clearly increasing numbers of Aboriginal people who are experiencing successful participation in mainstream education and employment, which arguably entails subscribing to something like the predominant work ethic. And, as Marcia Langton has pointed out in her 2012 Boyer Lectures, over the last two to three decades an Aboriginal middle class has emerged, largely unnoticed, along with the growth of Aboriginal businesses and corporations. Further, it is impossible to talk about Aboriginal societies and cultures today without talking about bicultural people.

Another change in recent decades is that the Aboriginal population also now includes many people who were part of the Stolen Generations, removed from their Aboriginal communities as children, and raised in white families, many without knowing about their Aboriginal heritage. Organisations such as Link-Up have worked to help many members of the Stolen Generations to find their Aboriginal families. But, without the sustained opportunity of childhood socialisation in an Aboriginal society, many such Aboriginal adults do not speak English in an Aboriginal way, unless or until they have considerable successful socialisation opportunities in Aboriginal communities as adults. Thus, it is likely that there are now more Aboriginal people who have not had the opportunity to grow up speaking English in an Aboriginal way than there were in the early 1980s, before the start of extensive work reuniting these Stolen Generations victims. (However, as statistics for language socialisation and use are notoriously very difficult to ascertain with any certainty of accuracy, this likelihood is impossible to verify.)

The twenty-first century is also a time of great social movement and fluidity. From anthropology and other social sciences, sociolinguists have been learning about the increasing complexity, plurality and hybridity of social groups and their ways of interacting. (This means that people typically belong to several social groups, some of which overlap and intersect, and there is increasing mixing between members of different groups.) Chapters 2–4 talk about Aboriginal culture and Aboriginal society, often using singular forms. In the twenty-first century it is more accurate, and less essentialist, to talk about Aboriginal cultures and Aboriginal societies, using plural forms.

There have also been changes in sociolinguistic approaches to intercultural communication, understood as communication between individuals from different cultural backgrounds. (The earlier term 'crosscultural communication' is mostly restricted now to the comparative study of communication in different sociocultural groups, without examination of actual interactions between individuals from the different groups.) The most important development in the study of intercultural communication is the realisation that earlier work paid insufficient attention to the power relationships involved. In this book, you will see this development most clearly in Chapters 7, 10 and 11. My current theoretical position is consistent with that explained by Ahearn (2012, p. 30) in this way: 'language, culture and social relations are so thoroughly intertwined that they must be studied in connection with one another'.

I hope that scholars and advanced students reading this book will be encouraged by the changes, gaps and unanswered questions they find here to conduct further research into Aboriginal ways of using English.

Further reading

about the history, development, vocabulary and structure of Aboriginal English: Arthur 1996; Kaldor & Malcolm 1991; Malcolm 2008a, 2008b; Malcolm & Grote 2007; Malcolm & Koscielecki 1997.

about Aboriginal English spoken as a second or additional language: Cooke 1996, 2009; Harkins 1994; Koch 1985, 1991, 2000, 2011.

about Aboriginal English in schools: Malcolm 1982, 1992, 2000; Malcolm et al. 1999; Malcolm & Rochecouste 2000; Malcolm & Sharifian 2002; Sharifian 2001, 2005; Sharifian, Rochecouste & Malcolm 2004; Sharifian & the Western Australia Department of Education (WADET) 2012; Western Australia Department of Education 2012.

about the theoretical approaches which inform this book: Ahearn 2012; Blommaert 2005; Conley & O'Barr 2005; Coupland 2001; Duranti 1997; Eades 2008; Ehrlich 2001; Gumperz 1982a; Holmes 2008; Hymes 1974; Matoesian 1993, 2001; Mesthrie et al. 2009; Piller 2011; Rampton 2001; Rampton et al. 2007; Sarangi 2001; Sidnell 2010; Swann et al. 2004; Woolard 1998.

about speakers of traditional Aboriginal languages in the legal process: Cooke 1995a, 1995b, 1995c, 1996, 1998, 2002, 2004, 2009; Goldflam 1995; Gray 2000; Henderson & Nash 2002; Mildren 1999; Neate 2003; Walsh 1994, 1999, 2008.

PART I:

Describing Aboriginal ways of using English

Chapter 2

'You gotta know how to talk...': ethnography of information seeking in Southeast Queensland Aboriginal society

First published in 1982, this chapter presents findings from my Southeast Queensland research about Aboriginal ways of using English to seek information. While it describes patterns of language use which have been found to also be relevant beyond Southeast Queensland, these patterns should not be taken as universal (see Section 1.5.2). Further, the chapter is not concerned with how bicultural Aboriginal people may interact with non-Aboriginal people. You will see in this chapter a few places where I wrote as if I was expecting readers to be middle class white Australians (using 'we', for example in Sections 2.4.3 and 2.6). My later writing is based on a more inclusive assumption.

2.1 Australian linguistics[1]

Linguistics has developed tremendously in Australia in the last ten years. It is largely based on a transformational approach to language and linguistic description. For the most part, grammars of Australian languages reflect Chomsky's dictum (1965, p. 3) that

> Linguistic theory is concerned primarily with an ideal speaker–listener, in a completely homogeneous speech community, who knows its language perfectly and is unaffected by such grammatically irrelevant conditions as memory limitations, distractions, shifts of attention and interest, and errors (random or characteristic) in applying his knowledge of the language in actual performance.

First published as Eades, D 1982, '"You gotta know how to talk...": information seeking in Southeast Queensland Aboriginal society', *Australian Journal of Linguistics*, vol. 2, no. 1, pp. 61–82. Reprinted in *Cross cultural encounters: Communication and mis-communication*, ed. J Pride, River Seine Publications, Melbourne, pp. 91–109.

The linguist typically selects the 'best' speaker — one who is conveniently located, has time, will concentrate, stay sober, etc., one who is judged by the linguist to be fluent in the language of study, 'uncontaminated by English', one who 'doesn't mix [their] languages' and one who responds profitably to elicitation of complex grammatical structures, such as relative clauses. While linguists often check material gained from their 'best speaker' with other speakers, the grammar written is usually a description of the linguistic rules of this 'best speaker' in a context of elicitation. The description usually concerns only rules of grammar while ignoring rules of use. This fieldwork strategy is used by most linguists in Australia, whether the work has theoretical goals or practical goals (as in bilingual education or Bible translation, for example).

Recent developments in linguistics based on the way speakers use language have caused people to ask just what our standard description of language represents. For example, Scollon writes of a linguistic description of the Fort Chipewyan Athabaskan language in Alberta (done in 1928 by Li): 'It clearly does not reflect very closely the way people at Fort Chipewyan speak to each other' (1979, p. 241). He points out that the informant used to dictate continuous texts, which he then went over and repronounced according to the linguist's standardisation and orthography. The informant in this way developed a special style of language through working with the linguist, and the resulting grammar in fact describes 'a normative, literary language'. Most of the grammars of Australian languages are of a similar nature. Unfortunately, it is rare for linguists to reveal in print details of their methodology, such as how many people they worked with and in what contexts, whether by elicitation or text gathering, or participation, and how they overcame the problems of incomplete data. However, my contacts and personal communication with Australian linguists over the last nine years indicate an approach similar to that described by Scollon. This approach is demonstrated in Sutton and Walsh's

Since this chapter was written three decades ago, there have been many developments in linguistic recognition of the social dimensions of language use. For example, linguistic studies of Aboriginal English go beyond the analysis of grammatical competence, to examine pragmatics, cultural conceptualisation, and applications to education and the law. And in the language renewal work being carried out all over Australia, linguists working in conjunction with Indigenous people are often incorporating social dimensions of language use in the core of their work on traditional languages.

(1979) *Revised linguistic fieldwork manual for Australia,* which gives techniques for interviews with the teacher (a terminological equivalent of the 'best' speaker) as the basic methodology for the linguist. Scollon's comment can be applied here too: the resulting grammar 'clearly does not reflect very closely the way people...speak to each other'. Undoubtedly the most scholarly and comprehensive grammar of an Australian language is Dixon's (1977) *A grammar of Yidiny* – yet he states quite openly (p. 29) that 'The writer never heard Yidiny spoken spontaneously', even though he does comment (p. 113) on 'normal conversational style' based on what speakers told him about Yidiny conversations.

The fieldwork methodology I have characterised for Australia and the resulting grammars do form a good basis for the theoretical work carried out by linguists. Blake and Dixon (1979, p. 3) outline the challenges offered by Australian languages as: (i) reconstructing earlier stages of Australian languages; and (ii) understanding the variety of ergative case systems, grammatical hierarchies and other linguistic structures, which is 'essential for an appreciation of human language as a whole and as a prerequisite to the formulation of any hypothesis of universal grammar'. Almost as an afterthought, they include the understanding of 'the relationship between the social organization and the culture of the speakers and the development of their languages', mentioning here bilingualism and avoidance languages.

The preoccupation with grammatical competence, in Chomsky's sense, has had some regrettable results for linguistic description in Australia. The first problem is caused by the linguists' assumption that the language under study fulfils the same sociocommunicative functions as their own language. This assumption has led linguists to incorrectly regard some languages as dead. For example, some multilingual speakers, who use English in almost all contexts, do speak an Aboriginal language in some restricted contexts, such as excluding outsiders (police, researchers or the like). But the interview method with 'best' speakers fails to reveal this restricted use of the Aboriginal language. Clearly we cannot describe a language as dead simply because we cannot elicit it. Many factors, ranging from the personal relationship between linguist and speakers to the social function of the languages, affect the linguist's ability to have access to languages. A functional community-based study of speakers' variations in performance shows that a language is not dead until it ceases to serve any function.

The second problem stems from the failure to take into account the significance of many variations in performance and the social dimensions of speaking. Keesing (1974, p. 89) has pointed out that the emphasis on competence 'has progressively narrowed the database of linguistic inquiry so that a large edifice teeters precariously on a thin edge of intuition'. By focusing on the rules of competence to the exclusion of variations in performance, linguists see language as a well-bounded static entity. This reification of languages causes problems. In Southeast Queensland, for instance, it is impossible to know exactly how to distinguish one language from another. Different families speak closely related languages for which they use the same language name. But their languages, while very similar, do have significant differences in vocabulary and grammar. Such factors as multilingualism, social varieties of language and many small family differences in vocabulary, cannot be satisfactorily handled within a framework restricted to grammatical competence.

Grayshon (1977, p. 31) likewise argues the need for a description of languages according to function rather than form, contrasting the traditional 'is' approach to language with the 'does' approach, which 'assumes a dynamic (dialectical) 2-sided condition of language'. The 'does' approach sees language as 'a collaborative act requiring interchangeable speaker–hearer relationships which themselves are the product of complex social relationships which are patterned and organized by social processes'. He argues that, owing to the complex nature of such social relationships, language is in reality never static or uniform.

The main theoretical thrust which takes a 'does' approach to language is the ethnography of speaking, advocated by Dell Hymes in the 1960s. The ethnography of speaking takes speakers (warm-blooded humans) as its starting-point, rather than the abstract entity language. It looks at who says what to whom, where, when, how, why, etc.

In the last three decades several other 'does' approaches to language have been developed, including interactional sociolinguistics, linguistic ethnography and Conversion Analysis (see Section 1.5.1).

My work in Southeast Queensland is with people whose use of Aboriginal language (or 'Lingo') appears to be limited to chastising someone or talking about certain taboo topics such as pregnancy, urinating, etc. Varieties of Standard English are spoken as the first language of all these people, but an investigation of the social dimensions of speaking reveals important elements of Aboriginality in areas barely studied in Australia, one of which is discussed in this chapter.

See Section 1.2 for discussion of issues involved in labelling varieties of English spoken by Aboriginal people. Also note that 'Lingo' is often used by Aboriginal people to refer to a traditional Aboriginal language.

2.2 The Southeast Queensland Aboriginal (SEQAB) study

Between 1973 and 1977 I carried out linguistic salvage work on the New South Wales coast. Within the traditional 'is' approach to language, I looked for best speakers or rememberers of language, tried to elicit the sorts of things I thought one should say in an Aboriginal language and wrote grammatical descriptions.

On coming to Queensland in 1978 I decided to wait until requested to do linguistic work by Aboriginal speakers. The request came (through John von Sturmer and Bruce Rigsby) from Michael Williams, an Aborigine of the Gooreng Gooreng people of Southeast Queensland, around Miriam Vale (north of Bundaberg). Williams is carrying out extensive research on the social history, language and culture of his people and I am assisting, focusing specifically on all aspects of language and speaking. I have found a great difference between this type of fieldwork and my earlier solo work. The Aborigines identify with and appreciate Williams' motivation in undertaking this research and I am rightly seen as his assistant. Williams directs and organises fieldwork which usually involves us both in research into social history. My conversational studies derive from the context of this research in addition to participation in family day-to-day business. As my involvement is in a non-directive capacity, I am in a good position to study conversations. Williams' style of fieldwork is quite different from my own previous work and will be discussed below. My theoretical focus has shifted to that of the ethnography of speaking. In investigating how Williams and his relatives use speaking to fulfil social functions, I have become aware of significant differences in the use of English between these people and middle class white Australians.

For discussion of the now outdated expressions SEQAB and MCWA, see Sections 1.3 and 1.5.2. Also note that the term 'informant' has been replaced in recent decades with 'teacher' (see Section 2.1) or 'consultant', to refer to speakers who work with linguists researching their language.

At this point it is important to characterise the people under study: Southeast Queensland Aborigines ('SEQAB people'), i.e. people who identify as Aboriginal and who come from the general Southeast Queensland area. This is not a closed group, but covers a wide-ranging number of people. They can be discussed under one label by virtue of their identity as Aborigines from the same geographical region, and their similarities in culture, lifestyles and speaking. In this part of Australia today there is [often] no clear-cut identity in terms of 'tribal' or language groups such as Gooreng Gooreng or Wakka Wakka. Identity here is in terms of Aboriginality and geographical region. In the ethnography of speaking I present here, it is contemporary Aboriginality which is the essential element. While this study is not primarily a comparative work, I shall draw attention to certain significant differences between the norms of speaking in SEQAB society and in my own 'MCWA' (middle class white Australia) society. More precisely I shall be concerned with differences in styles of speaking not so much between MCWA and SEQAB people as between MCWA and SEQAB contexts. For a SEQAB person may in fact choose to use MCWA rules of grammar and rules of use when talking in an MCWA context, such as a meeting. For simplicity, however, I shall generally refer simply to 'SEQAB speakers' with the understanding, unless otherwise specified, that they are speaking in a SEQAB context.

2.3 Questions and information seeking

In this chapter I shall be concerned with information seeking, an important aspect of the exchange of information for both SEQAB and MCWA people. While we use language to fulfil many functions, information exchange is one of the most widespread functions of speaking throughout the world. However, conversations in English with or between SEQAB people quickly reveal significant differences in the way information seeking takes place and the form it takes.

For example, in my own experience in trying to question Aborigines I have found, time and again, that they are confused, disfluent or noncompliant when questioned by means of an interrogative sentence like 'Were you very young?', the most usual type of question for MCWA speakers. Questions in the form of a declarative with question intonation are more successful, witness such exchanges as (1) and (2):[2]

(1) DE: Were you very young then?
A: Eh?

Some thirty years after I wrote this, it seems that many Aboriginal people are now not confused, disfluent or noncompliant when questioned with interrogative sentences such as example 1. However, the formation of Yes-No questions with declarative (or statement form) plus question (or rising) intonation remains very common with Aboriginal speakers of English.

DE: You were very young?
A: I was about 14.

(2) DE: Your husband was a Butchella man?
A: He was a Butchella.
DE: And where was he from, again?
A: Beg pardon.
DE: He was from further south was he?
A: He's, he's from here, not far from X station.

In (2) I was attempting to find out information on A's late husband, which would be relevant to earlier conversations about languages spoken in A's family. I began with the appropriate SEQAB type of question, hence successfully obtained an answer. I then reverted to the interrogative type, perfectly acceptable in MCWA conversations, but quite inappropriate here, as evidenced by the response *Beg pardon*. I switched to the SEQAB strategy of presenting information for confirmation (the information being selected, in fact, by guessing) and this strategy was again successful, as we can see from A's final response. (This strategy can also be used by MCWA speakers, but the important point is that for SEQAB speakers it is the normal strategy.)

It might be thought that the difference between SEQAB and MCWA questions is merely a difference in linguistic strategy. For example, the Van Leer Language Development Programme, devised and developed by the Queensland Department of Education for use in Aboriginal community schools, refers to Aboriginal English 'uninverted question forms' like *They can get it? (eh?)* contrasting with Standard English 'Can they get it?' (Dwyer 1974, p. 17). The two types differ, however, in more than their syntactic form, for the first involves checking inferred information. And this linguistic strategy of presenting known or inferred information for verification, clarification or further information reflects sociocultural aspects of SEQAB society, which are discussed below.

I define information seeking as a speech function aimed at eliciting information from the addressee. This function can be fulfilled directly (by means of questions) or indirectly (for example by making a provocative statement). While it seems quite likely that all societies use speaking for information seeking, it is true that there are culturally bound constraints on which verbal strategies are appropriate in what contexts. It is important to remember that questions can be used to fulfil other social functions as well. For example the MCWA question 'Have you got a knife?' could be used as a request for a knife, thus as a 'question-directive' (Ervin-Tripp 1976). In the present chapter, however, I shall be concerned only with the use of questions in information seeking.

2.4 Sociocultural aspects of information seeking

2.4.1 INTERPERSONAL RELATIONSHIPS

For MCWA society, information seeking plays an important role in interpersonal interactions. For example, when friends meet after a brief or long absence, questions are asked: 'Where have you been?', 'What have you been doing?', etc. People are insulted if they are not asked the right questions about a new job, trip, or house, for example. Strangers meeting in a social setting such as a cocktail party get to know each other mainly through the medium of information seeking, frequently by means of a direct question: 'Where do you work?', 'Where do you come from?', 'Why did you move here?'. In fact, where two MCWA people are meeting, it is considered impolite for a person to speak about themselves, rather than ask questions about the other person. We shall see below that this norm of interaction doesn't apply in SEQAB contexts. Information seeking is an important element of interpersonal relationships in MCWA. Where a person's relationship with another is close, however, questions are often not needed to compel interaction, though they remain important in information exchange, as we will see below.

When SEQAB friends meet after a brief or long absence, they exchange information to share in incidents of their lives that have occurred since their last meeting. Unlike a parallel MCWA situation, the friends/relatives tend not to ask each other questions, such as 'What have you been up to?', 'How's the kids?'. Rather, each speaker volunteers the information about themselves. Similarly when Aboriginal people meet for the first time, though they frequently ask 'orientation questions', especially about people, in order to establish how to relate to each other (see Section 2.5.1 below), it is uncommon for them to ask personal questions of each other. Having ascertained the nature of the relationship (whether through kin or affiliation with certain geographical, family or political groups), each speaker then talks about themselves without questioning by the other in a way which, for MCWA society, might be considered rude or self-centred.

It is not surprising that information seeking plays such an important role in speaking in MCWA society — a large-scale, complex and individualistic society, where so much information is available, and where a person's relationships with others are often undefined. Here, information seeking plays an important part in interpersonal relationships and the linguistic strategy of question serves to compel interaction and bind people together.

See Section 1.3 for discussion of the terms 'traditional' and 'non-traditional' in relation to Aboriginal societies, people and languages.

Traditional Aboriginal society, on the other hand, was and is based on small-scale groups. Each person has a particular kin relationship with every other person with whom they come into contact — if not a blood relationship, then by extension, a classificatory kinship relation. These kin relationships play a crucial part in all interaction. Haviland (1979a, 1979b) describes the types of speaking for Guugu–Yimidhirr, ranging from no speech at all with mother-in-laws, respectful words for brother-in-laws, through to polite and everyday style for many relatives, to a joking, vulgar relationship between grandfather and grandson. Reciprocity is clearly established and all interpersonal relationships are moderated by the kinship system. Clearly, then, the great need to compel interaction between people in MCWA society doesn't exist in traditional Aboriginal society.

The government no longer ignores cultural and social differences between non-traditional Aborigines and white Australians. However, the issue remains a complex one, and further research is warranted.

In the [more than] 200 years since white invasion of Australia, Aboriginal society in Southeast Queensland has changed dramatically. But despite the Queensland Government's determination to ignore cultural and social differences between non-traditional Aborigines and white Australians, there is, I claim, a great deal of Aboriginality in the culture of SEQAB people. There is a direct continuity between the types of relationships in traditional Aboriginal society and SEQAB society today. SEQAB people are related to each other through ties of on-going obligations. This is evidenced in such little known facts such as the way a SEQAB white-collar worker will regularly share their pay with relatives and their relatives' expectation that this will happen — compare the sharing of game in traditional Aboriginal society. This whole area of obligation and reciprocity (or debt relations) is central to the culture of non-traditional Aborigines, such as SEQAB people.

SEQAB society may also be contrasted with that of, for example, Gonja society in Africa, for which Goody (1978) provides an excellent study of the ethnography of questioning. She looks at the social functions which are fulfilled by questions, one of which corresponds to our information exchange function under study here. Gonja society is very hierarchical and people mainly ask information questions of those of a similar status. Goody explains this in terms of the power of questions to make commands. The syntactic structure of a question is formally incomplete and so a question begs a response. She claims (1978, p. 23) that questions are, universally, social devices for compelling interaction and they serve to bind two people in immediate reciprocity. Because of the strong command function of questions, Gonja students, for example, do not ask questions of their teachers. It seems that Aboriginal society differs greatly from Gonja society in that status is not fixed in Aboriginal society. Power derives not from hierarchy and position but from continuing rounds of negotiation. It is kin ties which bind people together and which ensure constant reciprocity in relationships. Verbal strategies are not needed to fulfil this function.

We have a contrast then between a status-oriented society such as Goody describes and a non-hierarchical society such as SEQAB society. In much of Gonja interaction, questions are inappropriate because of the command function involved. In much of SEQAB interaction, as we will see below, questions are inappropriate, not because of factors of command and status, but largely because they are unnecessary. SEQAB ties of obligation [often] obviate the use of questions and their inherent command function. We shall see in Section 2.5 that the constraints on the use of questions in SEQAB society are dependent not on the status of speakers, but on the nature of information. The functions of questioning and directives are bound up with permanent relationships and a sense of the right time to say and do things. Questions and commands are frequently either unnecessary or regarded as abruptly rude. Because of on-going debt relationships [many] SEQAB people make few direct social demands on each other. In many contexts, linguistic commands are inappropriate and, furthermore, often go unheeded.

2.4.2 OBLIGATION TO ANSWER

For MCWA society most information seeking involves direct questions and the addressee, generally speaking, is under an obligation to answer — cf. Keenan and Ochs (discussing middle class western society in 1979, p. 147): 'we assume that our conversational partner will provide the information relevant to our needs if he has it, unless there are specific mitigating circumstances'. Such circumstances include talking to a psychiatrist about their patient, or to a priest about someone he confesses. Or we may tease or joke with someone by not providing the information required. Or again certain topics — such as one's sex-life or income — may be considered too personal to be questioned on. But under most circumstances an MCWA person feels more or less obliged to answer a question (and incidentally also to comply with a request or command). To avoid answering is to risk being called uncooperative, or anti-social, or being likened to a politician. We shall see below that this norm of social interaction does not apply to SEQAB society. This situation of being generally obliged to answer a question is clearly linked in MCWA to the use of the question to compel interaction.

In SEQAB society, by contrast, where people are bound through ties of on-going obligation, this obligation, generally speaking, does not include the need to give information. There is thus no obligation on the addressee to answer a question. I will expand on this point in Section 2.5, in discussing the SEQAB social constraints on information seeking.

2.4.3 THE TRANSMISSION OF INFORMATION

Not only is information seeking essential to personal interaction in MCWA society, but information and knowledge are also of vital importance. A high premium is placed on acquiring knowledge — for example, we encourage children to have enquiring minds, to search for truth. Similarly through many media — oral, written, electronic, etc. — we are preoccupied with spreading information. And it is information seeking, with a high proportion of direct questions, which serves an important role in the acquisition of knowledge and the spread of information. Questioning is institutionalised in many ways in MCWA society. For example, public buildings, such as shops and offices, are full of enquiry desks and information booths. Media, in particular TV and radio, use the interview technique in providing information. Quiz programmes and questionnaires are further indications of the significant function of questioning in MCWA.

Direct questioning is also an essential strategy in western education, both formal and informal. Goody (1978) mentions the work of several people studying the use of questions by mothers in their interaction with infants and children. Western mothers address questions to preverbal infants, which they answer themselves as a way of provoking interaction with the infant. This question–answer strategy is also used in teaching children, as in exchanges like 'What's that? — Truck', and the like. At least in primary school, the question–answer technique forms the basis of much of the transference of knowledge.

In Aboriginal society, on the other hand, knowledge is not a free and easily acquired good. Knowledge is acquired or passed on as a part of social interaction and is subject to strong controls in many instances. For example, much knowledge of religious or ritual matters is strictly controlled so that only initiated men may know certain songs, stories and places (see Keen 1994 on the controls on religious knowledge which operate within a total economy of knowledge in Aboriginal society in Northeast Arnhem Land).

Basil Sansom (1980) demonstrates the controls on information of a day-to-day nature in a study of Aborigines of Darwin and its hinterland. To oversimplify Sansom's rich and dynamic ethnography, we can say that information in the camp is transmitted through involvement. He describes in Chapter 5 [of his book] the difficulties of finding out information about an event which occurred while he was absent from the camp. People are involved in events ('happenings') either as actor or as witness. Much information simply is not available to a non-participant after the event. Sansom (1980, p. 84) outlines rules to govern the retailing of information that has been gained by witnessing. These rules amount to a 'ban on reporting' of daily business at camp. While it is possible to witness events, one does not generally report on these events. In this way, he points out, 'the present, not the past, is open to inspection'. However, it is permitted to 'give the word' or tell of a communal camp verdict of an event. One example he gives is of the verdict 'Violet bin divorce Lionel after fightin''. The news of this change in the state of affairs is given, but without details of what happened in the events which caused it. However, while such day-to-day happenings cannot be reported at a later date, it is quite possible for many people to witness such happenings in the camp. (This is possibly the reverse of the situation in MCWA.) Despite these 'ban on reporting' rules, it is possible, though very difficult, to get details of some events. To have access to such information 'one has, in short, to learn the strategies for subverting the rule'. Sansom's work clearly demonstrates that the Aboriginal society he studied exercises strong controls on the transmission of information. From his work it appears that the strategy of direct questioning is frequently inappropriate for eliciting information.

We can see a parallel between Sansom's study of a Darwin fringe camp and Stephen Harris's (1984) research on traditional Aboriginal teaching and learning strategies at Milingimbi (see also Harris 1977). Both illustrate how information is transmitted through participation in Aboriginal society. Harris demonstrates that Aboriginal learning takes place in real-life situations and involves context-specific skills, such as digging for yams or a sacred dance. He contrasts this observation-and-imitation method of passing on knowledge with the western style of context-free verbal instruction, which heavily depends on questioning. He shows that the emphasis in Aboriginal teaching and learning is on observation and participation.

Harris also studies sociolinguistic rules of interpersonal speech, from the crosscultural perspectives of teachers in the western style Milingimbi school. His observations and conclusions are quite significant for my study, especially as he appears to be one of the few people to have written about such matters in the Australian context. I will refer to some of Harris's sociolinguistic rules below in comparison with my findings in SEQAB society. Keen, Sansom and Harris all demonstrate the importance of the *rights* to knowledge, be it religious, special or everyday knowledge. All knowledge is considered an inalienable part of relationships between people and has no value of its own separate from these relationships. We see examples of the continuity of traditional Aboriginal societies such as SEQAB society. These Aborigines are noted for their lack of cooperation with MCWA question strategies in passing on knowledge.

The inadequacy of MCWA education for such Aboriginal children is blatantly obvious and well documented. School teachers often complain that Aboriginal children do not participate in classroom activities involving questioning (and the children are often said to be uncooperative or lazy or verbally deficient). A white lawyer with the Aboriginal and Torres Strait Island Legal Service has explained to me that a lot of his problems and his clients' failures stem from Aborigines' misunderstanding of, or refusal to comply with, the questioning process inherent in the legal system. And the absence of Aborigines from TV quiz programmes, for example, reflects more than educational disadvantage.

An example of Aboriginal aversion to questionnaires was recently brought to my attention. It concerns an Australia-wide body whose total client group consists of Aboriginal and Islander people. Researchers in the organisation needed information from local Aboriginal staff around Australia. Aboriginal researchers were concerned from the start at the inappropriateness and ineffectiveness of written questionnaires, saying *We'll find out a lot more if we go and have a talk with them*. White researchers saw such a method of finding information as unnecessary and too costly. Accordingly a questionnaire was sent to all local staff, with the suggestion that it only be used as a guideline for conversations with the aim of gaining the required information. Aboriginal researchers went to pains to write about the importance of explaining the need for information to clients, and following this up with communicating results to clients at a later date: 'Our method of gathering information should be casual in approach and avoid direct question and answer situations.' However, the whole attempt at information gathering failed, as local Aboriginal staff regarded the letter as a questionnaire in the MCWA context. Rather than use points from the questionnaire as guidelines for conversations, many local staff simply handed the questionnaires to individual clients to fill in. Such questionnaires proved to be of almost no use to the researchers, as respondents gave very limited information or refused to answer at all, writing 'none of your business', or the like. And by far the majority of the mailed letter/questionnaires were not returned. This example illustrates the primacy of spoken communication for Aboriginal people, as well as the inappropriateness of using MCWA survey techniques for information seeking in [many Aboriginal contexts]. Further demonstration here came when one of the Aboriginal researchers later talked in a hotel with one of the clients whom he remembered to have filled in one of these questionnaires in the manner described above. By sharing information on the subject of inquiry and communicating orally in an Aboriginal context, the researcher found out a great deal of information which this client had not given in the MCWA survey context.

2.5 Information seeking in SEQAB conversations

Having noted that there are essential sociocultural differences between MCWA and SEQAB societies in information seeking, I will now concentrate on the strategies used in SEQAB conversations. I first outline the three main social constraints on the transmission of information, and then discuss the linguistic strategies used in seeking the two major types of information: 'orientation information' and 'substantial information'.

2.5.1 SOCIAL CONSTRAINTS ON THE TRANSMISSION OF INFORMATION

The expectation that I would be able to give details of a 'rule' about access to information was an indication of my naivety, as well as the early 1980s view among many linguists that sociolinguistic patterning must be so regular as to be captured in this way. We have learnt that social interaction and contexts are much more complex, and we think now in terms of expectations or norms, rather than rules.

(a) In SEQAB society there are significant constraints on who can have legitimate access to certain information. At this stage of research I am not able to detail this rule, but I can give a few examples. One of the older knowledgeable SEQAB people has told Williams of a sacred site near his birthplace, but has warned him not to tell me. When Williams mentioned this place on a trip, the knowledgeable man said in Lingo: *Don't talk about it: the white woman can hear you.* (In fact, I was out of hearing: Williams later reported the incident to me but without details of the site, etc.) Similarly, this man knows the story belonging to the Aboriginal rock formation removed from Gooreng Gooreng territory to the University of Queensland some thirty years ago. However, he says this story is not for ladies, Aboriginal or not, to know. Conversely, in his social history research, Williams has always considered it significant that *People know me and respect Mum and Dad, so they'll tell me things.* And even everyday information, such as the story of a fight, may be withheld from certain people within the social group.

(b) Secondly, the person requiring information in the SEQAB situation is obliged to wait for the knowledgeable person to give the information in their own time (if indeed they give it at all). This is in contrast to MCWA society, where the person requiring information generally has the right to question another, who is under some obligation to comply. A widespread inability to perceive this cultural difference causes many problems in communication. Harris (1977, p. 442) talks about this social constraint on questioning in the Milingimbi context, observing that Aboriginal speakers 'feel little obligation to respond to direct questions', and that 'to get an answer is a privilege, not a right'. It is clear that this is a crosscultural extension of the SEQAB constraint.

Both of these social constraints on information seeking reflect the fact that for SEQAB people the interpersonal relationships are a significant factor in the way information is handled. As Harris (1977, p. 294) puts it, an Aboriginal learner is 'more person-oriented than information-oriented'.

(c) The third constraint further illustrates the way information exchange is subordinated to relationships between speakers. This constraint is that information exchange in SEQAB conversations is decidedly a two-way process, with both the knowledgeable person and the questioning person contributing information. The person requiring information must present some known, inferred or guessed information, in an appropriate mode. When and if the knowledgeable person decides to, they then present their information.

2.5.2 TYPES OF INFORMATION SEEKING AND ASSOCIATED LINGUISTIC STRATEGIES

There are two main types of information seeking, depending on whether the information sought is orientation information or substantial information. I will consider them in turn, examining the linguistic strategies used.

ORIENTATION INFORMATION. This is information which clarifies a topic (often the current topic of conversation). The information sought comprises background details about people especially, but also about the time, place and setting of some situation or narrated event.[3] The linguistic forms used to seek orientation information are as follows:

(a) A declarative clause with question intonation (or a following interrogative tag). Basically the questioner presents some proposition for confirmation (or correction). The following conversational extracts illustrate a questioning person filling in details of topics under discussion.

(3) A: Grandfather X used to live at Tirroan?
B: Thornhill.

(4) DE: You didn't know about it?
A: Mm, I didn't know about that.

In (3), A is trying to find out information about his grandfather. In (4) DE wants to know if A knew about a certain incident. The MCWA question 'Did you know about it?' would most likely be inappropriate here.

(b) An interrogative (direct question) is also used, though much less frequently:

(5) A: Were you there when Jack was born in the scrub?
B: No.

In (6) below, A is trying to find out about an old lady and where she fits in socially. She presents the information she knows and then asks a question.

(6) A: Old Grannie X — she was a full-blooded Aboriginal woman — who was she related to?

Orientation questions of this form are notably used when people meet each other, e.g., *Where are you going?* or the like:

(7) A: Where youse headin? Down to the creek?
B: No, just wanna go up the back there.

Here, B has just walked into her grandmother's house: the first words A addresses to her are to question where she is going next.

Over the years that I have done salvage linguistic studies of Aboriginal languages whose function is drastically reduced, I have been struck by the way people remember these greeting questions in language. On many such occasions when I have been talking to people about language, they recall a little vocabulary and then 'what you say if you meet someone' — for example a Gooreng Gooreng speaker recalling vocabulary produced the following sequence of sentences completely without elicitation:

(8) *Woonju ngin yun.gim?*
'Where are you going?'
Yuluhm town-gu nguy yun.gim.
'I'm going to Rockhampton.'
Woonju ngihn booguy woowun?
'When are you coming back?'
O booluroo.
'In two days' time.'

I have similar examples which frequently occurred with the Gumbaynggir speaker I worked with in Northern New South Wales. On another tape I recorded with a SEQAB man talking generally about Aborigines in the old days, language had not been mentioned until he said: *When I'd meet you I'd say 'Wunyi gubuy', 'Where are you going?'* It now appears clear to me that in

SEQAB society, phrases such as *Where are you going*?, *Where did you come from?* are interactionally equivalent to 'Hullo', 'Hi', 'Gidday', etc., in MCWA society. (It also appears quite possible that this is true through a much wider region of Aboriginal Australia.) SEQAB people most frequently greet each other with an orientation question when they meet. Further, it is common for a SEQAB person sitting on the verandah or steps of their house to call out *Where you going?* to another SEQAB acquaintance or relative who walks past the house, in a manner similar to an MCWA person calling out 'Hullo'. (In the light of this observation, it would be revealing to know how SEQAB speakers greet each other on the telephone. Most of the SEQAB people I work with do not have telephones in their homes and hence I have not witnessed these interactions. However, it is interesting here that an older SEQAB man who lives in Brisbane and sometimes phones me to have a talk always tells me where he is. He often tells me to phone him on a certain day and always asks then where I am.

These observations about telephone communication are relevant to the early 1980s, before mobile phones, and at a time when many people had no home phone. I am unaware of any research or published observations of twenty-first-century Aboriginal phone interactions.

It seems to me that these greeting routines are very aptly termed orientation questions. The questioner is finding out background details of the addressee's movement. The Gumbaynggir speaker also frequently explained the routine when an Aborigine travelled to a *new tribe*. This involved the newcomer being questioned about his homeland, his name and moiety, so that he could be slotted into the kinship of the *tribe* he was visiting and know his kin relationship to everyone. In this example, which the speaker often talked about, orientation questions are vital in locating the addressee in a sociospatial relationship with the questioning person(s). Similarly when SEQAB people today meet each other for the first time, each asks the other a series of orientation questions, such as *Where you from?*, *What's your name?*, *You got relations around here?*, to determine their social relationship and basis for interaction.

(c) The third main linguistic strategy used by SEQAB people in seeking orientation information consists of interjections and repetitions to encourage a speaker who has given some information to give further information – yeah, *mm*, *oh*, *what*?, and the like. These forms also fulfil a central function of audience participation in the narration of a story. In seeking orientation information, the questioning person essentially asks to be told more by using an audience participation interjection or by echoing the information just presented. (This strategy is also used by MCWA speakers, of course.)

A better label for this use of oh yeah *would be 'acknowledgment token'.*

In the following example, A is seeking background information about an old man, X. She starts by presenting his name and then uses a direct question (type b). The knowledgeable person, H, then gives her kin relationship to the man being discussed. A then uses a classic audience participation interjection, *Oh yeah* (type c), to provoke further background detail on the man:

(9) A: What about that old fella called X, who was he?
B: That's our old grandfather — my old great uncle really.
A: Oh yeah.
B: My great uncle — he used to be king of Y [district]...[4]

SUBSTANTIAL INFORMATION. The second type of information seeking in SEQAB conversations aims to elicit what I call 'substantial information'. It generally involves a change of topic and may seek explanation for some event or situation. In this type of information seeking, direct questions are inappropriate and unsuccessful, as the examples (10)–(12) illustrate:

(10) DE: What's the story about?
Result: everyone talking at once, great disfluencies, no significant information.
(11) DE: Do you know any stories in the language?
A: No, I forget about all the stories.
(12) A: Do you know anything about Grandfather X's father?
B: Oh no, not much.
A: Where did he come from?
B: Wouldn know.
IK: Station owner, was he?
A: He's something to do with the station up there.

In (10) a group of knowledgeable SEQAB people and several children had travelled with Williams and myself to a story place. It was a trip that had been talked about and was considered by all to be of obvious importance to the social history research Williams was conducting. There was (as Williams confirmed in discussion later) the general expectation that the knowledgeable people would tell the story, and I had a tape-recorder and camera to record the occasion. However, I sought to elicit the story — substantial information — by means of a direct question, unwittingly ignoring the appropriate SEQAB way of talking here. And the response indicates that my questioning was unsuccessful: no information was given. But later, after a fair amount of talk about the story place (orienting us all to the features of landscape, history, and so on), the story was told by a few of the knowledgeable people in their own time. (12) is interesting in that it shows a SEQAB man, A, putting himself in a non-SEQAB role and context, and using the MCWA linguistic strategy for eliciting substantial information. It is quite unsuccessful, although at a later date B did give information about Grandfather X's father. The other interesting thing about this example is IK's use of a SEQAB orientation question, which was successful.

The linguistic strategies used in substantial information seeking are:

(a) 'Triggering' — a technique consisting of devices, often followed by silence, intended to lead the knowledgeable person to impart information.[5] In the most common triggering strategy the person desiring substantial information makes a relevant statement, presenting something he already knows about the topic. This is followed often by silence and then by the knowledgeable person talking on that topic, if they desire. Thus in (13) A uses a trigger-statement to question his mother about the significance of L Lagoon.

(13) A: [He's] dreaming about L Lagoon.
B: Hoho — that's the Lagoon, went, took Mum fishin there one day — my mother.
A: Yeah.
B: N she couldn get a fish bite, ya know.
A, B: (laugh)
B: She was fishin, and I said — (to DE) see my mother was a full-blooded Aboriginal — I said, I said, 'you know mum', I said, 'this is where they threw all the old gooris [Aborigines] in', (laugh)...

In another form of triggering the person desiring substantial information presents some known information, this time as something he remembers or was told, and thus reminds the knowledgeable person of the specific topic:

(14) A: You know I can remember Grannie X used to live in a funny little house.
B: That's just how it was when Grannie X...

(15) A: Heard there was the biggest row at the pub last night.
B: Yeah, Joe got stuck into Fred and Bill. He was really drunk. Went and rang up Bert and Jim to come and help him kill Bill. (laugh)...

In (14), A was talking to an elderly aunt at Cherbourg, trying to find out what the Reserve was like in the early days; B responded to the trigger by giving a description of the house and then later in the conversation gave other details of the early days, in the general talk. In (15), A wanted to know about a fight at the hotel, but again elicited the information by means of a trigger statement, not a direct question like 'What happened at the pub last night?': as we have seen, such a strategy, while perfectly normal in MCWA conversations, is not appropriate in the SEQAB context.

(b) Interjections and repetitions — a strategy also used, as we have seen, in orientation information seeking:

(16) A: They used to call him Stinker because he used to go to the killing yard [abattoir],
B: Stinker. (giggle)
A: and carry all the runners [small intestines] home on his head.
C: Oh yeah.
A: You know, the runners of the cattle.
B: Yeah.
A: Hangin down over his head like this comin along, these policemen comin — he was comin along carrying the thing on his head, they said, 'Ah you know where Stinker — where this fella Stinker live?'. He said, 'Oh, him longa camp'. He was talking to Stinker.

(17) A: I hear them two — oh, Grannie was swearing something terrible at that old woman.
B: Grannie X used to swear bad, eh.

In (17) A then went on to give further information about the character of Grannie during the course of the next fifteen minutes of the conversation: the nature of this hectic lunchtime conversation with many participants makes it unsuitable for quoting here. Indeed, many instances of substantial information seeking do not lend themselves readily to quotation as they are spread over too long a time: as observed above, there is no obligation on the knowledgeable person to reply, or answer with the desired information,[6] and matters concerning the relationship between speakers may cause the knowledgeable person to put off giving the information till later.

Sometimes, where substantial information seeking is not effective, the questioning person will first seek orientation information, such as where a person comes from, who they live with, and later use a trigger to elicit substantial information.

While I claim that it is easy to identify contrasting MCWA and SEQAB approaches to information seeking, there is in fact a continuum ranging between the poles. When languages come into contact, there is often a great deal of variation between speakers in the extent to which the language of the dominant group affects that of the subordinate group. Similarly, with use of language there is a varying amount of influence between them. SEQAB speakers (particularly younger city people) who are involved in MCWA education, employment, finance, etc., employ a greater degree of direct question strategies than do older people in SEQAB rural communities. A striking example of a SEQAB person using MCWA norms here occurred during a (taped) discussion on language which was joined by a rather drunk SEQAB lady. She defied many SEQAB standards of greeting, information seeking and personal interaction by asking me a series of personal questions:

(18) Now what's this all about?
(To others about DE) Who dat one?
Now what you got dere?

Other SEQAB people in the group diverted this lady's attentions from me and joked about her drunkenness. It seemed that they were embarrassed by her breaking the social rules of speaking. This incident also parallels the situation in Cape Keerweer, western Cape York, where Aborigines are multilingual in various Aboriginal language codes and where 'English is especially the language of drunkenness and of violent arguments' (Sutton 1978, p. 170). Other anthropologists (C Anderson, I Keen, 1981, pers. comm.) report that English is often used by Aborigines in situations of drunkenness, or violent verbal abuse. It appears that in using English, the irate or drunk speaker is not just using

English grammar, but appropriate rules of use. In this example, she is able to ask personal questions, which could not be asked in a SEQAB speaking context.

2.6 Implications

I have shown that there are significant differences in ways of speaking involving information exchange between MCWA and SEQAB people. In MCWA, we place a high premium on knowledge for its own sake and information exchange through questioning is very free. In SEQAB society, much information is not freely available and information seeking is subject to strong social constraints. There are restrictions on who can have access to certain information and the knowledgeable person gives information only if they are the right person to do so. There is no obligation on the SEQAB speaker to respond to information seeking. As well as these social differences, there are linguistic differences, most notably in finding out substantial information, which reflect the SEQAB social rule that information seeking is based on some information known or inferred by the questioner. (It is most likely that the generalisations made here about information seeking in SEQAB society are applicable to other Aboriginal Australian contexts.)

Such significant differences have serious implications in all areas of communication between MCWA and SEQAB people. Some obvious areas are schools, law courts, Aboriginal advisory bodies and land-claims hearings, where the significant differences in communication between the Aboriginal and non-Aboriginal contexts are usually unnoticed or ignored.

One area of particular concern is that of anthropological, linguistic and historical fieldwork in Aboriginal Australia. Until very recently, all such research has been carried out by non-Aborigines, particularly MCWA researchers and their British and American counterparts. By its very nature, this fieldwork consists of whites gathering information from Aborigines and often involves whites questioning Aborigines. We have seen the inappropriateness of questions in many Aboriginal contexts and the strong social constraints on information seeking. Undoubtedly, some culturally sensitive fieldworkers have been aware of some aspects of these differences. I suggest it is very important for any fieldwork handbook or course for workers in Aboriginal Australia to include comments on the social rules of speaking, especially in the area of information exchange.

Clearly, using a SEQAB approach to information gathering is much more complex and time-consuming than the MCWA questioning approach. Firstly, it involves the researcher developing relationships with people, without specific end-points in mind. This takes time and may be difficult to slot into a schedule, report or MCWA organisational approach. Secondly, it requires the researcher to have sufficient known or inferred information on the topics of research to be able to present to the knowledgeable persons. Thirdly, it involves active participation, such as travelling to historically important areas, in order for people to disclose information. And finally it requires that the researcher find out who is the appropriate source for what information. Simply by selecting a particular informant the fieldworker may be excluding the possibility of finding out about certain areas. I suggest that it is optimal for researchers to work in liaison with an Aborigine whose group they are studying. Apart from the obvious political advantage, the Aboriginal liaison person can advise on which people to talk to about which topics, etc., and advise on a whole range of social norms for speaking.

Three decades after this was written, researchers are engaging in more collaborative approaches, 'founded on a process of meaningful engagement and reciprocity between the researcher and [Aboriginal] people' (AIATSIS 2012, p.1). See also WADET (2012).

In my fieldwork experience, a very common reply to direct questions about the old ways and language is *I don't know anything*. This could be an example of the Reduction Principle in conversation described by Syder and Pawley (1974), which involves a speaker's humility or self-diminution as a social convention. However, more significantly here, this response indicates the inappropriateness of the type of information seeking strategy being used. In Aboriginal society the passing of information doesn't result from a direct query. It is the result of normal two-way interaction between people.

It is not only Australian researchers who are insensitive to different social norms of information exchange. Roger Abrahams (1976, p. 3) has recently published several excellent studies of black talking in the USA. He mentions that here information is embedded in types of conversational routines, which involve a 'leading' statement, challenges and responses and which depend on the establishment of 'reciprocality'. He contrasts this style of information exchange with what he calls the 'survey culture' of white America, where there are few questions which cannot be asked directly. His comment about the typical question method in social science research is relevant to Australia: 'simply by asking questions (any questions) ... we have already committed an unconsidered ethnocentric act, for we have assumed that all people pass on information as we do'. Many Aborigines have a well-founded resentment towards white researchers. Aside from the whole area of cultural theft, there is great reaction to the MCWA questioning approach. Aborigines are questioned directly on personal matters and significant areas, by people with whom they have no close relationship and in a totally inappropriate manner. Many Aborigines also feel that researchers are concerned only with answers to their own questions, rather than information they have to offer. As one SEQAB person expressed it: *They come in with a whole lot of questions, instead of just sitting down and talking*. There is now a growing number of Aborigines involved in research, particularly since the first Aboriginal Oral History Conference in June 1979. White fieldworkers have a lot to learn from these people.

Before I had seriously tackled the ethnography of information seeking, I heard an excellent explanation of Williams' approach to fieldwork. Williams was talking to a white researcher who mentioned the possibility of attending a short course on interviewing techniques and questionnaires, preparatory to undertaking a research project similar in some ways to Williams'. Williams was disturbed by this approach and said: *You gotta know how to talk – have a broader knowledge of things*. He then explained that for him it is important to build up relationships with people before worrying about information. It is necessary to talk about things he has in common with knowledgeable people, which might be kids, experiences in a particular town or whatever. It became clear to me, as I witnessed the conversation, that Williams was describing the art of information gathering for SEQAB society: consider information exchange as a part of your relationship with someone, and for specific issues start with known information and share it, then use triggering devices and wait until the knowledgeable person is prepared to give their information. Furthermore, accept that the person may exercise their right to withhold the information.

As a final comment, let me say that the labels people use for speech events can be significant. Many white researchers, using MCWA norms for information exchange, aim for specific information in their fieldwork, and talk about it to 'informants' as well as colleagues, as 'asking some questions'. Williams, on the other hand, uses SEQAB norms of speaking discussed here, in which relationships between people take precedence over specific information. In over three years of fieldwork and research with Williams, I have never heard him talk about 'asking questions': he always talks to relatives and other Aborigines, as well as research colleagues, about *having a talk*.

NOTES

1. I am indebted to the Aboriginal people of Southeast Queensland who shared their culture and lives with me. In particular, my thanks go to Michael Williams and his relatives for enabling me to be involved in the social history research and for teaching me so much about Aboriginality. I am grateful to Ian Keen, Francesca Merlan, Bruce Rigsby, Basil Sansom, Michael Silverstein and Peter Sutton for reading earlier drafts of this chapter and for their encouragement and helpful criticism. Other colleagues have made helpful suggestions and comments, including Chris Anderson, Peter Eades, Peter Gillan, Rodney Huddleston, David Trigger and Myra Westphal.
2. Much of the conversational material on which this study is based has not been taped. However, all the quotations are from taped conversations. To preserve anonymity, persons are labelled either with fictitious names as in (15) or with initials as in (6); there is no necessary identity between speakers labelled 'A' in different quotations. The only non-SEQAB people are labelled by initials: DE (the writer) and IK (Ian Keen, anthropologist, University of Queensland). Similarly, place names are labelled 'X'.
3. I use the term 'orientation' in a similar fashion to Labov (1972) in his analysis of narrative.
4. The Gumbaynggir language from the New South Wales north coast has a non-inflecting word *kalang*, which I used to gloss as 'Interjection: Gee!'. It now appears to me that *kalang* very neatly fills the function of audience participation in conversation. Ian Keen (1981, pers. comm.) reports that the Yolngu word *maʔ* fulfils the same function.
5. The full functioning of silence in Aboriginal conversations is yet to be studied, but it is a significant factor in substantial information seeking. There appears to be a greater use of silence in SEQAB conversations than in MCWA conversations. Cf. Philips' (1976, p. 88) comment on Springs (American Indian) conversations: 'There is a tolerance for silences — silences which Anglos often rush into and fill'.
6. Again we may compare SEQAB conversations with conversations in Warm Springs, where there is no requirement 'that a question by one person be followed immediately by an answer or a promise of an answer from the addressee. It MAY be followed by an answer, but may also be followed by silence or by an utterance that bears no relationship to the question' (Hymes 1975, p. 33).

Chapter 3

Misunderstanding Aboriginal English: the role of sociocultural context

First published in 1984, this chapter discusses the way that many Aboriginal speakers of English as a first language talk about future actions. Although it describes commonly observed patterns of language use, it should not be read as describing the language and culture of all Aboriginal people in all parts of Australia. Further, it does not deal with how bicultural Aboriginal people may interact with non-Aboriginal people (see Section 1.5.2). Section 3.4 contained some over-generalisations and gender-exclusive terms. These have been updated by changes or additions, indicated in square brackets [ ].

3.1 Introduction[1]

Aboriginal people in much of southern Australia no longer speak 'traditional' Aboriginal languages on a regular, everyday basis. While some of these people speak varieties of a pidgin- or creole-like Aboriginal English, the major language variety used by many Aboriginal people today is grammatically very close to Standard English.[2] Linguistic work has understandably been focused on more remote Aboriginal groups who still speak 'traditional'[3] Aboriginal languages in most contexts, or, in southern Australia, on the few elderly speakers who retain competence in these languages. While this work has contributed greatly to an academic understanding of the nature of human languages, much applied work has also been carried out in remote Aboriginal contexts in bilingual education and Bible translation. However, in southern Australia there has been little applied linguistic work to date.

First published as Eades, D 1984, 'Misunderstanding Aboriginal English: the role of sociocultural context', in *Further applications of linguistics to Australian Aboriginal contexts*, eds G McKay & B Sommer, Applied Linguistics Association of Australia Occasional Papers, Melbourne, no. 8, pp. 24–33.

The almost complete exclusion from linguistic research of the English-speaking Aboriginal people in southern Australia has had some regrettable results. Firstly, the linguists' concern with non-English languages has supported widespread views, held by linguists, anthropologists and many other Australians, that the viability of Aboriginal people and their distinctive ways depends on such attributes as speaking a 'traditional' language (and singing 'traditional' songs). So, the focus by linguists on 'traditional' languages has supported the general, but, in my view, erroneous, Australian belief that Aboriginal culture and people are 'dying out'.

Section 1.2 discusses the terms 'Aboriginal English' and 'Aboriginal ways of speaking English'. In the last three decades, there has been considerable application of linguistic research in southern Australia, to education (see Chapter 1, Further Reading), and to a lesser extent to law (see Part 11). But much more remains to be done.

Secondly, the concentration by linguists on non-English-related Aboriginal languages, in association with their tendency to view language as a phenomenon independent of social interaction, has prevented them from considering tension and conflict between Aboriginal and non-Aboriginal people in rural and urban Australia as due in any way to significant differences in communication. Although both parties in a conversation, negotiation, meeting, or class speak English, they are frequently using language differently. Recent work by sociolinguists such as Gumperz (1982a, 1982b) provides a framework that can account for the fact, which is increasingly obvious in large-scale multi-ethnic societies, that 'speakers may have similar life styles, speak closely related dialects of the same language, and yet regularly fail to communicate' (Gumperz & Gumperz 1982, p. 13). Put simply, where participants in a conversation do not share culture, many of their expectations, understandings and interpretations of the conversation are not shared. It is not sufficient to have shared grammatical competence — much of our understanding of what people say depends, to a significant extent, on features of shared sociocultural competence.

An ethnographically based sociolinguistic analysis examines what people say in the context of their social relations and cultural context. It uses the ethnographic study of society as a necessary prerequisite for understanding language. It also assumes that we cannot understand the way people act and cultural systems without understanding language use. The dynamic relationship between what people say and its linguistic and sociocultural context forms the

While ethnographically based sociolinguistics remains a powerful explanatory tool, it needs to incorporate examination of power relationships, in order to account for much of what happens in interactions between Aboriginal and non-Aboriginal Australians (see Section 1.5.3).

basis of ethnographically based sociolinguistics. In this chapter I show how this kind of sociolinguistics is a powerful tool for explaining much of what happens in interactions between Aboriginal and non-Aboriginal Australians.

3.2 Context is crucial to understanding

In order for language users to communicate effectively we need to know much more than how to construct grammatical sentences. While it has long been a cliché in linguistics that 'meaning depends on context', much linguistic analysis virtually ignores context. Sociolinguistic analysis, on the other hand, holds that the relationship between what people say (or language form) and its interpretation and effect (or language function) depends crucially on aspects of context.

For example, I visit an old school friend and I greet him: 'Good morning Mr Miller'. To understand what I am saying here requires grammatical competence and an understanding of the referential function of elements of the utterance. But this is not sufficient to know what I mean, what is happening in the interaction between my friend and me, or how the utterance is intended to function. A great deal of contextual social, cultural and specific interpersonal knowledge is needed to understand my greeting. As I greet my old friend, am I joking, trying to create a distance or formality between us, signalling deference, expressing hostility?

An understanding of my utterance requires an understanding of my relationship with my friend, cultural expectations and norms (such as the situations when such a greeting is regarded as distant, formal or appropriately friendly), as well as my moods and intentions. At the same time, my utterance helps to create or change this relationship. My friend's interpretation, and subsequent verbal or other response, further creates our relationship. In this way, what we say to each other, which cannot be divorced from its context, both reflects and creates our social interaction and personal relationship.

I define context as the set of factors associated with an utterance of a linguistic form which affect its interpretation. This includes a wide range of factors which are briefly summarised here (for a fuller discussion see Eades 1983, ch 2).

Linguistic (or verbal) context includes such factors as the speech event of which the utterance is part, the choice of language or style of speaking, the utterances preceding and following, and such prosody conventions as stress, intonation, voice speed. What I call immediate physical context includes details of setting, location, time, activity type (see Levinson 1979) and topic. The social context covers participants as individuals and the relationships between participants. (Here I draw heavily on the work of Brown & Fraser 1979.) The 'individual participants' category comprises both the stable features (such as personality, interests and physical appearances) of the individual as an individual, and features such as class, ethnicity, age and sex of the individual as a member of a social category. The 'relationship between participants' category comprises interpersonal relationships such as liking and knowledge, and the role and category relations such as social power and social status. Finally, extra-situational context consists of what I call 'shared knowledge' — that is the knowledge and beliefs about the world which participants in conversations share or assume one another to share and which are necessary (but not necessarily sufficient) for speakers to interpret conversation. This shared knowledge can be restricted to the relationship between two people or can be knowledge within a small group or within a wide sociocultural group. Our understanding of what people say depends on all these features of context. Clearly, different features will be more crucial than others in different situations. The sociolinguistic analysis focuses on the most significant features affecting the verbal interaction being studied.

In this chapter I look briefly at one small area of language use among Aboriginal people in southern Australia — the use of language to talk about one's own future actions. Firstly (in Section 3.3), I introduce contemporary southern Aboriginal culture. In Section 3.4, I focus on distinctively Aboriginal notions of time, the predictability and control of the future, and the structure of social relations. These sociocultural features of shared knowledge are the most crucial aspects of context in the understanding of Aboriginal talk about one's future actions. Then, in Section 3.5, we see that both Aboriginal and non-Aboriginal people use identical grammatical forms in speaking about the future, but meanings are not [always] shared. An understanding of this difference in meaning provides an important explanation of one significant area of crosscultural tension and misunderstanding. As linguists working in Aboriginal contexts, we are led to ask how many other areas of such tension and misunderstanding can be explained by similar ethnographically based sociolinguistic analysis.

3.3 Aboriginal culture in southern Australia

Like the majority of other non-Aboriginal Australians, [non-Aboriginal] linguists have frequently failed to see the continuities of Aboriginal culture in southern Australia. Because these Aboriginal people appear to live quite like whites, there is a widespread general misunderstanding of the extent of their distinctively Aboriginal social organisation and culture. There is a general misconception that 'Aborigines on the white side of the rolling frontier lack culture, have no distinctive culture, have only some truncated version of European culture, or have only a culture of poverty' (Langton 1981, p. 17).

While we are looking in southern Australia for corroborees, 'traditional' Aboriginal languages, sacred stories and carved artefacts, we will find it very hard to see Aboriginal culture. But if we understand culture to be about the way people perceive the world, act on it and relate to others, then we can see in southern Australia today much evidence of Aboriginal culture that reflects both a continuity from pre-contact times, and a viable adaptation to the dramatic changes it has faced in the last 200 years [and more]. We can cite here briefly such factors as the obligation of a wide range of kin, attitudes to old people, child-rearing practices, attitudes to alcoholics, and ways of participation in Christian churches. (For a discussion of these matters see Eades 1983, ch 4.)

In this chapter I focus on one area of contemporary southern Aboriginal culture and social action — how people talk about their future actions. In order to understand what people mean when they talk about the future, we need first to look at Aboriginal views of time, and the extent to which the future can be predicted or affected.

3.4 Time and the future

[Many] Aboriginal people operate with different notions of time from whites. In pre-contact time, the passing of time was marked by seasonal, geographical and social events. Chronological, seriated time marking and reference were not used. [This] way of viewing time persists [in some ways] today, so that, for example, people talk about events which happened *when Johnny was as big as this little one now*, or *in the winter time*, or *last time Auntie Daisy was in town*, or less specifically, *a long time ago*.

Similarly, while many people now wear watches and have to use clock and calendar time within the mainstream Australian society, within their own Aboriginal in-group, future time reference is frequently either vague or tied to some seasonal or social event, such as *...when it's a bit cooler*, or *...after Billy comes home*.

[Many] Aboriginal people today are not much concerned with or interested in the measurement of time (e.g. by clocks and calendars), nor with regulating their lives by such. Within [some] Aboriginal [societies] the concept of punctuality [is not important], and while [many] people widely recognise this as a significant element in white society, they frequently ignore it in their dealings with whites. Thus, although there is a widespread stereotype among non-Aboriginal people of 'Aboriginal time' as implying 'always late', [some] Aboriginal people are, in fact, sometimes very early for specific white events such as a doctor's appointment or church service.

See Sections 1.5.3 and 4.2 for further discussion of this topic.

[Many] Aboriginal people, even in southern capital cities, are not embedded in the system of wage labour (Aboriginal unemployment in southern Australia [in the late 1970s was] estimated to be over 50 per cent by Altman and Nieuwenhuysen 1979, p. 125). And further, [many] Aboriginal people do not share the [stereotypical Protestant] work ethic. They work for economic survival where necessary, and to achieve social and political goals. Within many Aboriginal families there is still a relaxed, unscheduled approach to time and the feeling that what doesn't happen today will happen some other day. The highest values are placed on social and political relations, rather than for example, achieved status. Spending time with one's relatives is possibly the highest priority in Aboriginal life.

To understand the way Aboriginal people talk about future action, we need to understand Aboriginal perspectives on the predictability and control of the physical and social world. While not wishing to reproduce the stereotype of 'the-noble-savage-in-harmony-with-nature', I nevertheless claim that there are ways in which Aboriginal [world views] differ significantly from the [mainstream] world view, in that the former sees much of the world as unchangeable. Aboriginal scholars Eric Willmot, Michael Williams and Steve Albert[4] all contrast the European view of the physical world which needs to be conquered, constantly controlled and modified, with the Aboriginal view which acknowledges that [people have] no power or need to drastically control or modify it. In the European ethic, [people control] the world and science is constantly proving this, with technology in exponentially increasing power. In the Aboriginal ethic, the world was made by Ancestral Beings whose spirits must not be disturbed by changing the physical world. Not only is this world uncontrollable, but many aspects of the changing world are also, to a large extent, unpredictable in Aboriginal [societies] (such as the availability of specific resources).

Similarly, in Aboriginal social world[s] much of what happens can be neither predicted nor controlled. People's activities are [often] not organised by schedules. And furthermore, the society is not stratified or hierarchical. It can be argued that there are no permanent structural positions of authority in Aboriginal society (see Sansom 1980). Hamilton's (1981) study of traditional Aboriginal child-rearing shows how babies and young children are rarely subjected to routines, controlled or disciplined. It is only when children reach puberty that they are disciplined at all and expected to accept considerable social restrictions (such as the lack of personal choice in marriage partner). But, aside from such formally fixed prohibitions and restrictions in traditional contexts, Aboriginal society, even in southern Australia, has a very individualistic character, in which people, including children, are considered to be responsible for their own actions. This is seen clearly, for example, in the way alcoholics are treated in Aboriginal society. While people express disapproval of alcoholism, at the same time they laugh at drinkers' jokes, pass them another bottle, look after them when they are sick, and frequently make no efforts to change their drinking habit. People complain, but they still fully accept the drinkers, acknowledging that they are their own masters and in control of their own actions. Aboriginal people consider themselves to be responsible for their own actions and cannot control or predict with certainty the actions of others.

3.5 An example

In talking about their own future actions, Aboriginal people in Southeast Queensland[5] use verb forms which appear to be Standard English forms, e.g.

> I'll come and see you tomorrow.
> I want to come and see you tomorrow.
> They're going to the football.
> I might go and see him.

In Eades (1983, ch 7), I analyse the verbal auxiliaries used by Southeast Queensland Aboriginal people to talk about the future. In this chapter I look at one of these verbal auxiliaries — *will* — and illustrate it with one example. Interested readers are referred to the thesis chapter for a discussion of *will*, *gonna*, *might*, *wanna* and the present tense to talk about future action.

The following conversation is typical of interaction between two Aboriginal people:

> Fred: Auntie May and Jimmy are coming to town tomorrow.
> Kate: Yeah? They gonna stay at your place?[6]
> Fred: Yeah. They gonna stay for a few days.
> Kate: OK, I'll come over tomorrow.

Non-Aboriginal observers could well expect that they have understood this conversation. Fred is telling Kate about two relatives coming to town and staying at his place. Kate decides to come and see them the following day. What would generally not be known by non-Aboriginal people is that Kate's *I'll come over tomorrow* means something like, 'At the moment I intend to come over tomorrow, and if nothing better happens or no-one else turns up, then I will'.

My analysis of the future auxiliaries used by Aboriginal people in Southeast Queensland shows that *will* is used as a prediction of the future, which is always conditional. It is as if it includes an unspoken conditional clause, *if nothing else happens*. It is primarily used with a first person (*I*) as agent, because Aboriginal people can rarely make predictions about others. This is in marked contrast to white society, where such factors as the scheduled nature of [the] lifestyle related to the demands of wage labour society, as well as many authority structures, frequently enable a person to make a well-based prediction about another's future action, for example an employer or teacher.

The less definite form for prediction of future action is *gonna*, which is usually used for non-first person agents (*you*, *he*, etc.), because speakers can be less certain about the future actions of others than their own. It is also used where future action is posited in a question.

Although Kate's utterance above is a prediction about her own future action, it does not in any way commit her to carry out the future action, or to apologise or explain if she does not. However, a similar conversation between white Australian speakers would produce the expectation that if the speaker does not carry out the future action of the *will*-statement, then [this person] would, at some stage, provide some apology, excuse or explanation.

The difference just described may seem trivial at first glance. Aboriginal and non-Aboriginal speakers are using the same forms, to mean more or less the same thing. But in fact, the difference is very significant. Aboriginal people are widely regarded throughout Australia as unreliable with regard to events in the future. One of the most common criticisms of Aboriginal political movements by sympathetic (as well as opposing) whites is that Aboriginal people cannot make plans and cannot organise for future events. Whites also frequently complain of Aboriginal unreliability in keeping to earlier arrangements and commitments. We see this in social workers, employers, school teachers, as well as white people who interact with Aboriginal people as friends, rather than in these service roles.

We form judgments about people largely from their actions. And speaking is one of the most important actions in all societies. (So for example, my greeting of my old friend as 'Mr Miller' could lead him to judge me as being unfriendly.) When an Aboriginal speaker says *I'll come and see you tomorrow*, a non-Aboriginal acquaintance could well judge this person as unreliable if they do not turn up and furthermore give no apology or explanation that day, or later, at the next meeting. But the person was not in fact making a strong commitment. Repeated examples of this kind of misunderstanding over two centuries throughout southern Australia could well be a major reason for the non-Aboriginal view of Aboriginal people as unreliable. Although there is grammatical identity (in Southeast Queensland, at least) in the way in which Aboriginal and non-Aboriginal speakers talk about their own future actions, an understanding of what these utterances mean shows significant differences in attitudes and assumptions. An understanding of what speakers are saying requires an understanding of their conventional expectations and interpretations. This involves an understanding of the sociocultural context, which here includes notions of time and degrees of specificity of time, and the extent to which the future of both the physical and social world can be predicted.

3.6 Conclusion

Ethnographically based sociolinguistics, as outlined and briefly illustrated above, could be a powerful tool in Australia in the next twenty years at least. Crosscultural communication between English-speaking Aboriginal people and non-Aboriginal people is intensifying, not only in informal social settings, but also in political, governmental, educational and judicial arenas. While many Aboriginal people are competent bilingually and biculturally, many choose [whether consciously or unconsciously] to maintain Aboriginal ways of speaking and relating. While distinctively Aboriginal ways are maintained, and non-Aboriginal people are unaware that English is used in Aboriginal ways, there is considerable communication clash and interracial tension. There is much work to be done by sensitive sociolinguists to document, analyse and explain cultural differences between Aboriginal and non-Aboriginal people and the way this affects our understanding of what people say.

For more on bicultural communication see Section 1.5.2.

NOTES

1. I am indebted to the Aboriginal people of Southeast Queensland who have shared so much with me over the last five years. In particular, my thanks go to Michael Williams and his relatives, with whom I carried out the sociolinguistic research on which this chapter is based.
2 I use the term 'Standard English' to refer to the kind of English that is taught in schools, and used in the media, and which provides norms for correction.
3 I use the term 'traditional' to refer to languages which are clearly closely related to languages spoken in pre-contact Aboriginal societies. However, it should be pointed out that English-related Aboriginal language varieties show continuities from pre-contact Aboriginal languages. In this way, these English-based Aboriginal languages can [perhaps] be seen also as 'traditional' [although I restrict the use of this term to those Aboriginal languages which have been spoken since before British invasion and colonisation, and had no connection to English before this time].
4 The views of these scholars on Aboriginal philosophy and world view were presented in the first Aboriginal history course at Macquarie University 1982.
5 Although this example is drawn from my work with Aboriginal people in Southeast Queensland, it appears at this stage to typify language use in a wide range of southern Australian Aboriginal contexts.
6 Note the Aboriginal style of question, discussed in Chapter 2.

Chapter 4

They don't speak an Aboriginal language, or do they?

This chapter was first published in 1988 in a book focused on Aboriginal identity in 'settled Australia' (edited by Ian Keen). Keen used the term 'settled Australia' to refer to the 'closely settled regions of Australia' in which Aboriginal life has been 'most radically transformed by people of European origin' (p. 1), following Rowley (1971). Focusing on people living in Southeast Queensland, this chapter provides sociolinguistic evidence of Aboriginal social life and culture. It highlights the importance of indirectness in many daily interactions, looking specifically at how people use English for these communicative functions: seeking and giving information; making and refusing requests; and seeking and giving reasons for actions. This chapter largely ignores the ways in which bicultural Aboriginal people may interact with non-Aboriginal people, and it should not be read as describing the language and culture of all Aboriginal people in all parts of Australia.

4.1 Introduction[1]

Growing numbers of people in 'settled' Australia who identify as Aboriginal speak varieties of English as their first language. The fact that such people speak little or none of their traditional Aboriginal languages is often used by non-Aboriginal people as evidence that these people are 'not really Aboriginal'. Thus the choice of language variety plays an important role in questions of Aboriginal identity, and therefore in issues of needs and rights in areas such as politics, land rights and education.

First published as Eades, D 1988, 'They don't speak an Aboriginal language, or do they?', in *Being black: Aboriginal cultures in 'settled' Australia*, ed. I Keen, Aboriginal Studies Press, Canberra, pp. 97–115.

In this chapter, I draw on my research in Southeast Queensland, which sheds new light on the relationship between language and identity. While many Aboriginal people may speak English as their first language, the context of conversation has significant Aboriginal cultural and social aspects which lead to distinctively Aboriginal interpretations and meanings. While the chosen language code is frequently English, there are important continuities in the ways language is used. By focussing on aspects of language use I will illustrate some of these continuities, which are significant both in the issue of Aboriginal identity and also in developing more effective crosscultural communication.

Discussions of Aboriginal Australia in the discipline of sociolinguistics have mainly worked from the assumption that language reflects or expresses social and cultural realities. Studies have tended to be restricted to isolated topics in language use, most notably the two areas of kinship terminology and special language varieties. While these topics are important, a broader and interactive view of language illuminates new and important dimensions of cultural continuity. Interactional sociolinguistics works from the assumption that language is much more than a reflection or expression of society and culture; it is a dynamic and creative instrument of social action. Such a theoretical framework is a powerful tool in understanding why people interact with each other in the way they do, their intentions and interpretations. Such a theory can also explain aspects of crosscultural miscommunication in interactions where Aboriginal and non-Aboriginal speakers are using varieties of English.

The framework of this chapter is ethnographically based interactional sociolinguistics. The ethnographic study of society is a necessary pre-requisite for understanding language. We need to understand the sociocultural contexts of speakers and situations, and look beyond isolated instances of language use to the use of language within interactions. Language is impossible to separate from context — it is continually both reflecting and creating aspects of context.

4.2 Aboriginal people in Southeast Queensland

Almost all Aboriginal people in Southeast Queensland today are of mixed descent, and there is still much intermarriage with non-Aborigines. Non-Aboriginal people frequently fail to see beyond skin colour and superficial aspects of lifestyle (including choice of language), and hence mistakenly assume that Aboriginal identity in areas like Southeast Queensland is largely tokenistic.

But the sense of Aboriginal identity remains strong. Although a few people (as elsewhere in Australia) have found it necessary to deny their Aboriginal identity and origins, publicly at least, in order to escape anti-Aboriginal discrimination, it is rare for Aboriginal people to renounce their responsibilities and rights in their Aboriginal society.

Aboriginal people in Southeast Queensland belong to overlapping kin-based networks sharing social life, responsibilities and rights, a common history and culture, an experience of racism, and ethnic consciousness. Social relations are characterised by ongoing family commitments within groups. Barwick's summary of Aboriginal identity (1974, p. 154; 1988) is highly appropriate here: 'To be Aboriginal is to be born to, to belong to, to be loyal to a family.' When people talk about being Aboriginal, they invariably talk about Aboriginal family relationships. Place of residence, travel, social networks, leisure activities and personal loyalties all revolve in some way around one's kin, as other authors in Keen (1988) have found. It is significant that Aboriginal kin involves a wide network of people, many of whom are related only distantly in non-Aboriginal terms.

One of the most important obligations or expectations of kin is that they maintain contact. Although people participate in mainstream Australian social life in many day-to-day activities, they place the highest priority on seeing relatives. The most serious complaints and accusations about people's behaviour usually concern some aspect of family interaction, such as: *She never visits her people*; or *He talks bad to [swears at] his mother when he is drunk.* Such interactional failings generally cause much more concern and bad feeling than incidents such as an illegitimate pregnancy, being sacked from a job, or failing an exam.

While the greatest responsibility is frequently to the nuclear family, family responsibilities are generally applied within a wide range of kin. This applies to the maintaining of social contacts, but also to such areas as the rearing of children, the support of ill or very old people, and the sharing of material resources.

There are many examples of the way in which the wages and benefit payments of Aboriginal individuals are shared between related households. Direct continuity can be seen from pre-contact times, when extended families were provided for by the labour of some of their members, and a young man killing a kangaroo, for example, would be obliged to share certain portions with specific kin. What is more significant than the extent to which resources such as money, housing and car are shared, is the expectation that they will be shared.

This is certainly an area in which both Aboriginal and non-Aboriginal Australians perceive a great cultural difference. It is impossible adequately to understand Aboriginal values, attitudes, intentions and actions without understanding the fundamental pivot of social relationships, particularly between relatives.

When this chapter was first published (1988), many Australians could not afford a television, and many others could only afford a black-and-white set.

Many non-Aboriginal people, for example, find it hard to understand why Aboriginal households invariably have a television set (usually colour), despite serious poverty and extreme lack of material possessions in some instances. But this is an indication of the Aboriginal concern with entertainment not just as a private experience, but as a group activity, rather than, say, with labour saving devices or attractive furniture and furnishings. Perhaps a link could be drawn between contemporary Aboriginal television watching and pre-contact Aboriginal ceremonial life, in which there was generally great passive participation (Christie 1982). Contemporary Aboriginal television watching can also be described as passive participation in that people constantly interject during shows, address actors, and discuss programmes with each other.

Aboriginal unemployment – while much worse than that of the general population – is not nearly as high in 2013 as it was twenty-five years ago when this chapter was first published, with the claim that 'few Aboriginal people in Southeast Queensland subscribe to a work ethic', meaning the stereotypical Protestant work ethic. Further, there have been, and continue to be, many sociopolitical factors involved in Aboriginal unemployment, as highlighted in Marcia Langton's 2012 Boyer Lectures. While it is no longer accurate to say that 'few Aboriginal people in Southeast Queensland subscribe to the stereotypical Protestant work ethic', the generalisations about Aboriginal families subordinating financial and employment priorities to social relations remain relevant to many.

Similarly, contemporary Aboriginal attitudes to employment need to be understood in the light of the priority on developing, maintaining and strengthening complex and overlapping social relationships. Aboriginal unemployment is high. Few Aboriginal people in Southeast Queensland subscribe to [the stereotypical Protestant] work ethic, and although many people are employed at times, their participation is often peripheral. Many place no importance on continual

This is my first use of the term 'bicultural competence', although the concept is briefly introduced at the end of Section 2.2 (and see also Section 1.5.2). In later years I have preferred the term 'bicultural ability', following feedback that some people felt the use of the (sociolinguistic) term 'competence' could lead to negative value judgments. Further, it now seems naïve to speak about bicultural competence/ability in binary terms (as if people either have it or do not have it). The situation with bicultural people parallels that of bilingual and bidialectal people where there can be many kinds and degrees of ability.

employment, and work is generally regarded as an economic necessity, rather than as part of a lifetime plan. Because of the shared financial obligations within family networks, individual unemployment has neither the disastrous financial consequences nor the negative social stigma common to mainstream Australian society. Here again Aboriginal families subordinate financial and employment priorities to the important aspects of social relations.

Non-Aboriginal readers who have dealings with Aboriginal people may be surprised at some of the features discussed in this chapter. It is important to point out that the majority of Aborigines in 'settled' Australia are biculturally competent. Many people choose to operate within white norms in many of their dealings with non-Aborigines, and to use Aboriginal norms, such as those discussed in this chapter, in their own in-group interactions. However, this choice is by no means universal, and much crosscultural interaction is affected by different norms of interaction, in areas such as those discussed here.

4.3 Aboriginal languages in Southeast Queensland

Aboriginal people in Southeast Queensland today primarily speak varieties of English. There is probably no-one from this area of Australia who today speaks an Aboriginal language as a first (or primary) language. Many Aboriginal people are competent users of a number of varieties of English, from which they choose according to aspects of the conversational context.

See Section 1.2 for discussion of the terms 'Aboriginal English' and 'Aboriginal ways of speaking English'.

Many people speak Standard English, particularly in their interactions with white Australians in formal settings, such as education, government, health and legal arenas. However, while many Aboriginal people throughout Australia are fluent speakers of Standard English, cultural factors affecting language use can lead to differing interpretations, as I will show below. As well, most Aboriginal people speak different varieties of Aboriginal English in different Aboriginal contexts. But there is considerable variability in the Aboriginal English spoken in Southeast Queensland, as throughout Australia.

Aboriginal English reflects grammatically the structure of traditional Aboriginal languages, for example, the plural –s marking on nouns in English is frequently absent in Aboriginal English (e.g. *one dog*, *two dog*). This is a reflection of the traditional Aboriginal languages in which plural is rarely overtly marked. Such features have led to a widespread tendency among non-Aboriginal Australians to regard Aboriginal English as a deficient variety of English, but it is important to point out that Aboriginal English is in no way an inferior language. It is a perfectly adaptable, rule-governed language. Some grammatical variations are simpler than the corresponding Standard English structures, such as the plural markings on nouns, and the equational sentence structure which differs from Standard English equivalents by the absence of a verb *to be* (e.g. *Where Johnny?*), but other variations are more complex. For example, the second person pronoun in Standard English is *you*, regardless of its reference to singular or non-singular participants, but, in Aboriginal English, there is a distinction between: *you* (second person singular); *you two*, *you-n(h)im* (second person dual); and *you mob* (second person plural). These pronouns also reflect the grammatical category distinctions of traditional Aboriginal languages.

Many Aboriginal people, speaking varieties of both Standard English and Aboriginal English, use Aboriginal language words [many of which are found in quite a few languages], for example:

> Move your big *jinung* [foot].
> Dog *goonung* [faeces] over there.
> Look out — *boolimun* [policemen] coming.

This style of speaking is common throughout Australia and is an important 'badge' of Aboriginal identity (see Schwab 1988).

The traditional Aboriginal languages (such as Gooreng Gooreng, Wakka Wakka, Wuilli Wuilli, Kabi Kabi and Butchella) are still spoken in some restricted contexts, mainly by older people. For several generations people were actively discouraged from, and on some government reserves even punished for, using their Aboriginal languages. Today it is quite rare for non-Aborigines to hear

Aboriginal languages being spoken in Southeast Queensland. However, Lingo (the local Aboriginal name for these languages) is still fulfilling a social function. It is used mainly by older people, either to chastise someone, or else to exclude someone from their conversation — be they a non-Aboriginal researcher, a policeman, or an Aborigine from another part of Queensland. It is also used as a polite, euphemistic form of language to talk about private topics such as pregnancy or urinating. It is not uncommon for older people to switch from speaking English to short but fluent conversations in Lingo and then back into English. These traditional Aboriginal languages in Southeast Queensland are thus not dead, even though they may be barely elicitable by linguists. They are fulfilling a social function in some restricted contexts.

4.4 Language as a part of culture

The Aboriginal priority on developing, maintaining and strengthening social relationships is both reflected in, and created by, the way people speak to each other, whether the language variety is English, Aboriginal English or Lingo.

We saw above that it is important for Aboriginal people to know a wide-ranging group of relatives, to know in detail how they are related and to maintain contact with many relatives. There are several aspects of language use which indicate the importance of these family obligations. It will be seen from discussion of these aspects that they do more than indicate the importance of these obligations, or reflect an existing reality. It is partly through the use of certain ways of speaking that these family obligations are actually fulfilled and maintained. These ways of speaking are creative social actions integral to the continuity of Aboriginal society and culture. This creative aspect of language usage is illustrated here with kinship terms of address, and the conversational avoidance of certain relatives.

4.4.1 USE OF KIN TERMS

Within the extended family, there is widespread use of English terms of address, such as *cuz* (cousin), *auntie* and *uncle*. Unlike the situation in most non-Aboriginal Australian families, the use of these terms is not restricted to children. *Auntie* and *uncle* tend to be used between any Aboriginal adults and their higher generation relatives. Some young Aboriginal adults, particularly those who marry non-Aboriginal spouses, stop using *auntie* and *uncle* and this causes considerable concern. Such behaviour [is sometimes seen as] not only a lack of respect for older relatives, but also cultural breakdown. It is important in Aboriginal culture to acknowledge respect due to older people, even by mature adults. Age [often] brings power and wisdom in Aboriginal culture in 'settled' Australia, just as in traditionally oriented Australia (Berndt & Berndt 1964).

While it is generally English kin terms that are used, there are some continuities with traditional language kin categories and terms of address, such as the following examples, discussed by Williams (1981), which are English translations of traditional labels: *cousin brother* is used sometimes by parallel cousins to address their male parallel cousins; and *daughter* is used by some children to address their great-grandmother.

The use of *cuz* appears to be frequent between same-generation relatives, no matter how distant. Its use is an important part of ongoing Aboriginal culture in places like Southeast Queensland, where Aboriginal people live and work in such a large-scale society. Links with one's own kin are still seen as important and as able to transcend non-Aboriginal social structures into which Aboriginal people are drawn. For example in bureaucratically structured Aboriginal organisations and government departments Aboriginal people work, have meetings, and decide policies with a wide range of other Aboriginal people from all over Australia. But within these bureaucratic structures and ways of operating many elements of Aboriginal culture persist. One such element is the loyalty to kin. Thus the use of the term of address *cuz* in a meeting or a tutorial in a tertiary institution, for instance, both maintains and reminds Aboriginal participants of a speaker's relationship to another participant and the accompanying rights and responsibilities. Whereas in pre-colonial times this might have encompassed food provision and child-rearing, in the 1980s it includes such dimensions as loyalty in voting, and assistance with assignment work, as well as financial and family responsibilities.

4.4.2 AVOIDANCE BEHAVIOUR

It is not only the actual words people use which reflect and create continuities of Aboriginal culture. In contemporary Aboriginal society, we see continuities of traditional norms concerning who an individual can speak to and in what ways.

Avoidance behaviour between particular in-laws in Aboriginal societies is well documented in the anthropological literature (e.g. Berndt & Berndt 1964). In many Aboriginal societies special language varieties were used between certain relatives (see Dixon 1971; Harris 1970). Haviland (1979a, 1979b) describes avoidance speech behaviour between certain relatives in Hopevale (a North Queensland community) as part of a range of avoidance behaviours which includes eye contact, posture, and restrictions on physical contact and on the sharing of food and possessions.

Older people in Southeast Queensland today remember that there was strict avoidance between a man and his mother-in-law until about the 1950s. They remember that in their childhood a man would never directly address, face toward, or give food to, his mother-in-law. Conversations between a man and his mother-in-law would take place through a third, intermediary person in a stylised way. One woman told me how her mother never ate at the family table when her husband was present. On these occasions she ate at the small table made specially by her husband for his mother-in-law to eat at.

While many Aboriginal families today no longer observe such strict avoidance, there is still some continuity in that many men avoid direct conversations with their mothers-in-law. The literature would indicate reasons to interpret such avoidance as not simply identical with the frequent mainstream antagonism, but as based on long standing Aboriginal traditions of respect-based avoidance. One such form that I have frequently observed in a particular country town concerns a man in his sixties with a bad leg who often walks about two kilometres to town. On the way he often passes his mother-in-law's house where he sometimes rests. However, he never enters the house, but rests in the shed out the back. They rarely, if ever, speak to each other.

We have glimpsed the way Aboriginal culture is created and reflected through ways of speaking. To put it another way, the use of language is an integral part of social action which is distinctively Aboriginal. Even though English is the language spoken by Aboriginal people in many parts of Australia, social aspects of the way it is used reflect and help to maintain and create a culture which is Aboriginal and which shows continuities with traditional Aboriginal cultures.

4.5 Further examination of the language-culture relationship

Ethnographically based interactional sociolinguistics enables us to go beyond the realm of kinship terminology and avoidance languages in the examination of the language–culture relationship and the continuity of Aboriginal culture. In this section I focus on the way Aboriginal people in Southeast Queensland use English to achieve certain social ends — namely making and refusing requests, seeking and giving information, and seeking and giving reasons for actions. But to understand these interrelated uses of language we first need some insight into aspects of the sociocultural context of speakers. We will look first at the public nature of Aboriginal social life, and the role of indirectness in social interactions.

4.5.1 THE ROLE OF INDIRECTNESS

Aboriginal social life is very public. Traditional Aboriginal society has no walls and, as Hamilton (1981, p. 97) puts it, 'No particular value [is] placed on privacy in camp'. Although Aboriginal people in 'settled' Australia live in quite different physical settings from those in traditional Australia, their social life is still very public. In the cities, towns and reserves people live very close to one another and their day-to-day activities are public. Small houses accommodate large families, or many members of an extended family, and by non-Aboriginal standards are frequently over-crowded. There is a communal, non-private nature to this style of living. As well, much day-to-day living takes place in open, outside areas, such as the main street of towns, in public places, and (in country towns particularly) on the verandahs of houses. The importance of verandahs in country town and reserve Aboriginal social life cannot be over-emphasised. Here people regularly sit for long periods, observing the comings and goings of others around them and passing on reports of other people's activities. Modes of transport are highly public too. Because people often walk, they are easily observed and they often bear reports between households. Cars frequently travel with full passenger loads, stopping at different houses to exchange passengers and news. The fact that many cars are also noisy enables people's movements to be easily observed. As well as this close lifestyle in physical, spatial terms, Aboriginal people live close lives socially, through complex and wide-ranging kin ties which are constantly maintained and strengthened in social interaction.

In such a public society, we can ask whether there is any privacy at all. To answer this question we need to look at norms and expectations of Aboriginal relationships. Here we find a dimension of personal privacy not common in non-Aboriginal Australia. The Aboriginal way of interacting indirectly preserves a considerable degree of personal privacy. In a number of aspects of conversation, Aboriginal people tend to be much more indirect than non-Aboriginal people. Even where the same language variety (e.g. Standard English) is used, there are cultural differences in usage which both reflect and continually create and maintain indirectness in social interactions.

Several researchers have discussed the norm in traditional Aboriginal societies of avoiding direct confrontation and respecting a greater personal privacy than is usual in non-Aboriginal society. Von Sturmer (1981, p. 29) says that for whites talking to Aborigines, 'the need for caution and circumspection' is 'the primary consideration'. Similarly, Harris (1984) reports that one of the most significant factors of conversations in Milingimbi (Arnhem Land) is the avoidance of direct verbal confrontation. The work of Liberman (1981; 1982a; 1982b, p. 1) examines the way Western Desert Aborigines structure discussions so that consensus can be preserved:

> The preservation of this consensus is achieved by the unassertiveness of participants, avoidance of direct argumentation, a deferral of topics which will produce disharmony, and above all, by an objectification of discourse which is effected by a serial production of summary accounts of the participants' deliberations.

I have observed similar conversational strategies among Aboriginal people in Southeast Queensland. In many interactions these people do not express a firm or biased opinion, even if they hold it. They may discuss a topic generally while gauging others' views, before stating their own. If people find their views on a topic to be at odds with others in a conversation, they will tend to understate their own. In minimising confrontation and argument, the speaker leaves open the possibility for further comfortable discussion. What Liberman (1982b, p. 2) explains as 'a strict refusal to force a way of thinking upon others' can also appear as a refusal to state one's position openly in a particular discussion. Thus, many meetings in which Aboriginal and non-Aboriginal people discuss contentious issues involves more than the expected crosscultural tension. Part of the tension is due to the different ways in which different or conflicting viewpoints are presented. It is an appropriate communicative strategy in European–Australian meetings to present clearly a viewpoint which is directly contrary to that of the previous speaker. Aboriginal speakers are more likely to present some similar viewpoint first, leaving the more significant conflicting viewpoint for a later opportunity. Because of the differences in timing, misunderstanding often occurs. Aboriginal speakers often feel they are not given enough time to speak, and to develop their viewpoint. As well they often feel that non-Aboriginal participants are confrontationist in the way they present their ideas. Non-Aboriginal speakers often feel that Aboriginal speakers are not clear in expressing their views — Aboriginal indirectness and circumspection is often interpreted as inarticulateness and the lack of a logical argument.

Von Sturmer's (1981, p. 29) discussion of Aboriginal caution and circumspection also points out the strategy of 'not presenting oneself too forcefully and not linking oneself too closely with one's own ideas'. He discusses the use of the expression *might be* (as a modal qualifier) to distance the speaker from the certainty of the idea he is presenting. Similarly Aboriginal speakers often preface their views with comments such as *This is just what I think*. Disclaimers such as these point to a fundamental cultural view that an Aboriginal person can speak only for themselves. Western-style democracy and notions of representation impose many difficulties on Aboriginal ways of expressing opinions.

The importance of indirectness in much daily conversational interaction is shown by examining the way Aboriginal people in Southeast Queensland use English for the following communicative functions: to seek and give information, to make and refuse requests, and to seek and give reasons.

4.5.2 SEEKING AND GIVING INFORMATION

In Chapter 2 I have discussed the ways in which Aboriginal people in Southeast Queensland obtain information. To summarise briefly, information-seeking is part of a two-way exchange in which people give information in order to get information. A distinction is made between orientation information and substantial information. Orientation information is defined as 'information which clarifies a topic' (often the current topic of conversation). The information sought comprises background details about people especially, but also about the time, place and setting of some situation or narrated event (see Section 2.5).

Direct questions are used to elicit orientation information, for example: *Where you from?*, or *Who's his mother?*. However, the form of the question frequently presents certain information, but with question intonation (or a following interrogative tag). This form of question, referred to in some studies of Aboriginal English as 'uninverted question forms' (e.g. Dwyer 1974, p. 17), is a linguistic strategy consistent with the indirectness typical of much Aboriginal conversation. Rather than directly ask for information, the questioner presents some proposition for confirmation or correction, for example: *That's his brother?*

or *Grandfather used to live at Tirroan?*. These orientation questions play an important interactional role in Aboriginal society. They are an essential part of the development and maintenance of social links. In constantly finding out about another's kin, movements, and country, an Aboriginal person is creating or maintaining closeness. Such a process is common between Aboriginal people all over Australia, whether in English, or English related languages, or traditional Aboriginal languages.

In Chapter 2 we saw that the common Aboriginal question, *Where are you going?* (or its language equivalent such as *Woonju ngin yun.gim* in Gooreng Gooreng) is interactionally equivalent to 'Hullo', 'Hi' or 'Gidday' in non-Aboriginal Australia. It is common for Aboriginal people to greet each other with this question. Orientation questions serve an important role in developing and maintaining social links, in locating participants in a conversation in a sociospatial relationship, and indeed in finding out information. We will see further that orientation questions can also be intended and interpreted in other ways, for example, as requests or inquiries after the reasons for actions.

While questions can be used to seek orientation information, they are not used to seek substantial information, such as important personal details, a full account of an event, or the explanation of some event or situation. In these situations indirect strategies are used: the speaker contributes some of their own knowledge on a topic and then leaves a silence, to lead the person with the knowledge to impart information. Important aspects of substantial information-seeking are the two-way exchange of information, the positive, non-awkward use of silence, and often considerable time delays (frequently several days) between the initiation of substantial information-seeking and the imparting of information.

4.5.3 MAKING AND REFUSING REQUESTS

[Many] Aboriginal people rarely make direct requests. The most common ways of asking someone either to do something, or to give or loan something, involve indirect, multifunctional forms. That is, a question might serve several of the functions outlined above, including that of a request. For example, [a common] Aboriginal way of asking for a ride is to ask a car owner an orientation question, such as *You going to town?* or *What time are you leaving?*. These questions are multifunctional, structurally ambiguous and, depending on the relationship between speakers, communicatively ambiguous. That is, these questions can be interpreted as part of the information seeking involved in sociospatial orientation, but they can also be interpreted as a request for a ride. Appropriate interpretation cannot be made without understanding the relationship between speakers. But even if speakers understand such questions as requests for a ride, the ambiguity enables a person to refuse a request in a similar indirect fashion, for example by saying, *might be later*, or *not sure*. In this way, Aboriginal people can work out requests and refusals without directly exposing their motives.

Such indirect strategies are of course not restricted to Aboriginal conversations. Non-Aboriginal people use such ways of making requests and refusals in sensitive situations. What is significant about the Aboriginal use of these strategies is that they are not restricted to sensitive situations, but are the usual everyday ways of interaction in which indirectness is the norm.

4.5.4 SEEKING AND GIVING REASONS

One of the most striking features of language use by [many] Aboriginal people in Southeast Queensland is the virtual absence of the reason-seeking question 'why'. People use *why* and *what for* to make complaints, as in: *What you come to me for? I got no money*. But there is no direct way of questioning a person's reasons. However, this is not to say that Aboriginal people are not curious, as they are constantly using ways of speaking to find out reasons for states of affairs. In seeking reasons, people elicit statements of fact, which they accumulate over time and interpret as reasons. The multifunctional forms discussed above also serve to seek reasons for actions. In seeking information, speakers are also seeking the evidence with which they can assume reasons for the actions of others.

For example, in trying to find out why a teenage girl was late home, her grannie would never ask: *Why were you late home last night?*. Instead, she would begin by establishing her granddaughter's whereabouts: *Where you went last night?*; or by assuming her whereabouts and querying this fact: *You were at the pub last night?*. Then, to find out why the granddaughter was at the pub, her grannie would ask: *Bill there too?*. By using a series of orientation questions, the old woman would establish reasons for the granddaughter arriving home late. There is no obligation on Aboriginal speakers to answer questions such as these, however the granddaughter would be well aware that her grannie was trying to establish reasons for her actions and she would usually give some answers to enable her grannie to establish some acceptable reasons. But the responsibility is on the person interpreting reasons, and the person being questioned does not have to account directly for their reasons. Again multifunctional forms make the requests for reasons indirect and ambiguous and give people considerable privacy. They are never confronted with an inescapable request for a reason, such as the question 'why'.

It is clear that strategies for seeking reasons for actions are indirect. A further technique which lessens direct verbal contact is the inquiry about reasons by a third person. Again the style of questioning is basically the presenting of an assumed fact or facts to a third person in an interrogative mode. Of course, this third person may then assume this fact to be true, and pass it on to a fourth person and so on. Indeed, because reasons are assumed so regularly, unfounded explanations are frequently circulated. However, because these explanations are expressed as facts or assumed facts, rather than as facts with undeniable reasons, speakers are not held accountable.

In reporting facts learned from another party, Aboriginal speakers have a range of expressions available which indicate the speculative nature of the reporting statement. When the speaker is disclaiming responsibility for the truth of the statement, one of the following is frequently used:

> *must have* — as in *He must have been after that woman*;
> *must be* — as in *They must be still at the pub*;
> *reckons* — as in *Kit reckons that man's still at the pub*; and
> *might be* — as in *They gone fishin? Might be.*
> (These qualifying forms are also used to protect one's commitment to future action; see Eades 1983.)

Non-verbal actions, such as observation, are important strategies for finding out reasons for the actions of others. In [some Aboriginal societies], there [appear to be] no sanctions against direct observation of the observable actions of others, including staring. The situation is rather the reverse in white society where there is a strong prohibition against staring at the observable actions of others. This prohibition is further supported by the privatised nature of white society. Much interaction takes place in enclosed areas and is secluded from public observation, as indicated by the expression concerning 'the four walls'. However, there is a wide range of contexts in which it is quite appropriate to question others' actions and reasons directly. On the other hand, in Aboriginal society people have direct and uninterrupted observational access to many day-to-day interactions, but the direct questioning of reasons is prohibited.

Just as the seeking of reasons uses multifunctional forms, so too does the expression of reasons. While the Standard English reason connectors, such as *because* and *to*, are sometimes used by Aboriginal speakers, it is much more common to give reasons for actions simply as statements, or by using the multifunctional connector *and*. For example, a woman advising another woman to be careful on a long trip, and to keep the driver awake, said,

> *You get too tired, you wanna camp on the road you know. Don't travel, he might go to sleep, he must be knocked up too you know. Camp on the road. I'll give you a stick. You give him a poke in the ribs, keep him awake.*

This extract could be translated with Standard English reason connectors as,

> If you get too tired, you should camp on the road you know. Don't travel, because he might go to sleep, because he must be knocked up too you know, so camp on the road. I'll give you a stick so you can give him a poke in the ribs to keep him awake.

As there is frequently no unambiguous linguistic marker of reason, Aboriginal speakers depend on aspects of context to interpret statements as reasons. Specifically they rely on that element of context which is derived from their sharing of experiences and knowledge.

Linguistic forms which express reasons, then, also serve other communicative functions at the same time. In particular, while giving information, speakers are also expressing reasons for action. Being structurally (but not always pragmatically) ambiguous, this way of expressing reasons leaves speakers not directly accountable for their motives. In Aboriginal conversations the responsibility for the interpretation of an utterance as a reason rests with the hearer. The speaker has no responsibility to encode an utterance as a reason. The hearer must interpret structurally ambiguous utterances in the light of knowledge shared with the speaker, but the speaker is free to keep utterances pragmatically ambiguous and leave the hearer with insufficient knowledge to disambiguate.

Thus in the expression of motives and reasons, speakers have a great personal freedom and privacy. It is the responsibility of hearers to infer causal links between statements. If hearers do not share enough knowledge with the speaker to do so, they need to initiate investigations, in the indirect ways discussed above.

AN EXAMPLE

To illustrate the seeking and giving of reasons, let me quote at some length an interaction which I witnessed and audio-recorded in a country town in Southeast Queensland. It is a good example of Aboriginal indirectness in the giving and seeking of reasons. Central to the Aboriginal style of seeking reasons are:

1. observations of movements, preferably from some public position — in this example, the verandah;
2. the gathering of evidence over time;
3. indirect questioning which overtly does not query anything more than the orientation of participants to events;
4. the norm that a person being questioned has no obligation to provide information, and can subvert the questioning with non-cooperative replies, such as untruths and, in this example, vague replies or silence; and
5. the repetition of assumed and observed facts to a third person.

Features 1 and 5 above are part of the public nature of Aboriginal life, while features 3 and 4 contribute to the privacy of Aboriginal individuals.

In a house where I frequently stayed in a small country town, Janey (an elderly woman) had been keenly observing the movements of Sally (her teenage granddaughter)[2]. In gathering evidence and making assumptions, Janey had made at least a few factual errors of which I was aware. For example, one day Sally was in town for quite a longer period of time than usual. Janey remarked to me, *She must have met Tom.* Now Janey was encouraging Sally to marry Tom, so she was pleased with any evidence of their being together. However, when Sally came home she told me she had had lunch with a girl friend. It seemed she had not seen Tom at all. A few days later Janey and I went out early in the morning. When we returned in the mid afternoon, no-one was home. Janey told me, *Sally must have gone out with Tom.* We resumed our positions on the front verandah and observed the comings and goings in the town. After some time we saw Molly's (Sally's sister's) car coming up the road. Janey was surprised because Molly's car usually came to bring Sally home. Janey said to me, *There Molly. Where Sally? Sally sitting there? Have a look.* I confirmed that Sally was there. When the car pulled up, Sally came up to the verandah and immediately told us, *I won on the races today.* This was followed by a short conversation on Sally's winnings in which the first person singular pronoun was used several times, indicating that her actions were not with Tom. In fact, Tom was not mentioned at all.

In the next exchange, which is quoted below, Janey (J) tried to establish the reason why Sally (S) didn't go with Tom. Janey's linguistic strategy was that of orientation questioning. In Turns 1 and 3 she queries assumed information; in Turn 5 she repeats information given by Sally; and in Turn 7 she uses a standard form of question (discussed in Chapter 2). Janey begins:

1. J: Oh youself, youself went there?
2. S: Yeah.
3. J: Didn you go with Tom out there?
4. S: No, he went fishin with Mick.
5. J: Tom did?
6. S: Yeah.
7. J: Where they went?
8. S: I dunno – somewhere.
9. J: Oh.

Janey was successful in finding out a reason why Sally and Tom did not go out together, but she was not successful in finding out why Tom went fishing. Sally successfully avoided giving any further information with her non-committal answer in Turn 8. (Note that while the relationship between grandmother and granddaughter in Aboriginal society places the granddaughter under certain obligations, such as cooking for her grandmother, they do not extend to giving information. The right to deny information appears to cut cross all kin obligations.)

The conversation turned to Janey telling Sally about our day and then the three of us played with Sally's baby. But the reason for Sally and Tom not going out together was still a concern to Janey. After some time, when Sally took her baby inside to bath her, Janey said to me in a surprised tone, *Wonder she didn go with Tom*. Later that afternoon Tom (T) arrived and Janey was able to continue her indirect investigations. Again she used orientation questioning, filling in background details in Turn 10 and using the audience participation strategy of repetition in Turn 14. Again the person being questioned (Tom) was under no obligation to provide factual information. Janey asks:

10. J: Catch any fish, Tom?
11. T: No, I didn get there.
12. J: Eh?
13. T: I didn get there.
14. J: You didn go there?
15. T: No.
16. J: Oh, I thought you went with Mick and Anne.
(Silence)

Tom made no further comment and then had a very quiet conversation with Sally on the steps of the verandah, which Janey observed. Later Janey joked with me about *them two fighting*. Her comments to me about the situation were made in an ambiguous causal manner, but knowing the Southeast Queensland Aboriginal mode of giving reasons, I understood that Janey had determined the reason Sally and Tom had not gone out together was because they were having a disagreement.

4.6 Conclusion

Many non-Aboriginal people feel that people like Janey and her family are 'not really Aboriginal', because of their relatively light skin colour and superficial similarity to many non-Aboriginal Australians in such aspects as language, dress, housing and employment. A traditional linguistic or static sociolinguistic analysis would do little to demonstrate continuities in Aboriginal ways of believing and acting in places like Southeast Queensland. But, ironically, while many people in 'settled' Australia deny any real or distinctive Aboriginality, many people, both Aboriginal and non-Aboriginal, perceive communication differences and difficulties (see Chapter 3). For example, Aboriginal people often complain that whites are rude, nosey, impatient and ask too many questions. And whites often complain that Aboriginal people are shy, ignorant, slow and uncooperative.

In this chapter, I have used ethnographic interactional sociolinguistics to explain some of these differences, thus providing evidence of continuing Aboriginality in Southeast Queensland. Furthermore, I have shown that it is impossible to understand language without understanding its social and cultural context. This chapter has examined some significant aspects of the social and cultural context of Aboriginal people in Southeast Queensland today, which reflect continuities from traditional Aboriginal cultures. These aspects, such as the importance of responsibilities to kin, the priority of social relationships, and the need for indirectness in interactions, are both reflected in, and continually created by, the ways in which people interact. Speaking is an important part of such interaction. It is in everyday conversational interaction, such as the giving and seeking of reasons for actions, that we can see significant evidence of Aboriginal cultural continuity. Understanding such cultural continuity is essential to any effective communication between Aboriginal and non-Aboriginal people in 'settled' Australia.

NOTES

1. This chapter is based on the research for my PhD thesis (Eades 1983) which was carried out between 1978 and 1983 with a number of Aboriginal families in Southeast Queensland. I am indebted to the people who shared their culture and lives with me. In particular, my thanks go to Michael Williams and his relatives for enabling me to be involved in the family research and for teaching me so much about Aboriginality. Many colleagues provided comments on my writings, and in particular I am grateful to Ian Keen for his encouragement and helpful criticism on both the thesis and this chapter.
2. All personal names in this chapter are pseudonyms.

Chapter 5

Aboriginal English

This chapter was first published in 1993 — the International Year of the World's Indigenous Peoples — as a short introduction to Aboriginal English for primary school teachers of English. Thus, this chapter is unable to provide scholarly depth, and it generalises from research at that time that had investigated varieties of Aboriginal English in parts of Western Australia, the Northern Territory, Queensland and New South Wales. An example of the use of 'strategic essentialism', discussed in Section 1.5.2, this chapter should not be read as describing the language and culture of all Aboriginal people in all parts of Australia. Further, in discussing commonly found patterns of language and communication among Aboriginal people who speak varieties of English as their first language, this chapter largely ignores the ways in which bicultural Aboriginal people may interact with non-Aboriginal people. Readers are referred to the work of Ian Malcolm and Farzad Sharifian and their colleagues for important work on Aboriginal English in education, which goes considerably beyond this introductory chapter (see Chapter 1, Further Reading).

5.1 Introduction

Appropriately, in the International Year of the World's Indigenous Peoples, this PEN (*Primary English Notes*) focuses on a number of issues concerning Aboriginal children and English language teaching in primary schools — namely:

- What English language skills and strengths do Aboriginal children bring to school?

First published as: Eades, D 1993, 'Aboriginal English', *Primary English Notes* (PEN) 93, Primary English Teachers Association, Sydney.

- What are the English language needs of these children in our primary schools?
- In what ways is their English different from the English of other Australian primary school children?
- To what extent can these differences shed light on a variety of difficulties that teachers may experience in teaching Aboriginal children?

In answering these questions, I shall offer an explanation of dialectal differences between Aboriginal English and Standard Australian English (referring to them by the abbreviations AE and SE respectively). Even if you are not teaching Aboriginal children, most of you will be teaching English and so are likely to be interested in finding out more about the linguistic diversity of Australian dialects of English.

5.2 What are dialectal differences?

Have you ever heard an Aboriginal person saying something like the following sentences?

This a ard one.
E in ospital.

Speakers of SE would express these sentences differently:

'This is a hard one.'
'He's in hospital.'
or
'He is in hospital.'

The original version of this chapter used an apostrophe to indicate omitted h *in AE words like* 'ard *(= SE 'hard'). Linguists have moved away from this convention. While it might make it easier for SE readers to recognise the word, it evokes a deficit view of AE. That is, it encourages a view that AE speakers have left out a sound, rather than a view of two equal and closely related versions of the word.*

The differences are small, and it is rare for a non-Aboriginal listener to be confused by such variations. However, the Aboriginal person's way of speaking is often considered to be 'bad English', 'lazy English' or 'incorrect English'; you might think that he or she has left out an important little word, or a part of a word or a sound. That's an interesting reaction, because it's exactly what a speaker of Standard American English would think on hearing the SE versions. The Standard American English versions of these sentences would be:

> 'This is a hard one.'
> 'He's in the hospital.' or 'He is in the hospital.'

Because SE speakers don't pronounce the –r– sound in the word 'hard' and don't use the word 'the' when talking about going to hospital in general, the SE versions will sound funny or incorrect to many speakers of American English.

These examples show us that little differences between ways of speaking English are often specific to a particular social or regional group. They are differences of dialect, and one of the tasks of linguists is to examine dialectal variation in different kinds of English all over the world.

It should be noted that the term 'dialect' is used here in a neutral way, as it always is by linguists. It does not have pejorative connotations, and it does not refer to kinds of English that are without a literary tradition or are spoken by uneducated people. Rather it refers to different ways of saying the same thing that are shared by social or regional groups of people. A dialect is a variety of language that:

- can be understood by speakers of other varieties of the same language; and
- differs from other varieties of the same language in systematic ways (these differences can be found in sounds, grammar, words and their meanings, and language use).

Australian dialects of English include Standard Australian English, Aboriginal English and non-standard Australian English. Examples of other dialects of English are Standard British English, Scottish English, Irish English, Standard American English and Black American English. Aboriginal English, like the other dialects of English, is not the same over all the region in which it is spoken; in other words, there are regional differences. Standard English (whether Australian, British or American) has no linguistic status or characteristic which separates it from all of the other dialects of English. It is simply the dialect of English which is spoken by the more powerful, dominant groups in society, and which has therefore become the language of education, the media, government and the law. Or, as Trudgill (1983, p. 17) puts it:

> Standard English is that variety of English which is usually used in print, and which is normally taught in schools and to

non-native speakers learning the language. It is also the variety which is normally spoken by educated people, and used in news broadcasts and other similar situations. The difference between standard and non-standard, it should be noted, has nothing in principle to do with differences between formal and colloquial language, or with concepts such as 'bad language'. Standard English has colloquial as well as formal variants, and standard English speakers swear as much as others.

5.3 What is Aboriginal English?

Aboriginal English is the name given to dialects of English which are spoken by Aboriginal people and which differ from Standard English in systematic ways. The historical development of Aboriginal English is fascinating because it demonstrates how Aboriginal people have adapted their ways of communicating to English. It is impossible to give more than a simplified summary of the development here, but interested readers are referred to Kaldor and Malcolm (1991).

It seems that there were about 250 languages spoken in this country before the British invasion, with at least 600 distinct dialects. The differences between neighbouring languages were often similar to the differences between, say, English and Spanish. And the languages were complex, with the 'easy' ones matching Latin in their complexity!

The great majority of the invaders were reluctant to learn any of the Aboriginal languages. So, from the time of their first contacts with the British, Aboriginal people began to use some English in their dealings with them (Troy 1993). With Aboriginal and British people trying to communicate with each other in English, a simplified kind of language developed, used only between Aboriginal and non-Aboriginal people in situations of limited contact. This kind of English is referred to as 'pidgin English'. Within a few generations this pidgin began to develop an important communicative function between different Aboriginal groups who did not have a shared traditional language, and so it expanded linguistically. The social and linguistic development of early pidgin gave birth to Aboriginal dialects of English all over the country, as well as to two creole languages in some northern areas.

In some areas, however, it appears that Aboriginal English developed not from pidgin English but from the Aboriginalisation of English as speakers learnt the language. In other words, Aboriginal people in areas where there was no pidgin language made English into an Aboriginal English by bringing into it accents, grammar and ways of speaking from their traditional languages. It should be noted that it is linguistically inaccurate and derogatory to use the term 'pidgin English' to refer to the kinds of English spoken by Aboriginal people today.

While most of the rest of this chapter is about Aboriginal dialects of English, a brief account of the creole languages mentioned above is included at the end. A creole language is a type of language which develops when a pidgin language expands its structures and functions to become the first language of speakers, not just a language of contact between people who do not share the same first language. To distinguish the Aboriginal creole from other creoles which have arisen in similar circumstances in other parts of the world, it has been given the distinctive name 'Kriol'.

5.4 But isn't it just uneducated English?

Since this article was first published, it's been pointed out that the heading in this section is misleading. It would have been better to omit the word 'just'. I never intended to imply that AE is 'uneducated English', and my meaning would have been clearer if I had used quotation marks around 'just uneducated English' to signal that it is the (mistaken) belief of some people.

A more recent report on Aboriginal languages (HRSCATSIA 2012) estimates that there are currently 'about 18 languages' which are 'strong', in the sense of being spoken by significant numbers of people across all age groups.

To people not trained in linguistic and sociolinguistic analysis, it might appear that Aboriginal English is simply an uneducated variety of English. However, this would be an erroneous assumption, for while there are a number of features (particularly grammatical features) which AE shares with other non-standard varieties of English, there are many others which are distinctively Aboriginal. These features testify to the fact that Aboriginal ways of using language and communicating have survived and remained strong – despite the extinction of traditional languages all over the continent. (It is estimated that of the original 250 Aboriginal languages, only about 90 survive in any form, and only 20 of these are in a 'relatively healthy state' (Schmidt 1990).)

5.5 Is it the same all over Australia?

It would be an oversimplification to speak of one dialect of AE, just as it would be to speak of one dialect of British English (one has only to think of the differences in grammar, sound systems, and vocabulary between Cockney and 'Geordie' English). There are a number of AE dialects, or, more accurately, there is a continuum of AE dialects, ranging from close to SE at one extreme to close to Kriol at the other. Increasingly the terms 'light' and 'heavy' are being used to refer to these extremes. Heavy AE is spoken mainly in the more remote areas, where it is influenced by Kriol, while light varieties of AE are spoken mainly in metropolitan, urban and rural areas. AE is spoken throughout Australia, as either the first or second language of the great majority of Aboriginal people. It is thought to be the first language of most Aboriginal people in the areas where traditional languages and Kriol are not spoken. While there have been some studies of AE in Western Australia, Queensland, New South Wales and the Northern Territory, there are still many areas, including notably the Torres Strait Islands, about which little detail is available.

Just as in pre-contact times Aboriginal people spoke a number of languages and dialects, contemporary speakers of AE are often bilingual or bidialectal. In the more remote areas many Aboriginal people speak AE in interactions with non-Aboriginals, and Kriol or traditional languages in interactions with other Aboriginal people. In the less remote areas many speak a light AE, or even SE, in interactions with non-Aboriginals, and a heavier AE in Aboriginal interactions. Thus non-Aboriginals who have dealings with Aboriginal people in official domains, such as employment or education, may not always encounter their use of Aboriginal varieties of English. For the same reason it would be wrong to assume that Aboriginal spokespeople or leaders with a high profile in mainstream society are not AE speakers. Frequently they are people who can choose the variety of English which best suits their purpose. Like bilingual speakers, they can use their linguistic and communicative skills to participate effectively both in their own communities and in mainstream society. [See discussion of bicultural Aboriginal speakers of English in Section 1.5.2.]

5.6 Aboriginal English and identity

Aboriginal English plays an important role in the maintenance and assertion of Aboriginal identity. As the linguistic situation before the British invasion shows, Aboriginal people have long used language and speech as markers of group identity. I have already remarked that Aboriginal ways of communicating remain strong, and AE signals Aboriginality in many subtle ways. The accent, vocabulary and grammatical patterns of AE enable Aboriginal people from all over the country to recognise other Aboriginal people, even in contexts where visible markers of identity are not present. Moreover, distinctively Aboriginal ways of using English (such as the indirectness discussed below) give Aboriginal people a feeling of being comfortable with each other, and a rich non-verbal communication system is widely used as well.

5.7 Features of Aboriginal English

Following recent work by Ian Malcolm, Farzad Sharifian and their colleagues, we should add to these aspects of language: cultural conceptualisations, or the way that the meanings in Aboriginal English words are deeply rooted in Aboriginal cultures (see Chapter 1 Further Reading).

If we are we going to understand the language skills which Aboriginal children bring to school, as well as their English language needs, then we need to understand how AE differs from SE. Differences are found in all aspects of language: i.e. phonology (or accent and pronunciation), morpho-syntax (or grammar), lexico-semantics (or words and their meaning), and pragmatics (or the way that language is used in sociocultural contexts). Examples of these differences are given below.

As I have explained, AE is really a continuum of dialects. Certain features are distributed very widely through all dialects, while other features are localised within certain regions, or somewhere along the continuum from heavy to light varieties. In the examples which follow, the symbol (H) indicates that the feature is usually found only in heavy AE, whereas the unlabelled features are widely found in AE varieties around the country. Interested readers are referred to Kaldor and Malcolm (1991) for information about the distribution of AE features.

5.7.1 PHONOLOGY (ACCENT AND PRONUNCIATION)

Many varieties of AE have no *h* sound at the beginning of the word.

AE *Enry's at.* SE 'Henry's hat'.

This feature is largely the result of the influence of traditional Aboriginal languages, which have no *h* sound. Over the generations, Aboriginal speakers have learnt English with an Aboriginal accent. So when they have learnt SE words which start with an 'h' sound, the Aboriginal accent has produced them without it. It's likely that this pronunciation was also influenced by the accent of many of the early non-Aboriginal Australians (especially Cockney and Irish convicts), and it coincides with some other non-standard varieties of English. Thus it is a mistake for teachers to assume that the pronunciation of words without 'h' is uneducated English. It is as much a part of the Aboriginal accent as the 'cute' vowel pronunciations of French speakers of English are part of the French accent, and it should be recognised and respected as a feature of which many Aboriginal people are proud. However, it can cause misunderstanding, as in the example below:

AE *Elen* SE 'Helen' different from 'Ellen'

(H) Aboriginal languages rarely have 'f', 'v' or 'th' sounds, and so the heavier varieties of AE often change these sounds in English words to other consonants. The most common changes are these:

AE	SE equivalent
p or *b*	'f'
b or *p*	'v'
t or *d*	'th'

This feature can sometimes cause misunderstanding, as in the following example:

AE *We ad a bight.* SE 'We had a fight'.
different from SE 'We had a bite'.

5.7.2 MORPHO-SYNTAX (GRAMMAR)

To express possession, many varieties of AE simply juxtapose the possessor and the possessed. By contrast, to express possession in SE the possessor noun receives the suffix –s.

AE	SE
I can't see that man car.	'I can't see the [or that] man's car'.
Where Tom house?	'Where is Tom's house?'

Note that this grammatical construction parallels the expression of possession in Aboriginal traditional languages. It's also worth noting that these languages rarely have an –s sound. It would be inaccurate to describe this feature of AE in terms of speakers 'dropping off the SE possessive -s suffix'.

(H) In the heavy varieties of AE, *he* (or *e)* is used to mean either 'he' or 'she'. This feature can cause misunderstanding, as in the following example:

AE	SE
E come from Perth.	'He/She comes from Perth'.

But of course the context often prevents such misunderstanding, as in the following example:

Q. *Your mother lives where?*
A. *Before up in Cairns, now e down Brisbane.*

5.7.3 LEXICO-SEMANTICS (WORDS AND THEIR MEANING)

In the area of lexicon or vocabulary there is often specific regional variation. So, for example, the word for policeman in parts of New South Wales and Queensland is *boolimun,* in other parts of New South Wales it is *gandjibal* (sometimes spelt *gunjibul),* in Perth it is *monartch,* in Geraldton it is *mardanyuwa,* and so on. All around the country, this is one of the words which remain current the longest, well after almost all of the Aboriginal language of the area has died. *Mardanyuwa* means 'person with chains'. *Boolimun* and *gandjibal* were originally borrowed from English 'policeman' and 'constable' respectively and incorporated into Aboriginal languages. Thus they have come into AE as Aboriginal words with an English history.

There are also some English words used with different meanings in AE. For example, the SE word *mother* means 'the woman who gave birth to a person, or her equivalent'.

But in many varieties of AE the word *mother* means 'the woman who gave birth to a person, and that woman's sisters'. This shows a continuity from the kinship organisation of traditionally oriented societies, where a mother's sister is often treated as a mother, and a single word would translate into SE both as 'mother' and 'mother's sister'. Some other examples are:

AE	SE
country	'land'
growl	'scold'
lingo	'Aboriginal language'
grow [a child] up	'raise [a child]'
camp	'home'
charge	'alcohol'

An interesting lexico-semantic feature of AE is the word *deadly,* which would translate into SE as something like 'really good'. It appears that this is a word which is spreading from AE into general Australian teenage slang.

5.7.4 PRAGMATICS (THE WAY THAT LANGUAGE IS USED IN SOCIOCULTURAL CONTEXTS)

See Section 1.2 for discussion of the terms 'Aboriginal English' and 'Aboriginal ways of speaking English'.

The area of pragmatics is where we frequently see the most persistent features of AE. In metropolitan and urban areas particularly, Aboriginal speakers often use linguistic forms which are very close to, or even identical with, SE. However, there are significant aspects of meaning which are not shared with speakers of SE because of sociocultural differences — in other words, the same utterance may have different meanings in AE and SE because of these differences. For similar reasons Aboriginal speakers may use English in different ways.

A good example of the pragmatics of AE can be seen in the way that people find out information. AE speakers use direct questions to seek certain information, such as clarification of reasonably public details about a person (e.g. *Where e from?).* But in situations where Aboriginal people want to find out more substantial or personal information, they [often] do not use direct questions. It is important for Aboriginal people not to embarrass others by putting them 'on the spot'. So they volunteer some of their own information, hinting at what they are trying to find out. Information is sought as part of a two-way exchange. Being silent, and waiting until others are ready to share their knowledge, are also central to Aboriginal ways of seeking any substantial information.

Although people in mainstream Australian society can recognise these ways of seeking information, they use them only in sensitive situations. But in

Aboriginal interactions they are the everyday strategies for seeking substantial information — they are part of the sociocultural context. Aboriginal societies in Australia are based on small-scale interaction between people who know each other and are often related to each other. Information is sought as part of an exchange between people who are in a reciprocal, ongoing relationship. Nonetheless, information or knowledge is often not freely accessible; certain people have rights to certain knowledge.

By contrast, mainstream Australian society is a large-scale society where information is highly valued and much information and knowledge is assumed to be freely accessible. There is also a deep-rooted assumption that if a person needs to find something out, then direct questions are appropriate and effective. The direct question is central to communication in most mainstream Australian institutions, including education, the media and the law. In fact [the question has been] 'institutionalised' in interviews, enquiry counters and questionnaires.

Furthermore, direct questioning is so central to western notions of how to teach children that parents and other care givers often communicate with babies, long before they can talk, by asking questions and then answering them on the baby's behalf. For example:

> Who's that? Daddy.
> Where's Mummy? Gone to work.
> Why are you crying? Oh, you're hungry!

This paragraph needs further research before it can be verified in this overgeneralised form. (See Section 1.5.2.)

However, this conversational pattern doesn't appear to be characteristic of interaction between Aboriginal people and their babies. Much of their interaction is physical, and the question-answer format is not central to verbal interaction. It is much more important to teach Aboriginal babies who their relatives are by telling them things like:

> *This your auntie.*
> *That your cousin brother.* (SE father's brother's son)

Thus there are significant differences in the way English is used within Aboriginal and mainstream societies in Australia, and they can cause serious misunderstandings, of which teachers are often unaware. To take one further example, silence in AE conversations is frequently a sign of comfortable interaction and is not interpreted as a breakdown in communication. [Many] Aboriginal people [often] like to use silence while they develop their relationship with another person, or simply while they think about what they are going to say. However, in the mainstream use of English in Australia (as in many western countries), silence in a conversation is an indication that something is going wrong. People try to avoid silences, and, if one develops, there are efforts to fill it. So, even though silence has the same linguistic form (or sounds the same) in both AE and SE, it does not have the same meaning.

5.8 The English language skills of Aboriginal children

Aboriginal children all over Australia come to school as fluent and competent communicators. Many of them speak a variety of AE, which we have seen is quite like SE in many respects, as well as being quite like some other varieties of (non-standard) English. But AE differs from these other varieties of English in its expression of Aboriginality in many different ways, including accent, grammar, vocabulary and language use. It is a totally adequate tool of communication, which expresses and maintains Aboriginal identity. While some Aboriginal children will also have developed some bidialectal and bicultural skills, for others their entry to school will present them with the first situation in which they have this need or opportunity. Most Aboriginal children also come to school with a good knowledge of a wide range of relatives, and of how to behave with them and what to call them. They have learnt that respectful behaviour often requires indirectness and that this includes the polite and comfortable use of silence in many situations.

Teachers who are unaware of Aboriginal ways of using English often wrongly stereotype Aboriginal children's language use as 'bad English', in need of remediation. Moreover they are often ignorant of the conversational and storytelling skills which these children have developed in their home environment. A monocultural classroom will fail to provide the opportunity for many Aboriginal children to use and develop their language skills. For example, they often find themselves excluded by mainstream assumptions about the use of silence and appropriate ways of finding things out.

5.9 Implications for communication in the classroom

When they start school, Aboriginal children have to learn to interact in the dominant question–answer pattern, which we have seen to be much more direct than the patterns they are generally used to. They are also quite likely to find that the silence which is used frequently and positively in Aboriginal conversations is interrupted by teachers, who misinterpret it as a sign that the children are ignorant, shy or unwilling to cooperate. We need to understand that the Aboriginal response to a question will often start with silence, not because of ignorance, but because this is the Aboriginal way of communicating. Another important cultural difference concerns eye contact. In many Aboriginal societies it is considered quite rude to look another person in the eye, especially if that person is older, whereas in mainstream society direct eye contact is usually taken as a sign of respect and honesty.

Further discussion of the pragmatic features of AE can be found in Eades (1992). This handbook was written specifically for lawyers, but many of its practical suggestions for more effective communication with Aboriginal people may also be useful to teachers. Another helpful reference is an excellent article by Malcolm (1982) [and see Chapter 1 Further Reading].

5.10 Further implications for education

It is only since the 1960s that AE has been recognised by linguists and some educators as a valid, rule-governed variety of English which differs significantly from SE in a number of ways. There is still a widespread lack of acceptance of AE, often based on ignorance. In areas where AE does not sound very different from SE, both Aboriginal and non-Aboriginal speakers are often unaware of the subtle but crucial differences between the two dialects. But though people tend to think that there is no real difference between AE and non-standard English, we have already seen that the pragmatic differences are often crucial to communication.

Since this chapter was written in 1993, several states have worked on bidialectal programs. The leader in this area is Western Australia, where the Department of Education produced a thirteen-volume resource for teachers in 2012, titled Tracks to Two Way Learning *(WADET 2012).*

Education systems in Australia still have a long way to go in recognising the home language of Aboriginal children and accommodating the special needs of Aboriginal speakers of English.

Few would deny that these children have the right to learn SE, which is after all a prerequisite for equal participation in areas such as employment and further education. Yet AE-speaking children should also have the right to education in their own dialect, and to learn SE as a second dialect. However, the development of bidialectal programs, which teach SE to speakers of AE, is far from adequate (Malcolm 1992). Moreover the training of teachers to recognise both AE and the needs of its speakers has hardly begun. Aboriginal children are still being wrongly classified as 'slow learners', in large part because of their different ways of communicating, and in particular because of their different ways of responding to teachers' questions.

In Australia, we could take warning from a situation which developed in the United States from a similar issue. In Ann Arbor, Michigan, Black parents at an elementary school in a low-income housing area took the School District Board to court in 1979 in a landmark case. The parents alleged that the School Board had failed to recognise the language difficulties faced by their children and had failed to educate them accordingly. The children were all speakers of the Black American dialect of English (known as Black English Vernacular, BEV, or, more recently, African-American English), which, like AE, is a significantly different dialect of English. The children, who were achieving very poorly at school, were classified as 'learning disabled' or in need of speech therapy. The parents' case depended on establishing that BEV was sufficiently different from SE to constitute a barrier to learning. With the help of linguists, they were successful in showing that it was. The judge ordered that the School District must recognise BEV, must develop a program to help teachers to recognise it, and must offer teachers methods of using that knowledge in teaching Black children SE (Chambers 1983). The implications of this American case are surely significant for teachers of AE-speaking students in Australia.

For more recent discussion of African-American English in education see Green (2002, especially ch 8). On bidialectal education, see Wolfram et al. 1999, Nero 2006; Siegel 2010; and WADET 2012.

5.11 The creole languages

While this chapter has been mainly concerned with the kinds of English spoken by Aboriginal people around Australia, it should also include a brief account of two new Australian languages which are related to English but are *not* dialects of English.

It is widely agreed that these two creole languages are the fastest growing Indigenous languages in terms of numbers of speakers (although it is impossible to estimate current numbers of speakers).

Kriol is spoken widely in northern Australia, in the Kimberley region of Western Australia, and in the Barkly Tableland region of the Northern Territory. It also extends into the Gulf of Carpentaria region of Queensland. It developed at the beginning of this century and is estimated to have at least 15,000 speakers (Schmidt 1990). Like AE, it developed out of the early pidgin English, but, unlike AE, it is a separate language from English and is often not understandable to speakers of SE.

Another creole language is spoken by up to 15,000 people throughout the Torres Strait Islands and by Torres Strait Islanders on the mainland (Shnukal 1988). This language is called Torres Strait Creole or Broken, and sometimes Blaikman Tok or Big Thap. Its history is complex and involves Melanesian Pidgin English, spoken in Papua New Guinea, the Solomon Islands and Vanuatu. Like Kriol, it is a separate language from English and is often not understandable to speakers of SE. However, many speakers of Kriol and Torres Strait Creole also speak some variety of AE in communicating with non-Aboriginal people.

If you teach speakers of either of these two languages who are not also competent in SE, then you really need an ESL (English as a Second Language) program for them – don't make the mistake of thinking that they are speaking 'some kind of English'. Teachers of Kriol speakers in Western Australia are currently being trained to recognise the language, its major differences from English and the needs of its speakers through an in-service program called FELIKS (Fostering English Language in Kimberley Schools) (Hudson 1992; see also Berry & Hudson 1997).

5.12 Conclusion

The home language of many Aboriginal children throughout Australia is some kind of Aboriginal English. It is not 'bad English' or 'pidgin English' and it is in no way inferior to Standard English. Children who speak AE are fluent, articulate and creative users of language, just like children who speak SE. Furthermore, although the differences between AE and SE may not seem great in many areas, there are subtle differences, especially in the way that language is used, which are important to the identity of Aboriginal children. Respecting, valuing and understanding Aboriginal ways of using English is a significant step in respecting, valuing and understanding the identity and self-esteem of these children.

Another important step is the delivery of effective bidialectal education which starts from the children's home language (AE) and teaches them to be competent users of SE in appropriate situations. Such English teaching aims not to correct or replace the children's AE, but to show them how it differs from SE and teach them fluency in mainstream uses of SE.

PART II:

Focusing on the criminal justice process

Chapter 6

Language and the law: white Australia v Nancy

First published in 1993, this chapter tells the story of an Aboriginal woman's encounter with the criminal justice process. The story is fictional, but based on a number of real cases, and the chapter is organised so that students can learn about aspects of Aboriginal culture and ways of communicating that are relevant to the case. Although it describes commonly observed patterns of language use, this chapter should not be read as describing the language and culture of all Aboriginal people in all parts of Australia. Further, it does not deal with how bicultural Aboriginal people may interact with non-Aboriginal people (see Section 1.5.2).

6.1 Introduction

Nancy is a twenty-nine-year-old Aboriginal woman who lives in a country town in southern Queensland. In May 1990 she was charged with unlawful use of a motor vehicle. She pleaded guilty and was fined $500 and placed on a twelve-month good behaviour bond, but she was innocent. This story is fictional, but it is based on a wide range of real cases studied by the author from the early 1980s.

To understand what happened, we need to know about Nancy and her family — about their background and way of living, about their values and priorities. We need to know about their experience of being Aborigines in an Australian town, and about the differences between them and the non-Aboriginal people in the town. And, in particular, we need to know about the linguistic and cultural issues faced by Aboriginal people in their dealings with the law.

Section 6.2 paints a picture of the lives of many Australian Aborigines today, and some of the background which is essential to understanding their dealings with the legal system. Section 6.3, 'Understanding Nancy's Story', provides some of the cultural and linguistic information which is also essential

First published as Eades, D 1993, 'Language and the law: white Australia vs Nancy', in *Language and culture in Aboriginal Australia,* eds M Walsh & C Yallop, Aboriginal Studies Press, Canberra, pp. 181–190.

to this understanding. The chapter separates these two sections in order to encourage you to think about cultural and linguistic matters which are relevant to crosscultural communication in Australia today. Various parts of Section 6.2 are marked by letters (a), (b), and so on; Section 6.3 is divided into numbered subsections, each of which is particularly relevant to one or more of the parts of the second section marked by letters. When you have read the chapter, work out the puzzle of matching the numbered subsections in Section 6.3 with the relevant parts of Section 6.2. The chapter was written in such a way that you should be able to match each subsection with one letter – but you will doubtless see additional subsections which are also relevant in some instances.

6.2 Nancy's story

Nancy's family had always been proud of being Aboriginal, even in the generations when it was easier (and often safer) for people of mixed Aboriginal descent to hide it. Grannie Lizzie, who died when Nancy was ten years old, often talked of the 'dark ages' when she was growing up. She had been taken from her parents at the age of about seven, and sent to the girls' dormitory at the Cherbourg Aboriginal Reserve (about 200 kilometres northwest of Brisbane). Here she was forbidden to speak her Wakka Wakka language, and she was only allowed to see her mother and grandmother once a week. At the age of about thirteen years, Lizzie was sent out west as a domestic on a large property. Although she was housed, fed and clothed, she had to work six-and-a-half long days a week, never receiving any payment. After trying to run away several times, Lizzie finally succeeded in getting back to Cherbourg, where she gave birth to her first child, whose father was the aggressive manager she had been determined to escape. At the age of twenty Lizzie gained the Reserve Superintendent's permission to marry another Cherbourg resident and move away from the reserve. She eventually had twelve children, the youngest of whom was her seventh daughter Maud. The children received limited schooling, because Aboriginal children were not allowed to attend school if non-Aboriginal parents objected to them being there.

When Maud gave birth to Nancy in 1962, her family was living in humpies on Sandy Creek, about ten kilometres east of the small town of Smithville. It was a happy place with lots of cousins growing up, despite the hard living conditions. There was no electricity, and the only water was what they carted from the creek. Her parents and aunts and uncles worked hard at whatever they could – mainly seasonal fruit and tobacco picking. At times the men worked for the railways, and had to live as far away as north Queensland for months at a time.

The year that Nancy started school was the year that the Australian government, acting on the result of a national referendum, allowed Aboriginal people to register as voters, and to be counted for the first time in the census of the population of Australia. But school was difficult for Nancy and her relatives in many ways. The white children laughed at them; and, when they learned about 'wild and savage natives', Nancy felt ashamed to be one of the dark people. And it was so hard to keep up with what was going on. The teacher asked so many questions and, when the children didn't answer, she thought they were stupid, or sulky, or both. (a)

There were other problems: Nancy often felt *shame*, and although the teacher seemed annoyed with her, she didn't know what she had done wrong. (b) (c)

And then the teacher was always telling her to speak 'proper English', not that 'bad, slovenly English, with the words left out'. (d)

Besides, it was hard to get to school, walking about ten kilometres every day. Sometimes it was too hot, sometimes Nancy just felt tired, and other times it was too exciting at home — especially when relations came to stay from Cherbourg. And then sometimes her relations would take her back to see her people, where she would stay for weeks at a time. (e)

In 1976, Nancy's family moved on to the Aboriginal reserve on the western outskirts of Smithville. They were one of the first families to be allocated a house to rent by the newly formed Aboriginal Housing Cooperative. When she was sixteen years old Nancy had her first child. During the next three years, while she stayed with her family on the reserve, two more children were born. In 1985 Nancy and her de facto husband Jim moved into town, where they still live today, renting a house through the Aboriginal Housing Cooperative. Now that they are in town the troubles with the police seem worse than they were on the reserve — maybe it was good to be out of sight, out there past the town dump. In town the police always seem to notice the usual family noise and the fights that happen from time to time, and often someone is arrested. (f)

But Nancy likes being in town: she can walk to the shops, and it is much easier for the children to get to school than it ever was for her. And she wants her children to have a good education. The hardest part is getting back out to the reserve to see her Mum and Dad, her brothers who still live there, and all her other relations. If one of the Murries in town is driving out, she can usually get a lift. But often she has to get a taxi. That's all right, unless it's that Harry driving the cab — he just hates blacks.

On Saturday, 5 May, Nancy was very pleased to see her cousin Charlie drive in from Jonesville, some eighty kilometres away. She guessed he'd borrowed a car from up there, and now he was offering to take Nancy and her kids out to see Mum. No good that he was drunk though — so Nancy drove. Suddenly the flashing blue light pulled her over, and before she knew it, Nancy was arrested for unlawful use of a motor vehicle.

In the police station, Nancy was scared. She had heard how one of her cousins had been beaten by one of the policemen in Jonesville just last year. She was scared that these two police officers would harass her like that. She was surprised to think that young Charlie would have taken that car, and she wondered whose it was, and where he had found it. She could hardly speak she was so scared. But she hardly had to speak — the policemen seemed to do all the talking. She wished she could read, to see what they were writing down. She told them what happened: she was at home, but she had been out to town earlier in the morning, after the boys left for football, whatever time that was; she came back, Charlie turned up and offered her a lift to the reserve. But there were so many questions that she didn't know what to do. (a)

Nancy was tired, scared and confused. She was worried about young Charlie too — she should help him; after all, his father had helped her so much when she had applied to the Housing Coop for the house. (g)

But then, when the policeman started to raise his voice, Nancy was terrified — it was just like the teachers all those years ago at school. The best thing would be to cooperate, so Nancy quickly said *yes* to the questions. (h)

The policeman calmed down, soon the questions were over, and he told her to see the Legal Aid man when he came to town the next week. In the Legal Aid office a few days later, there were more questions. Nancy was confused by the way that the lawyer was asking these questions. Here are some of the problems faced by Nancy in this legal interview. He asked lots of questions with 'or', like: 'Nancy, were you down at the creek that morning before you got a lift with Charlie, or were you at home all morning?'. To this Nancy answered *yes*. (i)

And he wanted prompt answers, so there was no time to think about them. (j)

She also felt as if most of the questions about time were too complicated, such as: 'What time did you go to town first?' and 'How soon after that did you return home?'. (k)

The lawyer seemed kind, and he explained to Nancy that she would have to go to Jonesville for the court case in four weeks' time. Nancy was really scared now. She had been to court before, two years ago, when she was fined $70 for swearing outside the hotel in Smithville late one night. (1)

At least she would be with her cousin Charlie. But the lawyer explained that Charlie would be going on a different day, in two weeks' time, because he was to plead 'guilty'. He had stolen the car, and he had told the police how it happened. He told the lawyer too. The lawyer would ask the magistrate to give him a community service order rather than a jail sentence. Everyone was very worried about the rising numbers of deaths of Aboriginal people in jails, particularly young men. It would be better for people like Charlie, who were not dangerous, to pay for their crime and help the community.

The lawyer explained it all to Nancy. If she genuinely had not known that Charlie had stolen the car, then she must plead 'not guilty'. Then she would go to court in four weeks' time, and answer the questions from the police prosecutor, and from her own lawyer. Nancy's head was spinning. She hated all their questions. Migeloos [white people] ask so many questions all the time – it's dangerous to answer them, and it's dangerous not to answer them. Nancy made up her mind.

Two weeks later Nancy was in court. The charge of knowingly driving a stolen motor vehicle was read out to her. She was asked 'How do you plead?'. Her answer was *Guilty, eh?*.

6.3 Understanding Nancy's story

(1) Aboriginal English can be regarded as a dialect of English in much the same way as Scottish English and American English. There are different ways of speaking Aboriginal English in different parts of the country, just as there are different ways of speaking American English in different parts of the United States. Think for example of the dialectal differences between American English and Australian English. In Australian English, we say 'She's in hospital', but to American English speakers this sounds a bit weird, and speakers of this dialect say 'She's in the hospital'. Neither dialect is right or wrong, but there are systematic differences between them. This is the same situation with the difference between Standard Australian English and Aboriginal English [see chapter 5 for further explanation].

Aboriginal English is also related to traditional Aboriginal languages. For example, in traditional Aboriginal languages (as in many other languages of the world) there is no equivalent of the English verb 'to be'. So the sentence *Geen junggoor* in Wakka Wakka (Nancy's Grannie Lizzie's language) would translate literally into English as 'Woman sick'. This grammatical structure has remained in many varieties of Aboriginal English and you may hear Aboriginal people say *woman sick* instead of Standard English 'the woman is sick'.

It is only since the late 1960s that Aboriginal English has been recognised as a distinct dialect of English with its own rules. Most non-Aboriginal Australians still mistakenly think that this dialect of English is 'bad English', or somehow inferior to Standard English, just because it has different rules.

(2) Aboriginal people are often uncomfortable about the way in which non-Aboriginal people ask them questions (see also Yallop's 1993 comments on the grammar of questions). This is because there are significant cultural differences between the two groups in the way that information is sought. While the direct question is central to most information seeking in mainstream Australian society, Aboriginal people throughout Australia, whether they speak a traditional language or Aboriginal English, frequently use a range of indirect means of finding out information.

For example, they make a hinting statement and wait for a response: *I'm wondering about what happened last night. I need to know about why you didn't do your homework*. Or they may volunteer information for confirmation or denial, such as: *It seems as if everyone went to the creek after school*, or *People might say that no-one likes the Maths teacher*, or *(I think) maybe no-one likes the Maths teacher*. Or they may tell people what they need to find out about, and then wait for a later occasion before receiving an answer.

It is clear that silence — giving people time — is important to all of these Aboriginal ways of finding out information.

Although some questions are used, it is considered rude in [some Aboriginal societies] to question people about many things, or to put them on the spot. Individual personal privacy is protected by the constraints on direct questions in many situations.

(3) Aboriginal people throughout Australia often answer *yes* or agree to whatever is being asked by a non-Aboriginal questioner, even if they do not understand the question. This phenomenon, which has been observed for many decades,

has recently been labelled 'gratuitous concurrence' (Liberman 1985). Liberman explains gratuitous concurrence as a way that Aboriginal people have developed to protect themselves in their interactions with non-Aboriginal Australians. It occurs particularly where the questioner, say a teacher or police officer, has authority over the Aboriginal person being questioned.

Thus, a very common strategy for Aborigines being asked a number of questions by non-Aborigines is to agree, regardless of either their understanding of the question or their belief about the truth or falsity of the proposition being questioned. Their apparent agreement often really means something like this: 'I think that if I say "yes" you will see that I am obliging, and socially amenable, and you will think well of me, and things will work out well between us.' This is undoubtedly one of the major problems facing Aboriginal people seeking justice in the legal system.

(4) Questions that ask the respondent to choose one of two alternatives are rarely found in the linguistic structure of traditional Aboriginal languages or in Aboriginal English. So such questions, known as either–or questions, may confuse the Aboriginal person being questioned, who often simply answers: *yes*.

This overgeneralisation about the structure of traditional Aboriginal languages was made on the basis of inadequate evidence, and needs further research. However, it is true that some Aboriginal speakers of English are confused by either–or questions, and answer yes *to such questions.*

(5) Silence is an important and positively valued part of many Aboriginal conversations. This is a difficult matter for most non-Aboriginal people to recognise and learn, because in western societies silence is so often negatively valued in conversations. Between people who are not close friends or family, silence in conversations or interviews is frequently an indication of some kind of communication breakdown. On the contrary, in Aboriginal societies silence usually indicates a participant's desire to think, or simply to enjoy the presence of others in a non-verbal way. Because Aboriginal people are so accustomed to using silence in conversation with other Aboriginal people, many are uncomfortable if they are not given the chance to use silence in their conversations or interviews with non-Aboriginal people.

This difference has serious implications for many interactions in mainstream Australian society where the question–answer method of seeking information is fundamental, such as employment interviews, doctor–patient interviews, school classrooms, and legal interviews, whether in the police station, the lawyer's office or the courtroom. Aboriginal silence in these settings can easily be interpreted as evasion, ignorance, confusion, insolence, or even guilt. In Australian courts of law, silence is not to be taken as admission of guilt, but it would be difficult for police officers, legal professionals or jurors to set aside strong cultural intuitions about the meaning of silence, especially if they were not aware of cultural differences in the use and interpretation of silence.

(6) Another important cultural difference in conversations concerns the use of eye contact. Direct eye contact is frequently avoided in Aboriginal interactions where it is seen as threatening or rude. Conversely, in much non-Aboriginal interaction in Australia, the avoidance of eye contact, especially by someone who has been asked a question, is interpreted as rudeness, evasion or dishonesty. This cultural difference in use and interpretation of eye communication can be very important in the classroom, as well as in police or courtroom interviews.

(7) Speakers of Aboriginal English, like speakers of traditional languages, often reckon time not by the clock or calendar, but in reference to some social or seasonal or climatic event. So, for example, an answer to the question 'When did that happen?', might be *just before Max turned up*, or *around sunrise*. When asked to give specific clock times, Aboriginal people often find it hard to be accurate and consistent.

(8) Many cultural values and practices which are important in traditional Aboriginal societies are still important in non-traditional Aboriginal societies, such as Nancy's. For example, responsibilities for child-rearing are shared among a wide group of relatives, and it is often considered beneficial for a child to move around between various relatives from the extended family.

(9) Another cultural value which is important in non-traditionally oriented Aboriginal societies, as in traditionally oriented societies, is loyalty to kin. Aboriginal people expect each other to be loyal to a wide extended family. In many ways Aboriginal cultural values emphasise the family group rather than the individual, and this is seen in many of the choices and actions of Aboriginal people.

(10) Another cultural practice which can be seen in Aboriginal societies throughout Australia is the preference for outdoor living and the expectation that people will see and hear much of what goes on in Aboriginal family life. Studies of traditionally oriented Aboriginal camps show that physical privacy is

a low priority. And in towns and cities today the same is often true. Small houses accommodate large families or many members of an extended family, and by non-Aboriginal standards they are frequently overcrowded. Much day-to-day living takes place in open, outside areas such as the main street of towns, in parks and other public places, or on the verandahs and in the yards of houses. The open way that many members of an Aboriginal family live in towns and suburbs often results in cultural clash with non-Aboriginal neighbours and police officers.

(11) One of the most common offences with which Aboriginal people are charged is that of using obscene language. Aboriginal people are particularly vulnerable to this charge because of their open lifestyle. But the very notion of 'obscene language' involves a significant area of cultural clash between contemporary Aboriginal and mainstream Australian societies. Simply put, what is widely considered to be obscene language in many sectors of mainstream Australian society is much less likely to be offensive in Aboriginal societies. Swearing, like fighting, is considered to be a normal part of Aboriginal social interaction, and in particular a necessary part of settling disputes. A further difference from most of non-Aboriginal Australia is that there is no gender distinction in this matter. That is, Aboriginal people do not generally consider swearing to be stronger or more offensive if it comes from a woman. [For more on swearing, see Langton 1988 and Eades 2008, pp. 67–71.]

(12) One of the strongest Aboriginal concepts is the feeling of *shame* which is felt when people are singled out in front of a group, whether it be for praise or for rebuke. This concept of *shame* has no simple equivalent in non-Aboriginal society, but it is like a mixture of embarrassment and fear. [For more on the Aboriginal concept of shame, see Harkins (1990) and Sharifian (2005).]

6.4 Conclusion (written in 2012)

Although this fictionalised account was drawn from cases in the 1980s, it is sadly still relevant to the experiences of many Aboriginal people in the criminal justice system. However, growing numbers of lawyers, judges and magistrates have some bicultural understanding (see Sections 7.3.2 and 7.4). See Section 10.4 for some recent positive developments with Indigenous sentencing courts.

Chapter 7

Aboriginal English in the criminal justice system

First published in 2007, this chapter provides an overview of language issues affecting Aboriginal speakers of English in their dealings with the criminal justice system. It discusses commonly found patterns of language and communication among Aboriginal people who speak varieties of English as their first language, and draws on some specific cases. However, this chapter should not be read as describing the language and culture of all Aboriginal people in all parts of Australia. Further, it does not deal with how bicultural Aboriginal people may interact with non-Aboriginal people (see Section 1.5.2). For relevant recent developments in Indigenous sentencing courts, see Section 10.4.

7.1 Aboriginal participation in the legal system[1]

Statistics for 2010 show that Indigenous people are imprisoned at 14 times the rate of the general population (age-adjusted figures), while Indigenous young people are in juvenile detention at 22 times the rate of the general population (SCRGSP 2011).

The participation of Aboriginal people in the criminal justice system in Australia has been one of considerable public discourse and concern over the past fifteen years, with Aboriginal people being greatly overrepresented in police custody and prison. Concerns over this situation contributed to the establishment of the Royal Commission into Aboriginal Deaths in Custody between 1987–1991, which made over 300 recommendations, addressing issues ranging from conditions in prisons, to far-reaching social, educational and health matters (RCIADC 1991).

First published as Eades, D 2007, 'Aboriginal English in the criminal justice system', in *The habitat of Australia's Aboriginal languages: past, present, and future*, eds G Leitner & I Malcolm, Mouton de Gruyter, Berlin, pp. 299–326.

In 1992, the national government allocated $400 million to federal agencies to support implementation of the recommendations. But still, the rate at which Aboriginal people are taken into police custody and imprisoned remains alarmingly high throughout the country. The Australian Bureau of Statistics (2004) reported that, as of 30 June 2004, the national imprisonment rate for Indigenous people was 11 times the rate for non-Indigenous people.[2] Further, while being overrepresented in police custody and prison, Aboriginal people are almost invisible in the legal profession.

The legal areas of greatest Aboriginal participation are the two areas of criminal justice and the tribunals which deal with Aboriginal land claims and, more recently, native title claims. In the more remote regions of Australia, 'traditional' Aboriginal languages play an important role in both of these areas of law. It is beyond the scope of this chapter to address issues affecting those who use traditional Aboriginal languages. (Readers are directed to important work by Cooke 1995a, 1995b, 1995c, 1996, 1998, 2002, 2004; Goldflam 1995; Henderson & Nash 2002; Mildren 1999; Neate 2003; and Walsh 1994).

In most of the country, Aboriginal participation in the legal system involves the use of varieties of English, and it is Aboriginal English in the criminal justice system which is the main focus of this chapter. Readers are referred to Malcolm and Grote (2007) about Aboriginal English generally. The current chapter discusses issues affecting Aboriginal English speakers in the criminal justice system, drawing on two sources: research and specific legal cases.

7.2 Aboriginal English and fabricated confessions

It appears that the first attention to Aboriginal English in the legal system was in two criminal cases — separated by almost thirty years — in which linguistic evidence about the kind of English spoken by an Aboriginal man was part of the defence in his murder trial. In the first of these two cases, that of Rupert Max Stuart in 1959, linguistic evidence was not accepted. In the second case, that of Kelvin Condren in the mid to late 1980s, linguistic evidence was ruled inadmissible by the highest court in Queensland, but this ruling was overturned by the High Court, and the evidence was ultimately accepted. The next two sections will briefly recount the way in which Aboriginal English was important in these two cases.

These two cases are discussed in more detail in Chapter 8.

7.2.1 THE STUART CASE

Rupert Max Stuart is an Aboriginal man from Central Australia, whose first language was Aranda and who spoke what would now be termed Aboriginal English in many interactions, including his police interview and courtroom hearings. In 1959, while he was in Ceduna in South Australia, he was convicted of the gruesome murder of a nine-year-old girl, and sentenced to be hanged. The murder conviction was made on the basis of a signed 'confession', which Stuart alleged was fabricated by the police. The linguist TGH Strehlow gave expert linguistic evidence to show that the language patterns in the answers attributed to Stuart in the 'confession' were not consistent with the way that he spoke English. The case proceeded through every possible criminal court in Australia, and even to the Privy Council in London (which until the 1980s was the highest appeal court for Australian state cases). Four successive appeals – all in 1959 – were unsuccessful: to the Full Court of the Supreme Court of South Australia in May, to the High Court in June, to the Executive Council of the South Australian Government in July for commutation of his death penalty, and to the Judicial Committee of the Privy Council in London later in July. Amid all the public and media pressure the South Australian Government appointed a Royal Commission which sat from August till October, concluding in December that the verdict against Stuart was wholly justified. However, the South Australian Cabinet had decided in October to recommend to the Governor that Stuart's death sentence be commuted to life. Strehlow's linguistic evidence was given first in an affidavit to the High Court in June, and then in a more detailed letter to the Attorney-General, and finally in evidence to the Royal Commission, but it was rejected in all instances.

After serving his life sentence, Stuart was released from prison, and returned to Central Australia, where he has become actively involved in Aboriginal organisations. He recently held the position of Chairman of the Central Land Council. His case was the subject of a documentary film titled *Broken English* (1993), and more recently the feature film *Black and white* (2002).

Strehlow's linguistic evidence in Stuart's case was the first time that a linguist had described features of any Aboriginal English variety. Using the term 'Northern Territory English' (NTE),[3] Strehlow outlined linguistic features found in the allegedly verbatim 'confession', which were very different from the way that Stuart spoke (for details, see Chapter 8). To support his assertion that Stuart did not speak the kind of English which was attributed to him in the ‘confession’, Strehlow tape-recorded a backtranslation session with Stuart. This involved Strehlow translating the ‘confession’ into Aranda (Stuart’s first language, which Strehlow also spoke fluently). Strehlow read this backtranslated Aranda version to Stuart clause by clause, as Stuart translated it into English. Strehlow expected this English reproduction would contain more Standard English than the original confession, but in fact it contained less.

For example, one feature that Strehlow described as characteristic of NTE[3] was the use of masculine third person pronoun (*he* or *him*) to refer to female as well as male referents. Stuart’s allegedly verbatim ‘confession’ included the two following examples of the Standard English third person feminine pronoun.[4]

64. She was standing in a pool of water playing.
77. She went unconscious.

But, in the backtranslation exercise, Stuart used expressions much more characteristic of NTE, namely:

64. ’E’s ... e was playin’ ... side on the water.
77. ’E went out.

The grammatical features of NTE that Strehlow reported on (which he found lacking in the ‘confession’) are features that have since been found in studies of Aboriginal English varieties throughout Australia (see for example Kaldor & Malcolm 1991 for Western Australia; Eades 1992 for Queensland; and Sharpe 1977 for the Northern Territory). While Strehlow limited his description to the English spoken by Aboriginal people in the Northern Territory, it is clear that the variety spoken by Stuart is consistent with varieties now known as Aboriginal English.

Strehlow also isolated some lexical items in the ‘confession’ that he says would not have been used by Stuart, including ‘unconscious’, ‘awoke’, ‘raped’, and ‘stared’. And the following sentences in the confession were singled out by Strehlow as implausible:

17. The Show was situated at the Ceduna oval.

23–4. The three of us sat down and drank a flagon of wine.

36. I put the half flagon in a sugar bag.
38–9. I left the bag with the flagon in it down behind the Picture Show wall.

Stuart's actual backtranslated 'equivalents' were:

17. That show was in Cedoona Opal.
23–4. Tree of us sit down, we drank a flagon o' wine.
36. I put that 'alf flagon in the sugar-bak.
38–9. I left that ... bag wid the flagon, uh, behind that pitcher-pitcher wall.

The Stuart case was widely known because of its role in the abolition of the death penalty in South Australia. It is also an important case for Aboriginal English in the legal system, but unfortunately, little was known about Strehlow's work in this case until after an eerily similar case in Queensland in the mid-1980s, namely Kelvin Condren's case (see below). Strehlow's work in Stuart's case on what he termed Northern Territory English, though never published in any academic forum, was ground-breaking. Judicial reactions revealed the view that speakers of English have the expertise required to make decisions about kinds of English, and that linguistic evidence was not required. Further, these reactions showed a deficit view common to 1950s discourse about language: they rebutted Strehlow's claims that Stuart spoke a *different* variety of English, on the basis that Stuart appeared to be fluent, and thus not a *deficient* speaker of English (see Chapter 8 for discussion of the judicial reaction to Strehlow's evidence in this case).

7.2.2 THE CONDREN CASE

Like Stuart, Kelvin Condren was convicted of a brutal murder on the basis of a signed 'confession' which he alleged was fabricated. His case took much longer than Stuart's, with a committal hearing in 1983, Supreme Court trial in 1984, appeal in the Queensland Court of Criminal Appeal (CCA) in 1987, High Court appeal in 1989, and second appeal in the Queensland CCA in 1990. This final appeal resulted in the quashing of his conviction and he was released from prison in 1990, after serving seven years of a life sentence. In 1995, Condren was awarded $400,000 by the Queensland Government as compensation for his wrongful imprisonment.

Although there were a number of parallels between Stuart's and Condren's cases, there were also differences (for details, see Chapter 8). Stuart's 'confession' was in the form of an allegedly dictated 850-word narrative statement, while

Condren's 'confession' was in the form of answers to 155 questions. And while Stuart spoke Aboriginal English as a second (or possibly third or fourth) language, for Condren it was his first language. Also, Condren's variety of Aboriginal English was lighter than Stuart's, showing less distinctiveness from general Australian English.

The linguistic analysis of the answers attributed to Condren in his alleged 'confession' focused on two main areas of discrepancy: answers to Yes–No questions, and answers which gave quantifiable specification. Yes–No questions are those that can logically be answered by either 'yes' or 'no', and in the 'confession' a large number of these contain an unsupported verbal auxiliary, as for example in the answer 'Yes, I did'. Such grammatical structures are generally uncharacteristic of many varieties of Aboriginal English, and specifically were almost non-existent in other interviews with Condren in legal settings. Thus, for example, the police interview contains allegedly verbatim answers such as:

Q52: When you hit her with the steel picket, did you aim for her head?
A: Yes, I did.
Q74: Was Patricia bleeding when you walked away?
A: Yes, she was.

But in other (tape-recorded) interviews with Condren in legal settings he does not use such grammatical structures. While the answers he gives in these interviews are not limited to Aboriginal varieties of English, they do not use the unsupported verbal auxiliary structure attributed to him in the confession. This is important, because, as explained above, this grammatical structure is uncharacteristic of many varieties of Aboriginal English, and was almost non-existent in the other interviews with Condren. The following two examples come from Condren's evidence to the Supreme Court during his trial:

Q18: Were they all Boydie's Special?
A: Yes, all Boydie's Special.
Q53: When you were hit in the mouth, did it do anything to you?
A: Yes.

But the grammatical structure with unsupported verbal auxiliary — which was found in a large number of Condren's 'confession' answers — is frequently found in some formal Australian English speech in interviews, such as the courtroom evidence of police officers.

In addition to these discrepancies in answer to Yes–No questions, there is a remarkable discrepancy in answer to many Wh-questions (the 'why', 'where', 'when', 'what' type questions). The answers attributed to Condren in many of these questions are characterised by considerable definiteness, frequent quantifiable specification (such as numbers), and frequent lack of the hesitation, qualification or approximation which characterised his answers to such questions in other legal interviews. For example, Question 61 in the police interview asked about a brutal attack on the victim:

Q61: When did you do this?
A: Quarter past four.

This contrasts with a widespread Aboriginal English pattern of giving such information in relational, rather than quantifiable terms, as seen in the following example. This comes from an interview carried out by this author and a lawyer, in which Condren was being asked questions about a recent nonhabitual event in the prison (a recent accident which Condren had witnessed in the prison laundry).

Q174: What day did this happen?
A: I don't know.
Q176: What time did it happen?
A: I don't know really, I know we's working — but I don't know — morning or in the afternoon.

As with Stuart's case some three decades earlier, the linguistic evidence in Condren's case concluded that the allegedly verbatim 'confession' could not have been an accurate transcription of exactly what had been said. There were too many glaring inconsistencies between the 'confession' on the one hand and the Aboriginal English speech patterns of the accused on the other, as found in other legal interviews with him, and as consistent with Aboriginal English generally.

But also, as with Stuart's case, initial judicial reaction to the linguistic evidence was negative, with the appeal court judges refusing to accept that there could be a specialised field of knowledge that could analyse the English of Aboriginal people. These judgments also revealed a lack of understanding of the social basis of language acquisition, insisting that because Condren's mother did not appear to have a very dark skin, then evidence about Aboriginal ways of using English could not be relevant to his case (see Chapter 8 for a discussion of these judgments).

The Stuart and Condren cases focused legal attention on the way in which a linguistic analysis of differences between Aboriginal English and Standard Australian English can help to provide clues about the fabrication of the confessions of Aboriginal people. It is impossible to know the extent of such fabrication, although there have been many allegations, and not only by Aboriginal defendants. But since the 1991 High Court ruling in *McKinney v The Queen* it is quite difficult for a confession to a serious crime to be admissible in an Australian court, unless it has been electronically recorded (see Eades 1997). Thus, this effectively removes the opportunity for police to fabricate a confession. However, I am aware of some instances where recording equipment has reportedly malfunctioned, but police have carried out an unrecorded interview and produced a confession. Linguistic evidence about Aboriginal English has been used in recent years in at least two such cases (I Malcolm, A Lissarague 2006, pers. comm.), but in these cases it has not been successful in having the confession disallowed as evidence in the trial.

7.3 Intercultural communication in the legal process

While the issue in the Stuart and Condren and related cases concerns police malpractice in relation to confessions, the linguistic issues which affect most of the Aboriginal participants in the legal process relate more generally to intercultural communication, or more specifically, intercultural *mis*communication. Given that success in any legal matter depends centrally on language use, then even small differences in language use have the potential to dramatically affect a person's fate in the legal process, as we will see.

The first published work to address intercultural communication with Aboriginal speakers of English in the legal process was not related to the criminal justice system, but to land claim hearings. This was the work of Harold Koch (1985, 1991) in the Northern Territory, which drew attention to a number of problems in communication which stem from differences – often unrecognised – in grammar, accent and word choice and meaning. Koch's study reports on the English used in land claim hearings by 'native speakers of Australian Aboriginal languages' (1985, p. 177), speaking some 'form of nonstandard English' in the land claim hearings. A similar study in 1991 includes a range of speakers, comprising some speakers of an interlanguage, some speakers of Kriol, and others who 'may have been native speakers of Aboriginal English' (Koch 1991, p. 96).[5]

In Koch's research, the main evidence of miscommunication lies in the official typewritten courtroom transcript, which contains a number of discrepancies.[6] Thus for example, when an Aboriginal witness said *Charcoal Jack properly his father*, meaning 'Charcoal Jack is his real father', it was heard (and transcribed) as ' ... probably his father' (1985, p. 180). This example shows the difficulties which can arise from both accent difference — as many Aboriginal English speakers do not distinguish the sounds *b* and *p* — and from lexical difference — as the word *properly* is used to mean 'genuine' in some Aboriginal English varieties. A small example such as this is just the tip of the iceberg of potential miscommunication between speakers of related varieties of English. It should be noted that this particular example could be quite important on its own, given the central role of establishing kin networks and genealogies, as well as knowledge of these, to the land claim process. Thus, the fact that participants in the legal process all appear to be speaking the same language belies the fact that seemingly small differences between varieties of the same language can cause considerable communication difficulties.

Since Koch's work with Northern Territory land claims, most of the research on Aboriginal English in the legal system has been carried out in Queensland and New South Wales, with speakers of light varieties of Aboriginal English, in the criminal justice system. As this research has been with speakers whose grammar, accent and vocabulary is quite similar to speakers of general Australian English, it has focused on pragmatic differences, that is, differences in communicative style. It is important to point out that this research is only a beginning: much more research is needed, particularly with speakers of heavy varieties of Aboriginal English, where not only pragmatics, but also accent, grammar and vocabulary are likely to be important.

Based largely on ethnography of communication research in Queensland in the 1980s, this author published several articles and book chapters in the early 1990s about features of Aboriginal English pragmatics likely to cause problems in the participation of Aboriginal people in the legal process (e.g. Eades 1994a). I will now briefly summarise some key pragmatic features of Aboriginal English that are important in legal contexts (this was also the topic of the handbook for lawyers, published in 1992 by the Queensland Law Society, Eades 1992).[7]

Interviews are widespread speech events in western societies, and they are central to the legal process, from police interviews, to lawyer–client interviews, and the whole of the courtroom procedure, both examination-in-chief and cross-examination. But just as corroborees are not events found in western societies (resembling aspects similar to western religious services, theatrical performances and parties, and yet not quite like any or all of these in detail), so too, interviews have not been part of the experience of Aboriginal societies until the last several decades. Of course, we have to be careful not to overgeneralise about the experiences of Aboriginal people, or to assume that there is only one Aboriginal culture or that it is static and not open to change. But for many Aboriginal societies around Australia, information seeking is typically much less direct, more time-consuming and involves much more reciprocity than one-sided interviews. This cultural difference in information seeking strategies is undoubtedly a major factor in the widespread Aboriginal difficulty with interviews, and in the hesitation, silence and disfluency which typifies much Aboriginal participation in interviews. Thus it is hardly surprising that for many Aboriginal people, participation in the legal process is quite difficult. Further, it seems most likely that the Aboriginal people with least experience and success in bicultural communication are the most likely to be involved in the criminal justice system.

For more on bicultural communication see Section 1.5.2.

Thus, a major problem for intercultural communication in the legal process results from the disjunction between interviews on the one hand, and typical Aboriginal ways of finding information on the other. Specifically, there are three major, general sources of misunderstanding which can often arise when Aboriginal English speakers participate in the legal system:

Firstly, typical responses to legal questions may be misinterpreted, especially where the non-Aboriginal questioner does not recognise aspects of Aboriginal culture and mistakenly assumes that the Aboriginal person being interviewed is speaking Standard English. For example a common Aboriginal response to inappropriate non-Aboriginal questioning is *I don't know,* or *I don't remember*. Often this is not a statement concerning the speaker's knowledge or memory, but it is a comment on the communicative strategy, and would translate into Standard English as something like: 'This is not an appropriate way for me to provide information of this nature.' This intercultural misinterpretation can have serious implications for an Aboriginal person's admissions concerning the seriousness of a crime.

Secondly, silence is an important and positively valued part of many Aboriginal conversations. Silence often indicates a participant's desire to think, or simply to enjoy the presence of others in a non-verbal way.[8] This is a difficult matter for most non-Aboriginal people to recognise and learn, because in western societies silence is so often negatively valued in conversations. For example, between people who are not close friends or family, silence in conversations or interviews is frequently an indication of some kind of communication breakdown. This difference has serious implications for police, lawyer, and courtroom interviews of Aboriginal people. Aboriginal silence in these settings can easily be interpreted as evasion, ignorance, confusion, insolence, or even guilt. According to law, silence should not be taken as admission of guilt, but it is difficult for police officers, legal professionals or jurors to set aside strong cultural intuitions about the meaning of silence, especially when they are not aware of cultural differences in the use and interpretation of silence. Further, a misunderstanding of Aboriginal ways of using silence can lead to lawyers interrupting an Aboriginal person's answer. Of course, we customarily define interruption as involving a second person starting to talk before the first speaker has finished talking. But if we accept that the first part of an Aboriginal answer often starts with silence, then to start the next question before the Aboriginal interviewee has had the time to speak is in effect to interrupt the first part of the answer.

Thirdly, possibly the most serious disadvantage experienced by Aboriginal English speakers is caused by the very common Aboriginal conversational pattern of freely agreeing to propositions put to them in Yes–No questions, regardless of their actual agreement, or even their understanding of the question. This interactional feature, which is found in Aboriginal conversations throughout Australia, has been named 'gratuitous concurrence' by Liberman (e.g. 1981, 1985), who explains it as

> a strategy of accommodation [that Aboriginal people have developed] to protect themselves in their interaction with Anglo Australians. Aborigines have found that the easiest method to deal with White people is to agree with whatever it is that the Anglo-Australians want and then to continue on with their own

> business. Frequently, one will find Aboriginal people agreeing with Anglo Australians even when they do not comprehend what it is they are agreeing with (Liberman 1981, pp. 248–249).

This phenomenon has long been recognised by people working with Aborigines (see for example Strehlow 1936, p. 334; Elkin 1947, p. 17; Lester 1974; Coldrey 1987, pp. 83–85; CJC 1996). One reason that this pragmatic feature is particularly prevalent in Aboriginal societies relates to the widespread cultural norm that harmony and agreement should be preserved at an immediate level, and differences can be worked out in due time. But the use of gratuitous concurrence in legal contexts can be very problematic for Aboriginal interviewees. Once a person has agreed to a proposition in a context such as a police interview, it can have life-changing consequences. It is likely that this pragmatic feature, which has been observed in intercultural communication in Aboriginal Australia for many decades, is also found in many other intercultural communication situations around the world (Gibbons 2003; Berk-Seligson 2009). Further, it is undoubtedly more prevalent in situations of power asymmetry, which characterise interactions in the legal process.

In my experience this strategy is particularly common where a considerable number of questions are being asked, the situation with both police and courtroom interviews. Undoubtedly, there are now a number of legal professionals who are aware of this Aboriginal strategy of gratuitous concurrence, and who exploit this strategy in their questioning of Aboriginal witnesses. Thus it is possible for this strategy to work even more strongly, either in favour of, or against, the Aboriginal witness.

The importance of an understanding of Aboriginal ways of using English to the effective functioning of the justice system is highlighted in the Queensland case of Robyn Kina, as the following section will demonstrate.

7.3.1 THE KINA CASE

Robyn Kina was an Aboriginal woman from Southeast Queensland, who was found guilty in 1988 of the stabbing murder of her de facto husband in Brisbane, and was sentenced to life imprisonment. In her trial, no evidence was given, by Kina or by any other person, about the horrific circumstances which led to her stabbing the victim in self-defence and reaction to provocation. In 1993 Kina successfully appealed against the conviction, on the grounds that her lawyers did not find out the necessary information from her to run her defence. Her conviction was quashed and she was released from prison (having served the equivalent of the sentence she would be likely to receive for manslaughter).

In Kina's 1993 appeal, there were three types of expert evidence: from a psychiatrist on the issue of repressed memory; from a social worker on the 'battered woman syndrome'; and from a sociolinguist (this author) about misunderstanding between Kina and her lawyers. The sociolinguistic evidence (which is discussed in detail in Eades 1996a, 2003b) showed how Kina's lawyers, who were not aware of Aboriginal English ways of speaking, lacked sufficient intercultural communication ability to find out her story and to adequately represent her at her trial. For example, not recognising that Aboriginal answers to questions often begin with considerable silence, the lawyers had been unsuccessful in their attempts to elicit her story. They reported that she had been very difficult to communicate with, and she reported that they had asked her questions, and not waited for the answers! As a result of this serious miscommunication, the jury at her trial had convicted her of murder in the absence of important evidence which should have been used in her defence. While we do not have taped or transcript data from her interviews with lawyers, we can deduce from a number of sources[9] that there was also a misunderstanding about the meaning of her *yes* answers to their questions and suggestions about the way she should proceed. That is, they mistakenly interpreted her answers of gratuitous concurrence as her agreement to their suggestions, for example, that she should not give evidence.

In finding that Kina's trial (in 1988) had involved a miscarriage of justice, the appeal court (in 1993) cited 'cultural, psychological and personal factors' which 'presented exceptional difficulties of communication between her legal representatives and the appellant' (*R v Kina*, pp. 35–36). In effect, the court accepted the sociolinguistic argument that Kina and her lawyers had suffered serious misunderstanding, which resulted in her wrongful murder conviction. This misunderstanding, it had been argued, was rooted in cultural differences in their uses of English, for example in the use of silence.

One of the shocking things about the wrongful conviction in Kina's case is that it was her own lawyers who failed her – it was not skilful manipulation of her evidence by an aggressive cross-examination. In fact she had given no evidence in her own defence, as her lawyers had not managed to find out her story, finding her 'extremely difficult to communicate with' (Eades 1996a, p. 219). It must be remembered that the trial had taken place in 1988, some years before the lawyers' handbook was written. Indeed, the judgments in Kina's 1993 appeal pointed out that none of her lawyers 'received any training or instructions concerning how to communicate or deal effectively with Aborigines' (*R v Kina*, p. 17).

7.3.2 INTERCULTURAL COMMUNICATION AWARENESS FOR LEGAL PROFESSIONALS

In discussing the implications of Kina's case on the day following the decision to quash her conviction, the state Attorney-General spoke about 'the need for the legal system to have knowledge of the problem of crosscultural communication and be sensitive to it' (ABC 1993).

This need has been addressed in a number of ways since then, for example in workshops for legal professionals, as well as articles in professional journals. The lawyers' handbook (Eades 1992) is reportedly widely used, in law schools and in offices of Aboriginal Legal Services and other lawyers who work with Aboriginal clients. It has been cited in judgments (e.g. *R v Aubrey* 1995), and extensively drawn on by the Queensland Criminal Justice Commission (CJC) in its report on Aboriginal witnesses in criminal courts (CJC 1996). In 2000 it was adapted by the Queensland Department of Justice to form the basis of its *Aboriginal English in the Courts* handbook, and it is the source for the section titled 'Dealing with Aboriginal Children' in that Department's guide for legal practitioners about juvenile justice (1997, pp. 9–11). Although based on Queensland research, and written for legal practitioners in that state, it has been cited as helpful and relevant to lawyers in Northern Australia (Lavery 1992, p. 13), and to the native title process nationally (Ritter & Garnett 1999, p. 3). Further, much of the chapter on 'Language and communication' of the 'Aboriginal Benchbook' published by the Australian Institute of Judicial Administration (Fryer-Smith 2008, ch 5) for West Australian judiciary is drawn from the lawyers' handbook.

In my experience, many legal professionals have been excited to learn about intercultural communication generally, and Aboriginal English specifically. A clear example of this comes from a 1992 hearing of the Queensland CJC. This hearing was part of an investigation of an allegation of police misconduct, and I was asked to appear as an expert witness. In addition to explaining some of the subtle ways in which communication patterns differ between Aboriginal and non-Aboriginal speakers of English, I was asked to advise the Commission specifically on more effective ways of hearing the evidence of Aboriginal witnesses to this tribunal. As part of this process, I listened to an Aboriginal woman being questioned by lawyers. This woman had originally approached the Commission wanting to tell her story (related to her witnessing of police misconduct in the matter under investigation), and no disadvantage could occur to her as a result of her evidence. However, under questioning by the lawyers, she provided very little information. The lawyers asked her questions, and she appeared unable to provide answers. I was then asked to advise the Commission about communication with this witness, in her absence. I recommended that the lawyers should wait after each question, until the witness answered. I explained that this means asking a question and then 'shutting up'. Given the uncomfortable feeling that this leaves with many (non-Aboriginal) people, I suggested that the interviewing lawyer could shuffle papers, or say something like 'there's no need to rush'. In answer to the Commission's question about 'how long should we wait?' I replied, 'until after the answer'.

Following a short adjournment, the witness was asked to return to the witness stand, and this revised style of questioning took place, with remarkable results. The same witness who had earlier that day appeared shy, difficult to communicate with, and of little help to the Commission's investigation, was now an articulate witness with a clear and important story to tell the Commission. The only significant change was that the interviewing lawyers allowed time for the silence which began quite a few of her answers to their questions.

7.4 Intercultural communication awareness and the delivery of justice?

The cases of Rupert Max Stuart, Kelvin Condren and Robyn Kina show that linguistic factors can play a key role in judicial outcomes. It appears that the early 1990s represented a turning point in some ways in the recognition of Aboriginal English in the legal system, and the understanding of its significance for the delivery of justice to Aboriginal people. But the rate of Aboriginal over-imprisonment remains high, as we have seen. Of course, there are multiple and complex factors involved in this (RCIADC 1991; Cunneen 2001). But if we focus on the role of Aboriginal English in the legal system, we can ask whether the apparent increase in awareness about Aboriginal ways of using English is resulting in a more equal delivery of justice to Aboriginal people. The answer to this question requires much more research, but we can already glimpse some developments which suggest that the answer might be summarised as 'only sometimes'.

7.4.1 THE MAPLETOWN STUDY

In the mid-1990s, the author carried out research in the District (intermediate) Court of a country town in New South Wales, referred to by the pseudonym of Mapletown (Eades 2000). Aboriginal people in this area speak a very light variety of Aboriginal English, and the study found few instances of miscommunication which could be attributed to dialectal differences in accent, grammar, vocabulary, or communicative style. What was striking about the Aboriginal evidence in these cases was both how little was said by the witnesses, and the ways in which they were silenced in direct examination.

The study found that some lawyers seemed to have a good understanding of some Aboriginal ways of using English. For example, some lawyers used their knowledge of the positive Aboriginal use of silence to the advantage of their clients. The example below comes from a sentencing hearing in the case of an Aboriginal defendant who has pleaded guilty to assault. In answering questions which can help to establish grounds for minimising the severity of his sentence, he is invited by his lawyer to show remorse for his actions to the judge:[10]

29. DC: And do you tell His Honour that you know you shouldn't- and that you're sorry for having done that?

30. W: Uh well- yeah- I am- sorry (6.7) when we're not- oh sorry- when we're not drinkin you know- we don't even fight or nothin- you know- when we're drinking it's a bit of a problem- it's one of them things- drinking.

The witness answers with a formulaic apology, and the very long 6.7 second silence which follows would not be allowed by many lawyers. But the power of the witness's silence, which is not interrupted by the lawyer (or judge), is evident, as it is followed by a personal, honest-sounding explanation which can be helpful to a typical defence strategy of suggesting that the most appropriate sentencing should include alcohol rehabilitation rather than a prison sentence.

But the study also found a number of instances in which Aboriginal witnesses were not allowed to tell their story by their own lawyer, and in some cases by the judge. This silencing of witnesses was brought about sometimes by interruption of the witness, and at other times by metalinguistic comments about how to answer a particular question, such as 'I don't think it's an answer to the question'. Perhaps the most important finding of this study related to the central role of Aboriginal culture in communication, as the silencing of Aboriginal witnesses appeared to occur particularly in situations where legal professionals (whether lawyer or judge) were seriously ignorant about fundamental aspects of the everyday cultural values and practices of Aboriginal people.

Readers are referred to Eades (2000) for discussion of examples which illustrate this point. That paper demonstrates how lawyers and judges are overly preoccupied with courtroom procedure, which is bound by rigid discourse patterns. It is the individual answers to questions which are the focus of the courtroom interaction, rather than the story which a witness is trying to present to the court. And the paper shows how an obsession with the question–answer discourse structure prevents lawyers and judges from realising how much they fail to understand about some of the Aboriginal witnesses and their evidence. This lack of understanding results not primarily from linguistic difference, but from cultural difference, compounded by limiting linguistic (discourse) practices.

The Mapletown study focused on the questioning of Aboriginal witnesses by their own lawyers in direct examination, or by the judge. The finding that witnesses were often silenced corresponded to a widespread feeling in the Aboriginal community that 'the court doesn't really want to hear what people have to say' (Eades 2000, p. 168). It was impossible to determine the impact of this silencing on the judicial outcomes for Aboriginal defendants. It may be possible that, while disempowering Aboriginal defendants in terms of having their voice heard in court, such silencing strategies actually work positively in terms of judicial outcomes.[11] That is, there may be strategic advantages for Aboriginal witnesses in saying very little in court in sentencing hearings, despite the frustrations at not being heard.[12]

7.4.2 THE PINKENBA CASE

Since this chapter was first published in 2007, my detailed research into the cross-examination in the Pinkenba case (Eades 2008) has provided some initial answers to this question (see also Chapter 11).

But what about the way that Aboriginal witnesses are treated in cross-examination, by lawyers for the opposing side? While there is no research that has addressed this question to date, serious concerns have been raised by a 1995 Queensland case, known as the Pinkenba case. Before discussing Aboriginal English in this case, we need a summary of the incident involved:

> Some time after midnight on 10 May 1994, three Aboriginal boys aged 12, 13 and 14 were walking around a shopping mall near the Brisbane downtown area. The boys were approached by six armed police officers who told them to get into three separate vehicles. They were then driven 14 kilometres out of town and abandoned in an industrial wasteland in Pinkenba near the mouth of the Brisbane River, from where they had to find their own way back.
>
> The boys were not charged with any offence, nor were they taken to any police station, and they were not (legally) in custody or under arrest. According to police, the young people were 'taken down to Pinkenba to reflect on their misdemeanours' (ABC 1996). Following the boys' complaint to the Aboriginal Legal Service, an investigation was conducted by the Criminal Justice Commission. This investigation recommended that criminal charges be laid against the six police officers. As a result, the police officers were charged that they had unlawfully deprived each of the boys of 'his personal liberty by carrying him away in a motor vehicle against his will'.
>
> In February 1995, the boys were prosecution witnesses in the committal hearing, which was the first stage in the trial process against the police officers.[13] Most of the four-day hearing consisted of evidence from the three boys, which included lengthy cross-examination by each of the two defence counsel who represented three of the police officers. The case centred on the issue of whether or not the boys had got into and travelled in the police cars against their will: no doubt was ever raised that they were approached and told to get in the police cars, and that they were taken to the industrial wasteland and abandoned there. The defence case was that the boys 'gave up their liberty' and that 'there's no offence of allowing a person to give up his liberty'.[14]

This, then, was a very serious and highly contested hearing, in which the only evidence against the police officers was that of the three Aboriginal boys, the victim–witnesses in the case. Although they were legally children, they had no protection or support such as is offered in Children's Court, because they were not defendants, but witnesses in an adult court. The cross-examination of the boys was devastating: these three young Aboriginal part-time street kids, with minimal successful participation in mainstream Australian institutions, such as education, were pitted against the two most highly paid and experienced criminal barristers in the state. It is hardly surprising that the boys were unable to maintain a consistent story under the barrage of cross-examination, which involved so much shouting at times that many legal professionals in the public gallery were amazed that the lawyers were not restrained or disallowed from using this haranguing behaviour.

Elsewhere, I have written about the linguistic strategies used by these two defence counsel to manipulate and misconstrue the evidence of the three boys (Eades 2002, 2003a, 2008). These strategies succeeded in the magistrate accepting defence counsels' construction of these victim–witnesses as criminals with 'no regard for the community', and the reinterpretation of the alleged abduction as the boys voluntarily giving up their liberty while the police took them for a ride.[15] As a result, the charges against the police officers were dropped.

The manipulation of Aboriginal ways of using English was central to this defence strategy, particularly the use of gratuitous concurrence and of silence (see Eades 2002, 2003a). The extract below provides a glimpse at the lawyers' exploitation of the Aboriginal tendency to gratuitous concurrence. This example is part of the successful strategy of constructing Barry (a pseudonym) as an unreliable witness, as a result of his being easily and skilfully pressured into conflicting answers by defence counsel (DC) on the central point of the whole hearing.

1. DC: And you knew (1.4) when you spoke to these six police in the Valley that you didn't have to go anywhere with them if you didn't want to, didn't you?

2. BARRY: (1.3) No.

3. DC: You knew that, Mr (1.2) Coley I'd suggest to you, PLEASE DO NOT LIE. YOU KNEW THAT YOU DIDN'T

HAVE TO GO ANYWHERE if you didn't want to, didn't you? (2.2) DIDN'T YOU? (2.2) DIDN'T YOU, MR COLEY?

4. BARRY: (1.3) Yeh.

5. DC: WHY DID YOU JUST LIE TO ME? WHY DID YOU JUST SAY 'NO' MR COLEY (4.4)? YOU WANT ME TO SUGGEST A REASON TO YOU MR COLEY? THE REASON WAS THIS, THAT YOU WANTED THIS COURT TO BELIEVE (2.1) THAT YOU THOUGHT YOU HAD TO GO WITH POLICE, ISN'T THAT SO?

6. BARRY: (1.2) Yeh.

7. DC: AND YOU LIED TO THE COURT, TRYING TO, TO (1.2) YOU LIED TO THE COURT TRYING TO PUT ONE OVER THE COURT, DIDN'T YOU?

8. BARRY: (1.8) °No°.

9. DC: THAT WAS YOUR REASON, MR COLEY WASN'T IT? (3.1) WASN'T IT? (3.2) WASN'T IT, MR COLEY?

10. BARRY: (1.9) Yeh=

11. DC: =YES. (2.9) BECAUSE YOU WANTED THE COURT TO THINK THAT YOU DIDN'T KNOW THAT YOU COULD TELL THESE POLICE YOU WEREN'T GOING ANYWHERE WITH THEM. THAT WAS THE REASON, WASN'T IT? (1.5) WASN'T IT?

12. BARRY: (0.6) Yes=

13. DC: =Yes.

This excerpt occurs after Barry (who is sarcastically addressed by this defence counsel as *Mr Coley*) has been on the witness stand for over ninety minutes on two consecutive days, most of it being cross-examination. Turn 1 in this example puts the proposition central to the defence argument: that the witness knew he did not have to go in the police car. The witness's answer of *No* (Turn 2) is not accepted by defence counsel, so he is harassed in Turn 3 until he does agree (in Turn 4). Of course, we cannot know what is in the witness's mind, but we can see the ideal situation for gratuitous concurrence, increased when defence counsel begins shouting angrily in Turn 3. The contradictory answers given by the witness in Turns 2 and 8 on the one hand, and Turns 4, 6, 10 and 12 on the other hand, are interpreted literally by defence counsel, to provide clear evidence that the witness is a liar (emphasised for the court with the theme of 'Why did you lie?', a frequently repeated 'chorus' throughout the cross-examination of all three boys).

The linguistic strategies of the cross-examining lawyers, which included the exploitation of Aboriginal English ways of communicating, in relation to gratuitous concurrence and silence for example, were very overt and effective. In deciding to drop the charges against the police officers, the magistrate's 450-word decision primarily amounted to a criticism of the boys, including the statement that they 'have no regard for members of the community, their property or even the justice system'. This criticism was largely based on their minimal answers to the cross-examination questions, many of which were haranguing, as we have seen above. The magistrate's decision caused a public outcry: it seemed to give the support of the legal system to the police removal of Aboriginal young people who were not charged with any crime and thus not under arrest. As a result of the appeal by the boys' families against the magistrate's decision, a judicial review was held: a judge read all of the evidence and decided that the magistrate's decision should be upheld. Indeed, the legal process did give legitimacy to the right of the police to remove Aboriginal young people in circumstances which were undeniably intimidatory, and a denial of liberty in ordinary terms, if not in legal terms.

And in this legitimisation of police removal of Aboriginal young people, the exploitation of Aboriginal English ways of communicating played a key role, as the example above demonstrates. It was disturbing to find out that the two defence counsel had at the Bar table a copy of the handbook for lawyers (Eades 1992). The handbook had been written to assist lawyers in more effective communication with Aboriginal witnesses. But, in the Pinkenba case, it appears to have been used upside-down, as it were. The provision of intercultural awareness for lawyers seems to have been used to make things worse in terms of intercultural communication. An understanding of Aboriginal ways of using English, such as the tendency to use gratuitous concurrence, appeared to provide the defence counsel with a powerful tool in the manipulation of the evidence of the Aboriginal boys.

Elsewhere I have discussed the implications of this case for our understanding of Aboriginal English in the legal system (e.g. Eades 2004a, 2004b, 2008). To briefly summarise this discussion, this case shows that there is much more involved in intercultural communication than differences in language varieties and their usage. Following Fairclough (1989), we need to go beyond the immediate situation of the courtroom, to the wider institutional and societal contexts, in order to understand the power relations that were operating within the courtroom.

Indeed, this case highlights the importance of power relations in intercultural communication, representing as it does a climax in the 200-year struggle between the state and the Aboriginal community over the rights of police officers to remove Aboriginal young people. To briefly summarise this: since British invasion in the late 1700s, the police force has been used to control the movements of Aboriginal young people. Until the 1960s, this included the now widely known process of forcibly removing children from their families, as part of successive government attempts to deal with 'the Aboriginal problem'. Although this practice is no longer carried out, it is clear from the work of criminologists that current policing practices construct Aboriginal young people as a 'law and order problem' (e.g. Cunneen 2001). Through selective policing, they are detained with much greater frequency than their non-Aboriginal counterparts. There has been increasing opposition from Aboriginal communities about the overpolicing of their young people, and the struggle between Aboriginal people and the police force is increasingly volatile.

Specifically in the city of Brisbane where the Pinkenba incident took place, there were several episodes in this struggle in the year preceding, including a street riot outside the police headquarters (for details see Eades 2004a, 2004b, 2008). Arguably, the Pinkenba committal hearing, in which the boys gave evidence, was charged with enormous political significance. The struggle between the police force and the Aboriginal community had moved from the streets to the courtroom, where language is a crucial weapon. Of course, it can be argued that this was an extreme case, but it is important to point out that it happened, and it was allowed to happen. The cross-examination of the three boys was taken as 'due process' and the proper functioning of the justice system, and indeed it was legitimised by the judicial review.

Criminologists such as Cunneen (e.g. 2001) have argued that the state continues to exercise neocolonial control over the movements of Aboriginal young people. The Pinkenba case highlights the central role of language practices in this process. Linguistic strategies, such as exploitation of the Aboriginal tendency to use gratuitous concurrence, have effects far more wide-reaching than just the courtroom interaction. They are central to the functioning of the criminal justice system, which, as we have seen, legitimises this control over the movements of Aboriginal young people. It is clear that differences between Aboriginal English and general Australian English are important in way in which the criminal justice system functions. And criminologists continue to raise concerns about the fairness of this system:

> Far from providing Indigenous Australians with a just and respected means of social control and protection, appropriate to their needs, the Australian criminal justice system remains an alien and discriminatory instrument of oppression, through which Indigenous people are harassed, subjected to unfair legal procedures, needlessly gaoled, and all too often die whilst in legal custody. (McRae, Nettheim & Beacroft 1997, p. 342)

7.5 Conclusion

This examination of Aboriginal English in the criminal justice system will conclude with a brief summary, followed by an outline of some of the important issues that remain to be addressed. Firstly, the summary:

1. Aboriginal English is an important language variety in the Australian legal system: it is being used around the country by a considerable number of Aboriginal people, whose experience of the criminal justice system remains one of disadvantage, if not discrimination.
2. Success in legal proceedings depends to a significant extent on skilful manipulation of language. Given that the language of the law is general Australian English, and that many non-Aboriginal Australians are unaware of differences between general Australian English and Aboriginal English, Aboriginal English speakers are clearly linguistically disadvantaged in legal contexts.

3. The recognition of Aboriginal English and an understanding of ways in which it differs from general Australian English can play a significant role in the delivery of justice, as we have seen in the Kina case.
4. In comparison, the cases of Stuart and Condren highlight the need for the education of legal professionals about Aboriginal English.
5. But the Pinkenba case demonstrates that education of legal professionals about Aboriginal English is not enough. The participation of Aboriginal people in the criminal justice system cannot be separated from sociopolitical issues involved in race relations in Australia.

Secondly, much remains to be researched about Aboriginal English in the legal system. We have seen that much of the research on this topic to date has focused on pragmatic aspects of light varieties of Aboriginal English. What about heavy varieties of Aboriginal English? What particular aspects of grammatical structures, accent and vocabulary, in addition to pragmatics, are likely to cause miscommunication in the legal process?

Recent research focused on educational settings has highlighted the ways in which the semantic system of Aboriginal English is deeply rooted in Aboriginal cultures (e.g. Sharifian 2001, 2007). What is the significance of this work for the ways in which Aboriginal English is used in the legal system? Further, the work of Sharifian and Malcolm and their colleagues shows that the ways in which Aboriginal English speakers tell stories may be very different from non-Aboriginal narrative organisation. 'Aboriginal English speakers may not rely very much on the chronological sequencing of the events in their narratives. Instead in Aboriginal English narratives, events may be ordered according to their importance among the schemas in the mind of the speaker' (in Sharifian, Rochecouste, Malcolm, Konigsberg & Collard 2004, p. 8). Again, what is the significance of this work for the ways in which Aboriginal English is used in the legal system?

Another important issue relates to Aboriginal comprehension in police interviews. The availability of video- or tape-recorded police interviews makes it possible for defence lawyers to carefully search for any evidence to suggest that their client did not fully comprehend their rights, and thus that their participation in a police interview was not completely voluntary. Several linguists have examined this issue in specific cases, involving speakers of traditional Aboriginal languages (e.g. Michael Cooke 2006, pers. comm.), Kriol (*R v Rankin*), and Aboriginal English speakers (Ian Malcolm 2006. pers. comm.). Much more work is warranted on this complex and important area.

Addressing questions and concerns such as these will not be a simple matter – like all language varieties, Aboriginal English is in the process of change. Further, it is likely that increasing numbers of Aboriginal English speakers are bidialectal to varying extents. That is, these people may have the linguistic ability to use general Australian English in their dealings with the law, while using Aboriginal English in many other contexts. But it can not be assumed that this is true of all speakers of Aboriginal English, especially those with little successful participation in general Australian society, for example through formal education or employment.

It is clear that Aboriginal English will continue to play an important role in the legal process, and it is hoped that further research and communication with the legal profession can play a role in bringing a more equitable justice system to Aboriginal people.

NOTES

1. This chapter draws on a number of previously published publications by the author, including Eades 1992, 1994a, 1996a, 2000, 2002, 2003a, 2004a, 2004b, and Chapter 8 of this volume.
2. The term 'Indigenous Australians' refers to descendants of the original inhabitants, both Aboriginal people, whose ancestry comes from throughout the whole country, and Torres Strait Islanders, from the islands between Queensland and Papua New Guinea. This chapter focuses on Aboriginal people, who number many more than Torres Strait Islanders, and who have assumed the greatest prominence in court cases involving Indigenous people (CJC 1996, p. xi).
3. In his earlier affidavit to the Attorney-General, Strehlow had referred to Stuart's English as 'pidgin English'. But his evidence to the Royal Commission used the more linguistically accurate and non-stigmatised label 'Northern Territory English' (see Section 8.4). It must be remembered that Strehlow's analysis in this case predates any linguistic work on Aboriginal English, and indeed on other ethnic varieties of English, such as African-American Vernacular English.
4. All examples from the Stuart and Condren cases are taken from Chapter 8 (first published in Eades 1995). The numbering is from the original transcripts [and Strehlow's use of apostrophes has not been edited, see textbox in Section 5.2].
5. Interlanguage refers to the linguistic system of language learners, which in such regions would include some English and some indigenous language forms and structures. It is not a stable, rule-governed language variety, and in this way is quite different from Aboriginal English and Kriol. Kriol is a full language, related to both the indigenous languages and Aboriginal English (see also Harris 2007).

6. See Walsh (1999) for a more detailed analysis of the processes involved in the production of transcripts of land claim hearings in northern Australia.
7. Part of the impetus for writing this handbook was provided by the problematic views on Aboriginal English which were revealed in the appeal court's judgment in Condren's case.
8. Similarities can be noted with the use of silence in Native American societies (Basso 1970; Philips 1976).
9. These sources include discussions with lawyers about their interview processes and pressures, observation of other lawyer interviews, affidavits from the lawyers involved, and Kina's comments and memories.
10. See the appendix for transcription conventions. All personal names in this chapter are pseudonyms, with the exception of Robyn Kina, Kelvin Condren and Rupert Max Stuart whose cases have been widely discussed in the media.
11. This dilemma is not unlike that discussed in Trinch's (2003) book about the transformations made by lawyers to the stories of Latina women in domestic violence cases in the United States.
12. Such frustration is of course not limited to Australian Aboriginal witnesses. Based on extensive ethnography of courtroom discourse in the United States over more than two decades, Conley and O'Barr (1990, p. 172) conclude that 'Perhaps the most common complaints of litigants at all levels of the legal process are that they did not get a proper opportunity to tell their story and that the judge did not get to the real facts in their case'.
13. *Crawford v Venardos & Ors*, Brisbane Magistrates' Court, 24 February 1995, unreported.
14. Quotations from this hearing are based on my transcription of official tape-recordings. It should also be pointed out that I was in court for most of the hearing, and was able to observe the event, as well as work with the tape-recording.
15. Arguably they were taken for a ride both literally and metaphorically.

Chapter 8

Aboriginal English on trial: the case for Stuart and Condren

Although this chapter was first published in 1995, it follows the later-published Chapter 7 in this book, as it goes in more depth into just one section of that chapter (Section 7.2). In this chapter you will read the story of two different Aboriginal men (in 1959 and 1987) who each alleged that their 'confession' to police in two different brutal murder cases was fabricated. In both cases, linguistic evidence about Aboriginal English played a significant role. When reading this chapter remember that its general comments about Australian linguistics and about legal rules concerning expert evidence were current in 1995 (and see text box in Section 8.7.2).

8.1 Introduction[1]

The question of the authenticity of 'confessions' allegedly typed verbatim by police officers is one that has been receiving much public attention in recent years. The famous British cases, known as the Birmingham Six and the Guildford Four, in which confessions were fabricated by the police, are well known in Australia. In this country there is no acquittal as famous as either of these two cases, but the widespread familiarity with such a practice has led to the coining of the much-used Australian term 'verbal', as in 'to verbal someone'. In the Macquarie Dictionary this is glossed as 'to represent (an accused person) as having made a statement containing admissions and presenting it to a court as evidence', although it should be pointed out that the term also has the implication that this representation is dishonest.

First published as Eades, D 1995, 'Aboriginal English on trial: the case for Stuart and Condren', in *Language in evidence: issues confronting Aboriginal and multicultural Australia*, ed. D Eades, University of New South Wales Press, Sydney, pp. 147–174.

Linguistic evidence has now been used in some Australian cases to assist the courts in investigating allegations of police verballing (or the fabrication of a police record of interview). See also Jensen (1995).

The present chapter examines two murder cases in which forensic linguistics was used to address the question of an alleged police verbal of an Aboriginal man. These two famous and controversial cases show an uncanny resemblance in some regards, despite their separation by almost thirty years. This chapter compares and contrasts the linguistic evidence in these two cases. We see that forensic linguistics has a longer history in Australia than is generally known, and we find that some of the themes and problems appear to have remained unchanged over three decades. And readers who are linguists may be surprised to find that forensic linguistics in fact provided the first linguistic description of Aboriginal English, predating any published work in this area.

'Forensic linguistics' was a new term in the early 1990s to refer to the presentation of expert linguistic evidence in court. Its use has developed more broadly to also include the linguistic study of language in the legal system.

8.2 Aboriginal English

Aboriginal English is the dialect of English spoken by most Aborigines today in its different varieties throughout the country. Like Scottish English or American English, it is generally understandable to speakers of Standard English. (Hereafter the abbreviation AE is used to refer to Aboriginal English and SE to refer to Standard Australian English.) Also, like these other dialects of English, AE is characterised by systematic differences from SE in all aspects of the language: phonology (or sounds and accent), morpho-syntax (or grammar), lexicon (or vocabulary), discourse structure (or connections between single utterances or sentences) and pragmatics (or language use in context).

As with any other dialect of English there are differences in AE, which generally relate to the speaker's social or geographical background. 'Lighter' varieties of AE (those closest to SE) are spoken by many people who do not also speak a 'traditional' language, especially those who live in less remote areas of Australia. 'Heavier' varieties of AE (those most distinct from SE) are spoken by many people who also speak a 'traditional' language, especially those who live in more remote areas of Australia. In this chapter we have an example of each of these varieties, with the accused in one case being a speaker of 'light' AE (Kelvin Condren) and the accused in the other case being a speaker of 'heavy' AE (Max Stuart).

The linguistic evidence in both the Stuart and the Condren cases depended on the analysis of dialectal differences between the subject's AE and the language attributed to him in the 'confession'. Stuart's case took place at a time when linguistic studies of AE were just beginning; in fact before there were any published studies of this dialect of English. In the linguistic evidence in Stuart's case, as we shall see, this variety is given the name Northern Territory English (although initially it is termed 'pidgin English'). It is clear that the kind of English spoken by Stuart and referred to in the linguistic evidence as Northern Territory English is the same as that now referred to as AE.

8.3 Background to the Condren case

Kelvin Condren is an Aboriginal man from north Queensland who served nearly seven years of a life sentence for the brutal murder of Patricia Carlton, in Mt Isa, a northwest Queensland town. Carlton (who was also Aboriginal) died in September 1983, less than 24 hours after being savagely attacked.

Condren was born in north Queensland in about 1960 and grew up in an extended Aboriginal family. His parents are both of mixed Aboriginal/European descent, from northwest Queensland. Despite his mixed descent, Condren's social life, residence and working life have been dominated by Aboriginal social patterns and interactions. As an adult he has lived in an Aboriginal community in Central Australia, an Aboriginal hostel and an Aboriginal detoxification centre in Townsville, his mother's home (also in Townsville) and an Aboriginal fringe camp at Mt Isa. Most of his social contacts have been with Aboriginal people and his participation in mainstream (white) institutions, such as education and employment, has been marginal and unsuccessful.

After nearly a year in prison awaiting his trial Condren was convicted of murder in 1984 and sentenced to life imprisonment. In 1987 he appealed unsuccessfully against his murder conviction in the highest Queensland court – the Court of Criminal Appeal. And his petition to the Governor of Queensland for a pardon in 1988 was also unsuccessful. In 1989 the High Court of Australia decided that the evidence, including the sociolinguistic evidence, was 'cogent, plausible, and relevant', and strongly recommended that Condren be allowed a new appeal. This new appeal was heard in April

1990, and on 26 June the Court of Criminal Appeal announced that Condren could have a retrial. But in considering the findings of the three judges in this new appeal, the Attorney-General ruled on 27 July that Condren's conviction be quashed. In this ruling the Attorney-General accepted the view of the third judge that the interests of justice would not be served by a retrial. Condren was released that day, after nearly seven years in prison. An inquiry held in 1992 by the Criminal Justice Commission of Queensland (CJC) found that there had been no wrongdoing by police officers involved in his arrest and interview (CJC 1992). In February 1995, the Queensland Government announced that it would award compensation to Condren for his seven years' imprisonment.

The Condren case is remarkable in a number of ways and the story received attention in numerous newspaper articles, in television current affairs shows and, more recently, in popular writing (Masters 1992; Brown & Wilson 1992). Many factors seem to argue against the possibility that Condren murdered Patricia Carlton. For example, the exact time of the attack on Carlton was not established but certain evidence indicated that it must have been after Condren was arrested for drunkenness and while he was being held in police custody. Also, another man confessed to the crime on a number of occasions. But despite these factors, and Condren's avowed innocence, he was convicted 'beyond reasonable doubt' and he was unsuccessful in several attempts to appeal against this conviction before it was finally quashed in July 1990. Why?

Condren was convicted on the basis of a signed 'confession', a transcript of a police record of interview (PRI) in which answers attributed to him clearly assert his guilt and describe in detail the brutal attack on Patricia Carlton which caused her death. But Condren maintains that he was 'verballed' in this police record of interview, and he appealed on the basis of this claim.

During Condren's trial and since then (CJC 1992, p. 31) the arresting officers insisted that the words attributed to him in the PRI were his exact words. I was approached by Condren's solicitors in 1986 and asked to examine the PRI in order to give a professional opinion as to whether this could really be a verbatim record of Condren's words. My conclusion was that it was not possible that all of the utterances attributed to him in this alleged 'confession' were verbatim reports of Condren's actual speech. [This conclusion was based on dialectal differences between SE and AE, and on a detailed sociolinguistic comparison of three different interviews undertaken by Condren. Consistent differences were found between his answers in the alleged 'confession', and his answers in the other two interviews, namely his answers at his Supreme Court trial, and in an interview I did with him at Stuart Prison in Townsville in 1986.]

In working on the Condren case I was unaware for several years of the striking resemblances between it and the Stuart case in South Australia almost thirty years earlier. Not only were there similarities in the nature of the appellant's claims but in the Stuart case, also, linguistic evidence concerning AE was used. This evidence was presented in writing in a letter to the South Australian Attorney-General in June 1959 (following a more general affidavit presented to the High Court in Melbourne, also in June), and orally to the Stuart Royal Commission in September and October of the same year. Amazingly, this evidence appeared to be unknown to Australian linguists (such as Dutton 1965) who produced the first published academic studies of AE in the late 1950s and early 1960s (confirmed by T Dutton 1991, pers. comm.). It appears that, despite Strehlow's linguistic work on AE, which was used in Stuart's case, his published work contains no more than two pages on this dialect (Strehlow 1947, pp. xviii–xix). (This brief discussion, which predates the Stuart case by twelve years, reflects an earlier stage of Strehlow's understanding of AE, which he refers to in this publication as 'Northern Territory pidgin English'.)

8.4 Background to the Stuart case

In contrast to the Condren case, in which I was directly involved, the sources for my study of Stuart's case are the three books that have been published about it. The historian K. Inglis published *The Stuart Case* in 1961 – it appears to be the least biased of the three books. The Crown Solicitor of South Australia during the time of the Stuart case, Sir Roderic Chamberlain, published *The Stuart Affair* in 1973. This book is understandably biased and has not been referred to much in my study. Then many years later, in 1987, T. Dixon, the prison chaplain, who had been a central player in Stuart's case, published *The Wizard of Alice*. Despite this book's obvious bias it has provided some useful data for the study, because of its lengthy quotations from the hearings.

Rupert Max Stuart is an Aboriginal man from Central Australia who served a life sentence for the rape and murder of a nine-year-old non-Aboriginal girl, Mary Hattam, at Thevenard, near Ceduna, on the coast of South Australia west of Adelaide, in December 1958.

Stuart is an initiated Western Aranda Aborigine who was born in 1932 on a pastoral station near Alice Springs and (up to the time of his arrest) spoke Aranda as his first language. His father was a fully descended Aranda man, while his mother had only one white grandparent. Stuart had no formal education before he was fourteen or fifteen, but he did have links with the Central Australian missions of Hermannsburg and Santa Teresa. Starting at the age of eleven years he worked as a casual labourer in several locations thousands of miles from Aranda land, as far away as Thursday Island.

Like Condren's case some thirty years later, Stuart's case received much media attention, as well as political debate. This was primarily because of its role in the campaign for the abolition of the death penalty in South Australia. Following a preliminary hearing in the Ceduna Police Court in January 1959, the trial in the Supreme Court in April found Stuart guilty and he was sentenced to hang. The case then proceeded through every possible criminal court in Australia. After an unsuccessful appeal in the Full Court of the Supreme Court of South Australia in May, the execution date was set for 22 May. An application for a High Court hearing stalled the execution, but this High Court appeal (in June) proved unsuccessful. Meanwhile there was tremendous public and political pressure on the South Australian Government to revoke the death penalty in all cases, and the Stuart case itself became a focus for this movement. In July Stuart unsuccessfully appealed to the Executive Council of the South Australian Government for commutation of his death penalty. His final legal avenue was the Judicial Committee of the Privy Council in London, which refused Stuart's petition in July.

Amid all the public and media pressure the South Australian Government announced a Royal Commission into the case on 30 July. The Royal Commission, which sat from August till October, announced in December that it found the verdict against Stuart wholly justified. However, in October the South Australian Cabinet had decided to recommend to the Governor that Stuart's death sentence be commuted to life. Stuart was released from prison in the early 1970s.

As with Condren almost thirty years later, Stuart was convicted primarily on the basis of a signed 'confession'. In Stuart's case there were actually two documents. The police record of the preliminary interrogation takes the form of questions and answers written some eighteen or nineteen hours after the interrogation (Inglis 1961, p. 233). Despite the police evidence to the Royal Commission in October that this was 'an endeavour to reproduce the conversation verbatim' (Inglis 1961, p. 234) we will not consider this document here. It would be ridiculous to give any credence to its alleged verbatim character.[2] It is the second document, the written 'confession', that was the subject of forensic linguistic analysis. This confession takes the form of an 850-word statement which the police alleged was typed at Stuart's dictation. The officers stated at several hearings that 'apart from the opening words and references to dates, the "confession" contained Stuart's actual words' (Inglis 1961, p. 183). (At different hearings the police officers concerned testified that the language in the 'confession' was Stuart's 'exact words' (Inglis 1961, p. 189) and that it was 'exactly his own words...his own narrative, word for word' (Dixon 1987, p. 269).

Again, as with Condren (CJC 1992, pp. 27–29), Stuart maintained that he had been assaulted and intimidated by the arresting police officers, and that the 'confession' was fabricated. As reported in the *Adelaide Advertiser,* Stuart's words to the Supreme Court were: *...Police hit me, choke me, make me said those words, said that I killed her* (Inglis 1961, p. 31).

This situation is one that contemporary forensic linguists would recognise as appropriate for the application of linguistic analysis. And this is also what Stuart's counsel saw in May 1959 when, seemingly prompted by the prison chaplain, Fr Tom Dixon, they sought the expertise of the linguist TGH Strehlow. Strehlow, whose father was a Lutheran pastor at the Central Australian Aboriginal mission of Hermannsburg, was the only white man brought up in Aranda society. Having grown up as a fluent speaker of Aranda (as well as German and English), he became a linguist and studied the Aranda language (see Strehlow 1947). Between 1936 and 1942 he was Deputy Director of Native Affairs in the southern half of the Northern Territory. Since 1946 he had been a lecturer in Australian Linguistics at the University of Adelaide (Dixon 1987, p. 90).

At Fr Dixon's request Strehlow agreed to go to the gaol to hear Stuart talk and to judge whether, in his view, the language of the confession rang true. (In addition to his detailed knowledge of the Aranda language Strehlow knew Stuart's family well.) Strehlow's reaction was unequivocal: 'In plain English,' Strehlow declared, 'my immediate reaction upon reading the police confession was — "Rupert Stuart just does not talk like that".' Further, he felt that:

> Far from bearing any resemblance to any statement ever made by an aboriginal or illiterate part-aboriginal person within my own experience, this succinct and purposeful typescript, in point

> of its contents and the arrangement of its subject matter, began to reveal itself as a document which could have been composed only by someone who was well versed in legal procedure and in the practice of giving court evidence. (in Inglis 1961, p. 45)

So in June Strehlow presented an affidavit to the High Court, in which he argued that the language of the 'confession' was not in the kind of English spoken by Stuart, which he termed in this affidavit 'pidgin English' and also 'pidgin or broken English'.

Later that month, in a more detailed letter to the Attorney General, Strehlow explained why he suspected the 'confession', providing numerous examples that he said were 'in complete opposition to all the stylistic and grammatical features of Northern Territory English' (Inglis 1961, p. 56). In this letter he went from talking about pidgin English to Northern Territory English. He said that Stuart had learned pidgin English as a boy, 'and later on he made some headway in the slightly improved form of it which bears a close resemblance to what may be termed 'Northern Territory English', i.e. the language spoken by most educated part-aboriginals' (Inglis 1961, p. 56).

It was in his evidence to the Royal Commission in September and October that Strehlow gave the greatest detail of the kind of English spoken by Aboriginal people in the Northern Territory. In this evidence he no longer used the term 'pidgin English', but referred to it consistently as 'Northern Territory English'. (Hereafter I will use the abbreviation NTE for Northern Territory English.)

It should be pointed out that the fact that Strehlow moved from the term 'pidgin English' to NTE is hardly surprising, as he was describing a relatively new variety of English which, in 1959, had no 'official' name in either academic or lay circles. Reactions to Strehlow's evidence indicate, again unsurprisingly, that very many white Australians perceived this variety of English simply as 'bad' English. One of the major developments in sociolinguistics since the late 1960s and early 1970s has been the recognition of Aboriginal English in Australia as a rule-governed variety of English (see for example Flint 1968; Brumby & Vaszolyi 1977; Sharpe 1977; Eagleson, Kaldor & Malcolm 1982). This parallels the recognition in America of the dialect of English spoken by African-Americans, frequently referred to as BEV (Black English Vernacular) (see for example Labov 1972; Chambers 1983).

To support his assertion that Stuart did not speak the kind of English which was attributed to him in the 'confession', Strehlow tape-recorded a special backtranslation session with Stuart, which he later went through with the Royal Commission. This had involved Strehlow translating the 'confession' into Aranda, which he read to Stuart clause by clause. Stuart then translated this into English for Strehlow. Strehlow said he would have expected the reproduction in English to be 'better' than the original 'confession'. (By 'better' he appears to have meant more Standard.) But in fact he found the backtranslated English to be 'worse'.

8.5 Differences in the linguistic evidence

Although the linguistic evidence in both the Stuart case and the Condren case concerned the alleged fabrication of a police interview with an AE speaker, the different form of the allegedly fabricated document in each case has led to some significant differences in the actual linguistic evidence used.

In Condren's case the 'confession' takes the form of answers to 155 questions, while in Stuart's case it is an 850-word statement, allegedly dictated to police without questions, and 'with no more than two or three interruptions' (Inglis 1961, p. 26). Thus an important part of the linguistic evidence in Condren's case concerned the linguistic structure of answers to questions, while in Stuart's case the evidence concerned particular grammatical constructions, and vocabulary, as well as the structure of the narrative.

Unlike the long, uninterrupted narrative attributed to Stuart, Condren's 'confession' consisted primarily of very short answers to questions. (Only one answer is more than one line long.) A major part of the linguistic evidence in Condren's case concerned answers to Yes–No questions; that is, questions that can logically be answered by either 'yes' or 'no'. A cause for great concern was the discrepancy between the answers attributed to Condren that included an unsupported verbal auxiliary, such as 'Yes, I did'. Such grammatical structures are [generally uncharacteristic of many varieties of Aboriginal English], and of Condren's answers in other interviews, but they occur very frequently in the allegedly verbatim police record of interview. (This issue is explained more fully in Eades 1988a, 1993.) The following examples illustrate the difference.

PRI Q52 When you hit her with the steel picket, did you aim for her head?

A. Yes, I did.

Q74 Was Patricia bleeding when you walked away?
A. Yes, she was.

Compare these answers attributed to Condren in the police record of interview, with two examples from the Voir Dire[3] (TVD) of his trial and then two examples from my interview with him in prison (CES):

TVD Q18 Were they all Boydie's Special?
A. Yes, all Boydie's Special.
Q53 When you were hit in the mouth, did it do anything to you?
A. Yes.
CES Q94 Is this the room you have Bible Study in?
A. Yeah.
Q191 Does she speak English well?
A. Yes, she speaks English.

Much of Strehlow's evidence in Stuart's case concerned grammatical features of the 'confession' that Strehlow found inconsistent with Stuart's use of English. Most of these features are characteristic of the 'heavy' AE (or NTE) spoken by Stuart, for whom Aranda was his first language; and AE was his second (or possibly third or fourth) language. These features were not relevant in the 'confession' of Condren, who spoke a rather 'light' variety of AE (as a first language).

Strehlow outlined a number of features that were common in NTE. For example, he pointed out that a feature of NTE was 'a confusion about the use of definite and indefinite articles' (Inglis 1961, p. 214). Stuart's allegedly verbatim 'confession' included the two following examples of the Standard English use of the article 'the':

26 Alan went back to the showground.
125 I slept at the Wheatboard.

(These and the examples below are taken from Dixon 1987, ch 54. The numbering of clauses is Strehlow's, as presented to the Royal Commission. [Strehlow's use of apostrophes has not been edited, see textbox in Section 5.2.])

But in the backtranslation exercise that Strehlow conducted with him Stuart used expressions much more characteristic of NTE, namely:

26 Alan went back to showground.
125 I slept in that Wheatboard.

Another feature highlighted in Strehlow's evidence was what he termed 'the use of "he" and "him" for females'. Stuart's allegedly verbatim 'confession' included the two following examples of the use of the Standard English third person feminine pronoun:

64 She was standing in a pool of water playing.
77 She went unconscious.

But in the backtranslation exercise Stuart again used expressions much more characteristic of NTE, namely:

64 'E's...e was playin'...side on the water.[4]
77 'E went out.

Two of the above examples also illustrate another feature of NTE, which was not highlighted by Strehlow but is apparent from examining the transcripts of evidence. That is, the 'confession' contains SE prepositions, such as 'in a pool of water' (64) and 'at the Wheatboard' (125). But, consistent with AE, Stuart's backtranslated forms contain non-standard prepositions: in these examples *side on the water* (64), and *in that Wheatboard* (125).

Strikingly, but not surprisingly, the grammatical features of NTE that Strehlow reported on in his evidence and found lacking in the 'confession' are features that have since been found in studies of AE throughout Australia (see for example Eagleson, Kaldor & Malcolm 1982 for Western Australia; Eades 1992 for Queensland; Sharpe 1977 for the Northern Territory). Studies of AE in the Northern Territory (such as Sharpe 1977, 1979; Koch 1985, 1991; Harkins 1994) do not refer to Strehlow's work on NTE.

Turning to the lexicon, Strehlow isolated some words in the 'confession' that he says would not have been used by Stuart, such as 'unconscious', 'awoke', 'stated', 'raped'. And the following sentences in the 'confession' were singled out by Strehlow as implausible:

17 The Show was situated at the Ceduna oval.
23–4 The three of us sat down and drank a flagon of wine.
36 I put the half flagon in a sugar bag.
38–9 I left the bag with the flagon in it down behind the Picture Show wall. (Inglis 1961, p. 56)

Stuart's actual backtranslated 'equivalents' were:

> 17 That show was in Cedoona Opal.
> 23–4 Tree of us sit down, we drank a flagon o' wine.
> 36 I put that 'alf flagon in the sugar-bak.
> 38–9 I left that...bag wid the flagon, uh, behind that pitcher-pitcher wall. (Dixon 1987, chapter 54)

As well as features of grammar and vocabulary, Strehlow was concerned with the discourse features of the 'confession' overall. He told the Royal Commission that 'the narrative had a conciseness and relevance not possible for somebody who had never been taught how to construct English prose' (Inglis 1961, p. 172). In this attention to the features of the narrative construction, Strehlow was ahead of linguistic work in Australia (and elsewhere) which was primarily concerned with the analysis of sentences and smaller units (such as phrases, words and sounds). He compared 'the whole composition' of Stuart's 'confession' with that of a narrative account Stuart gave to the Royal Commission concerning an earlier attack on a nurse in Alice Springs. In this comparison Strehlow focused on the connections between clauses, noting that NTE rarely used a main clause and subordinate clause but more frequently co-ordinate clauses joined with *and*. Strehlow found that in the nurse story Stuart had used *and* 21 times in 230 words, while in the 'confession' it appeared only 13 times in 850 words. Factors such as this led Strehlow to conclude: 'My opinion is that he could not have produced the document unaided. It is more than the sentences, it is the whole composition as well. I would discount it fairly heavily as a linguistic[ally accurate] document' (Dixon 1987, p. 321). In his letter to the Attorney-General, he had indicated that not only was it unbelievable that this was Stuart's composition but also that it had the structure and argument of a legal document: 'It is a completely damning document which sets out in their logical order only those facts and details which would be of use in a Court of Justice, and even here only to the police and to the prosecution' (Inglis 1961, p. 55).

8.6 Similarities in the linguistic evidence

Given the strong contrast in the way that the 'confessions' were taken from Stuart and Condren, and the fact that answers attributed to Condren were very short, one might expect to find little similarity in the actual linguistic evidence presented in these two cases.

But there is a striking parallel in the area of pragmatics, which can be defined here as the way in which language is used in context. In Stuart's case the concern was over expressions about time, while in Condren's case it included other specific expressions, such as size, number and distance, as well as time. In both cases the linguistic evidence concerned the way in which the accused allegedly used English to make specific reference to something. The use of numeric specification in the 'confessions' was held to be suspect in both cases.

It is relevant to explain how AE speakers give specific information, such as information about time and distance. Aboriginal specification in statements (including replies to questions) frequently refers to physical, social, geographical and climatic events and states of affairs. For example, time reference for past or future events [often] involves reference to a social event or situation, rather than clock time or calendar time (see Section 3.4). An answer to the question 'When did that happen?' might be *Not long before the sun went down, after Jack came home, before Auntie Nellie came.* Many traditional Aboriginal languages have names for two or three numerals only. Items, people and places are often listed or named rather than counted. Even where Aboriginal speakers use AE only, [many] tend to avoid the use of numbers, or to use them with hesitation or qualification.

But in both of these cases there is a striking discrepancy between AE patterns of giving specific information and the patterns found in the 'confessions'.

In Condren's 'confession' specific information is given in answer to WH-questions – that is, questions which can never be answered by 'yes' or 'no' and which are often signalled by an interrogative word or phrase, such as 'Who?', 'Where?', 'Why?', or 'How many?'. The 'confession' is remarkable for the way in which the answers attributed to him in reply to WH-questions show a specificity not consistent either with AE patterns of giving specific information or with answers to comparable questions in other interviews held with Condren. In contrast to these patterns, the answers attributed to Condren to WH-questions in his 'confession' are characterised by:

considerable definiteness;
frequent lack of hesitation, qualification or approximation; and
frequent quantifiable specification.

This contrast can be demonstrated by comparing a typical answer attributed to Condren in the PRI with an example from his trial and then three examples from my interview with him in prison.

PRI The following question was asked following a six-word answer describing a brutal sexual assault on the victim. Note particularly that the answer below shows no hesitation, qualification or approximation in the use of quantifiable specification.

Q61 When did you do this?
A. Quarter past four.

TVD In answer to a similar question in the trial Condren displays a characteristic typical of many AE speakers who, realising that the white questioner wants some kind of numeric specification, use two numbers not adjacent in the counting system. Notice also that Condren qualifies this specific answer in two ways, using *about* and *I think*.

Q16 How many flagons did you drink?
A. About twelve, I think, or seven.

CES During my interview with Condren in prison several specific questions were asked following his description of a recent accident in the prison laundry. Notice that his answers are vague, that he tries to specify the time in relation to an activity rather than clock time, and that when he does use numeric specification he hesitates and qualifies his answer.

Q174 What day did this happen?
A. I don't know.
Q175 How many days ago?
A. Um, about, about two weeks ago.
Q176 What time did it happen?
A. I don't really know, I know we's working – but I don't know – afternoon or in the morning.

The linguistic evidence concluded that AE patterns generally, as well as the specific factors of Condren's relative lack of experience with numeric specification, his extremely poor mathematical ability,[5] and the unprepared nature of the information supposedly given by him in the PRI, made it unbelievable that he would have answered all of the WH-questions in the words attributed to him in the PRI.

Turning to Stuart's 'confession', we find that a similar suspect pattern occurs, specifically in relation to the expression of time. But Stuart's 'confession' consists of a narrative, rather than answers to questions. What concerned Strehlow was the uncharacteristic 'obsession' with specifying clock time. In his letter to the Attorney-General, Strehlow stated that 'All Northern Territory aboriginals and part-aboriginals...showed when giving evidence an irritating vagueness about all dates and clock times...', 'yet in his alleged confession, the illiterate Stuart, who has never had any formal education of any sort, is depicted as a person with a perfect obsession for ascertaining clock times at short intervals and for thinking about days in [terms] of the calendar' (Inglis 1961, p. 54). Some of the time expressions that appear in the 'confession' are 'about 9 am', 'about 7.30 am', 'until 10 o'clock', 'about half past 11', 'one o'clock', 'about 2 hours', 'at 8 am', 'about 7 o'clock'.

Strehlow's evidence about time became a major issue in Stuart's case. It appeared that Strehlow was interpreted as saying that Stuart could not tell the time. So some point was made of examining and cross-examining Stuart during his evidence to the Royal Commission about his ability to read a watch. In fact, Strehlow never made claims about Stuart's ability to read a watch, but was talking about the way in which he would think about time and express time, for example when recalling incidents. Dixon (1987, p. 233) explained it in this way: 'The Commissioners deliberately and consistently failed to measure up to the distinction between reading the face of a clock with some rudimentary skill and using a clock to divide up the day with its activities and regulate his life by those readings.'

8.7 Reactions to the linguistic evidence

8.7.1 IN STUART'S CASE

A major problem for Strehlow in giving evidence was the lack of understanding or acceptance by the courts of the systematic and significant differences between Stuart's AE (or NTE) and Standard English. That such misunderstanding and disbelief existed in 1959 is hardly surprising, as it appears that Strehlow was really in the forefront of contemporary linguistic knowledge in his work in this area. (It also appears that he did not call on the support of linguistics colleagues.) But the fact that similar misunderstanding and disbelief were still operating at the time of Condren's case is much more problematic, given that it was nearly twenty years after the appearance of the first published studies of Aboriginal English and that this is a dialect of English now well recognised in the linguistics literature (see for example Dixon 1980).

Two main arguments were used to counter the usefulness of the linguistic evidence in Stuart's case. These arguments, which were interwoven, basically addressed two issues:

- Strehlow was not right in his assessment of the way that Stuart spoke, and its difference from SE; and
- Stuart was fluent and articulate.

The second of these arguments was in no way contradictory to Strehlow's evidence, as we will see, but this argument, linked with the first, was used to oppose it.

In relation to the first argument, one of the problems for Strehlow's evidence concerned the way in which he changed from initially referring to Stuart's speech as 'pidgin' English (in his affidavit to the High Court) to using the term 'Northern Territory English' (NTE) in later evidence. It has been pointed out above that Strehlow's development in terminology is hardly surprising given the fact that there was at that time no literature on, and no conventional label for, this kind of English. By the time he was cross-examined in the Royal Commission in October Strehlow was firm that Stuart's way of speaking, as displayed in his own evidence to the Royal Commission, was not pidgin English but NTE (Inglis 1961, p. 228). But, in unavoidable legal style, this seeming inconsistency in the linguistic evidence was seized upon by the prosecution and the Commissioners.

In order to assess Strehlow's claim that Stuart did not speak the kind of English found in the 'confession', a number of non-expert witnesses were asked their opinion about Stuart's English. But their evidence was primarily in relation to the second argument outlined above (which was not disputed by Strehlow), and yet it was used to address the first argument — to say that Strehlow was wrong in saying that Stuart spoke English in a different way from that expressed in the 'confession'. These non-expert witnesses included police officers, a taxi-driver, a welfare officer and prison warders, many of whom made statements such as 'Stuart spoke English quite well' and 'He speaks as an ordinary white person would speak...He gave a connected narrative without prompting' (Inglis 1961, p. 187). But the non-expert evidence on this question varied, with other witnesses saying that he spoke 'broken' or 'pidgin' English and that they sometimes had trouble understanding him. No other *linguist* was called upon to assess Stuart's language.

But Strehlow's evidence in fact was not concerned with how easy or difficult it was to understand Stuart's English, or with Stuart's fluency. He was focusing on the *patterned differences between Stuart's NTE and SE.* This focus was, somewhat understandably, not grasped by people not trained in linguistic analysis, despite Strehlow's clever attempts to explain. At the Royal Commission he compared Stuart with Eliza Doolittle in the popular George Bernard Shaw play *Pygmalion,* saying: 'It was not that Eliza Doolittle could not speak English, even adequately, but whether she spoke the same English as Professor Higgins. Eliza Doolittle was very fluent in her own language' (Dixon 1987, pp. 91–92). He also used a similar analogy with the language of Ray Lawler's well-known Australian play *Summer of the Seventeenth Doll* to reinforce his point that this was 'a certain kind of English'.

However, either not understanding or perhaps choosing to ignore this aspect of Strehlow's evidence, the prosecution and the Commissioners concentrated on Strehlow's earlier use of the term 'pidgin English' and took every opportunity to rebut any notion that Stuart was incoherent in English. At the time pidgin English was popularly seen to be an inadequate and incoherent means of communication.[6] In the generally recognised authority on Australian English at that time (Baker 1945), pidgin is described as a 'lingual bastardization' (p. 227). Strehlow's evidence to the Royal Commission was not about pidgin English but about 'a certain kind of English', namely NTE, whose grammatical features he described and illustrated. But legal reactions remained obsessed with what was referred to by Dixon as 'the old herring' about pidgin English (1987, p. 136) and 'this grand red-herring' (p. 91). Continuing the metaphor, Dixon pointed out that 'the smell of the eroding herring was to persist and permeate all the reports' (p. 136).

Stuart himself gave evidence to the Royal Commission and this gave the Commissioners the chance to rebut Strehlow's claims. It is clear that Stuart's evidence demonstrated all of the features of NTE cited by Strehlow, but the Commissioners were obviously expecting less subtle patterns to demonstrate that he spoke 'a certain type of English' or NTE. In answer to questions about Stuart's use of a few subordinate clauses and not many displaced personal pronouns in his Royal Commission evidence, Strehlow pointed out that his time in prison in the nine months since the 'confession' was taken would have led to some developments in his English. Strehlow felt that 'it would be a reflection on the warders' if this had not happened (Inglis 1961, p. 229). In current terminology Stuart was speaking a 'lighter' variety of AE than he had before his imprisonment.

When Stuart gave evidence to the Royal Commission the prosecutor stated that he was 'easy to handle in ordinary English', and later that 'it was obvious that Stuart understood everything that he was asked' (Chamberlain 1973, p. 205). However, it must be pointed out that this assessment was made by the prosecutor on the basis of a very large number of answers by Stuart which consisted of the one word *Yes* (or its variants *Yep* or *Yeah*). For example, at one stage in his evidence to the Royal Commission Stuart gave this one-word answer to thirty-seven consecutive questions. Cooke (1995a) discusses the problems in assuming understanding on the basis of very brief answers from Aboriginal witnesses for whom English is not the first language.

Furthermore, given the very widespread Aboriginal pattern of 'gratuitous concurrence', it would be most unwise to assume that a one-word *Yes* answer signalled Stuart's agreement with the proposition, let alone his understanding of it. Gratuitous concurrence is the common Aboriginal tendency to agree in response to a question asked by a white person, especially one in power, regardless of whether there is understanding of or agreement with the proposition (see Liberman 1985; Eades 1992.) Although the term is relatively new, this Aboriginal way of answering questions has long been recognised (see for example Strehlow 1936, p. 334; Elkin 1947, p. 176). And it appeared to be well known at the time of the Stuart Royal Commission. In an ABC News commentary at the time, Professor Julius Stone of Sydney University asked: 'Can a trial be said to be 'fair' when the accused is so ill-equipped in the language used, and so accustomed (as Stuart and other Aruntas apparently are) to acquiesce in white men's statements which they do not understand?' (Inglis 1961, p. 146).

The other relevant issue here is that the prosecutor (and others) assumed not only that Stuart understood what was going on but also that they understood Stuart. In the light of the work done on AE (for example Eades 1992; and chapter 4) it may well be that this was a false assumption. For example, Stuart's *yes* might not have been intended as agreement with a proposition.

As Strehlow's evidence appeared before a Royal Commission, rather than a court of law, there was no question as to its legal admissibility. Nonetheless, it appeared to be resolutely rejected. The Commissioners, in finding the verdict against Stuart wholly justified, disputed Strehlow's claim that Stuart spoke NTE. They produced no scientific or scholarly refutation of his expertise and appeared to have made no systematic study of the material presented by Strehlow.

However, they did annotate the written 'confession' in response to Strehlow's criticisms of words and structures found in it. In doing this they made comparisons between Stuart's evidence to the Royal Commission and points made by Strehlow about NTE. For example, they found a few answers to the Royal Commission in which Stuart had demonstrated 'correct' use of the definite article 'the'. But they also ignored the evidence of many answers that supported Strehlow's examples of features of NTE (such as non-Standard verb tenses), and they showed a lack of understanding of the basics of linguistic analysis. For example, the Commissioners' annotation refers to the interrogative preform 'where' as a preposition (Dixon 1987, p. 319).

Strehlow's reaction to the Commissioners' annotation exercise was: 'Clearly their Honours should have stuck to the law and refrained from dabbling in linguistic matters for which they had neither the requisite training nor experience. Their annotations are a sufficient monument of their linguistic frailties' (Dixon 1987, p. 319).

The Commissioners also ignored the fact that Stuart's evidence to the Royal Commission took the form of short answers to questions, many of them one-word answers. Thus they ignored Strehlow's evidence about the narrative structure of the 'confession'.

Although the Commissioners did not accept that 'the body of Stuart's confession was dictated verbatim' (Inglis 1961, p. 293), they found there was no need for expert linguistic evidence and they did not accept that Stuart spoke NTE. They found Strehlow's affidavit to the High Court and subsequent letter to the Attorney-General misleading (p. 295). They concluded that, 'even allowing for both an improvement in Stuart's English in [jail] and a tendency on the part of transcribers to ignore differences between Stuart's speech and normal usage', 'Stuart was more nearly capable of dictating the confession than Strehlow believed' (p. 295).

In their findings the Commissioners asserted that there was 'no truth in the suggestions that [Stuart's] knowledge and understanding of the English language was inadequate...His vocabulary is, no doubt, limited, but when he wishes he can speak English, not pidgin or what Mr Strehlow has described to us as 'NT English', but reasonably good English, that is to say, that he speaks English as it is commonly spoken by people who have had some but not a great deal of education' (Inglis 1961, p. 272).

In focusing on the question of whether or not Stuart spoke 'good English' the Commissioners failed to understand Strehlow's linguistic argument about the subtle but patterned differences between SE and NTE. Summing up the problem some years later, Strehlow wrote: 'Objections to the confession were based on linguistic grounds and on my knowledge of aboriginals when giving evidence in court cases in Alice Springs. I had never stated that Stuart could not understand English. I had attacked only the kind of English. But my critics, and the commissioners too, sought to confuse this vital distinction' (Dixon 1987, p. 319).

8.7.2 IN CONDREN'S CASE

In comparing the legal reaction to the linguistic evidence given in these two cases we find some continuity in thinking about Aboriginal ways of using English.

The Condren appeal was heard by three judges, and in making their judgments one judge concurred with the decision of another; thus there were effectively two judgments. (All following extracts from these judgments are from *R v Condren*.) The linguistic evidence was heard in full during the appeal, but the judgments ruled it as legally inadmissible.

Whereas in Stuart's case the issue of dialectal variation had been virtually ignored, a major concern in the Condren judgments was whether linguists can actually describe this dialectal variation. This concern is summarised in Judge Ambrose's statement (p. 297):

> It seems to me unlikely that there exists a specialized field of knowledge which qualifies an 'expert' within it to attribute 'unusual' characteristics to all 'aboriginals' (comprising persons of widely varying genealogical and cultural backgrounds) relevant to the issues which differ significantly from the 'usual' characteristics of persons generally in the community with respect to which of course expert evidence may not be given.

This concern appears to relate to one of the three main rules governing the presentation of expert evidence,[7] namely the 'field of expertise' rule. (See Eades

With changes to evidence rules in Australia beginning since 1995, it is now no longer necessary for an expert's knowledge to be based on a 'recognised field of expertise'. An expert must have specialised knowledge based on training, study or experience. Further, the common knowledge rule no longer holds.

1994b for a discussion of these rules.) The 'field of expertise' rule prevents a person from giving expert evidence if they are not considered by the court to be qualified as an expert or if their area of expertise is not considered to be 'scientific'.

All this led to a related concern in Condren's case that if there were no such specialised field of expertise, the linguistic evidence was merely opinion evidence and thus, as I understand it, contravened the common knowledge rule. This is a rule that prevents the use of expert evidence on any matter considered by the court to be common knowledge. In discussing this point Justice Macrossan stated that: '...evidence of what are said to be normal characteristics of Aboriginal speech and behaviour is no more admissible than evidence of any other aspect of normal human behaviour would be, or the normal behaviour of persons of Anglo-Saxon descent or the Australian community in general and is not a proper subject for expert testimony' (pp. 267–8). He also referred to a precedent in which a judge ruled against 'opinion evidence on matters of human nature'.

On this point the Condren judgment was similar to the conclusion of the Chairman of the Stuart Royal Commission, Chief Justice Sir Mellis Napier, who said: 'We do not think it is a matter for expert evidence testimony' (Dixon 1987, p. 319). In Stuart's case non-experts were called to counter Strehlow's expert evidence, while in Condren's case the expert evidence was ruled as inadmissible.

So the picture that emerges in this judgment so far is that, as in Stuart's case, the linguistic evidence did not convincingly show that Aboriginal English is a rule-governed dialect of English. And, as in Stuart's case, it did not show that linguistics can provide scientific information on the way in which dialects of English differ from each other. Nor did it show that this information is not common knowledge.

A third concern in the judgments in Condren's case involved the relevance of the speech of a group of people to the speech of an individual. Judge Ambrose (p. 297) ruled that the only issue before the jury was the characteristics of the appellant, not 'characteristics commonly found within a category of persons described as Aboriginal'. And similarly Judge Macrossan (p. 267) stated: 'The verbal response characteristics of a class is not a matter at issue but only the alleged responses of the applicant'. An examination of the judgments makes it clear that the linguistic evidence should have explained the fundamental sociolinguistic principle that an individual's speech is limited by the range of variation found within their speech community (see Labov 1988, p. 180).

With respect, one might question whether the same judgment would have been made if Condren had spoken no English, but only Russian, for example. In comparing his patterns of speech (in Russian) with those attributed to him in the PRI (in English), one would in fact have to compare two languages (Russian and English) which are known from their use by social groups, or 'categor[ies] of persons described as [English and Russian]'.[8]

In a distinctly ironic twist the reverse of this principle was later invoked by the Chairman of the Criminal Justice Commission to prevent me from giving specific linguistic evidence at the investigation in 1992 into Condren's complaint about his wrongful arrest (and related matters). Referring to the ruling by the Court of Criminal Appeal that this specific linguistic evidence was inadmissible, the Chairman restricted my evidence to general matters concerning the difficulties in interviewing Aboriginal people. I was prevented from giving any specific evidence about Condren and my linguistic analysis of his 'confession', and could answer only in general terms about what was effectively the 'verbal response characteristics of a class' of people, namely Aboriginal people.

Several other issues were raised in the judgments concerning the sociolinguistic evidence, which are not directly relevant to this discussion (such as the legal issues of whether this evidence was 'fresh evidence' and whether it addressed the ultimate issue).

One alarming aspect involves the judgments' discourse of race, which is no longer accepted in the social sciences, and has been disparagingly termed by some scholars 'the pathology of ethnicity'. For example, Judge Ambrose (p. 297) referred to the '...absence of any clear evidence as to the genealogy of the appellant and to the fact that neither of his parents were full-blooded Aboriginals'. Terms such as 'half-blooded', 'full-blooded' and 'of partly Aboriginal extraction' are used in the judgments in determining the usefulness of applying evidence about Aboriginal people to Condren specifically. Of course, this is quite different from the findings of the social sciences that it is socialisation and cultural factors, rather than genealogy, that are most important in accounting for behaviour – including speech behaviour.

This question of the extent of the Aboriginality of the accused, and thus the relevance of evidence about the way in which Aboriginal people speak English, appeared not to be at issue in Stuart's case.

In this respect the reactions to linguistic evidence in Condren's case were more complex than those raised against similar evidence in Stuart's case some thirty years earlier. But a major factor in the legal aversion to linguistic evidence in both cases was the unwillingness of the legal profession to accept that linguists have a specialised expertise that enables them to make fine-grained analyses of different ways of using English.

8.8 The significance of the linguistic evidence

8.8.1 TO THE LAW

Strehlow's involvement in Aboriginal legal issues was extensive. While he was Commonwealth Patrol Officer for the Northern Territory Administration between 1936 and 1942 he attended, in an official capacity, all trials in Alice Springs courts that involved Aboriginal people (Kirby 1980, p. 177), and he often gave expert evidence to the Northern Territory Supreme Court in matters involving Aborigines (Inglis 1961, pp. 44, 169). Early in this period he wrote about the difficulties facing Aboriginal witnesses (Strehlow 1936), and for many years he voiced strong concern in the debate over whether the Australian legal system should recognise and enforce Aboriginal customary laws (Kirby 1980). (The Australian Law Reform Commission in its report on this matter [ALRC 1986] recommended quite conservative measures in this regard, consistent with Strehlow's views.)

While his evidence in the Stuart case appeared to be relatively well known in the legal profession, as the above discussion has indicated, his actual linguistic expertise in analysing NTE and comparing it with the suspect 'confession' was not recognised. In a similar way, almost thirty years later, in the Condren case, linguistic expertise in analysing AE and comparing it with the suspect 'confession' was also not recognised. This was despite the growth in linguistics in Australia since 1959 to the position where it is now [i.e. in 1995] a well-recognised discipline at most universities, with eight full university departments, many positions in other universities, and a wealth of publications, conferences and degrees in linguistics.

Despite the failure of the linguistic evidence given in the two cases, the mere fact that such evidence has been presented is an important part of the growing attempts by linguists to have their evidence recognised as legally admissible (see Jensen 1995; Bowe & Storey 1995; Eades 1994b).

It is clear that linguistics can make little meaningful contribution to forensic science until this type of expertise is recognised by the legal profession. In considering legal reaction to linguistic expertise in the two cases, a comment made by a leading American forensic linguist seems apt: '...many judges do not understand the complexity of language, and they often feel that "language speaks for itself", and that juries do not need expert assistance in hearing it' (Shuy 1986, p. 59). But, like Chambers (1990, p. 23), I believe that as linguistic expert witnesses we 'should see our participation in the legal process as an opportunity for supplying some rigor to aspects of the law that have traditionally been vague or impressionistic'. In talking about dialectology and other social sciences Chambers goes on to say that our findings and methods should become more significant both in the legal setting and in challenging a 'legocentric' view of society. In this way Chambers sees that 'The law could be — and surely will become — an applied social science'.

The challenge before forensic linguists in Australia as elsewhere is to communicate with the legal profession in a useful way, so that the particular analytical skills of linguistics are recognised, and the complexity of language variation is acknowledged.

Despite positive developments in forensic linguistics since this chapter was first published, this challenge remains.

8.8.2 TO LINGUISTICS

The two cases have made a contribution to linguistics in two ways: in the application of linguistics to the law, specifically in forensic linguistics; and in the study of Aboriginal English.

The linguistic work on the Condren case was the first time in which forensic linguistic analysis was presented to the linguistic community, in terms of both annual conferences (Eades 1988b), and national publication (Eades 1988a). While several linguists had given expert evidence in courts (see Eades 1990, 1994b), it had been considered to be largely an aside to their genuine academic work. In the last few years, however, forensic linguistics in Australia has been gathering academic status with support from an annual workshop held since 1989 on Language and the

Forensic linguistics/linguistic study of language and the law has intensified since 1995, with biennial conferences of IAFL, twice-yearly publications of the journal now titled The International Journal of Speech, Language and the Law, *and a small but growing number of Australian scholars involved in research, consultancy and other applications. To read more about forensic linguistics see Coulthard & Johnson 2007, 2010; Eades 1994b, 1997, 2010; Gibbons 1994, 2003.*

Law at the national conference of the Australian Linguistics Society, and with the publication of the first Australian text on forensic linguistics (Gibbons 1994). This has paralleled overseas developments in the field, such as the establishment in 1993 of the International Association of Forensic Linguistics (IAFL) and the recent establishment of a new journal, *Forensic Linguistics: The International Journal of Speech, Language and the Law.*

The linguistic evidence in Stuart's case is most likely the first instance of forensic linguistics in Australia. Despite the ignorance of this work among the Australian linguistic community – until a conference workshop on Language and the Law more than thirty years later (Eades 1991b) – it still holds an important place in the history of forensic linguistics in this country.

Both of these cases have significant contributions to make to the recognition and analysis of Aboriginal English. Undoubtedly, the greatest impetus for the linguistic study of AE has come from educational linguists and from linguists concerned with the AE spoken by Aboriginal children in white schools (see for example Eagleson et al. 1982; Sharpe 1977; Flint 1968 [and for more recent work see Chapter 1 Further Reading]).

It appears that to a lesser extent the application of linguistics to the law can be recognised as a site for the development of these studies (see also Koch 1985, 1991). The discovery of Strehlow's work on the Stuart case has provided valuable historical information on features of AE spoken in the Northern Territory in the 1950s.

There appear to be three reasons why Strehlow never published the ground-breaking work on Aboriginal English that he did for this case. Firstly, at the time of his work in 1959 anthropological and linguistic work on non-traditionally oriented Aborigines was almost non-existent (but see Fink 1957; Reay & Sitlington 1948). The concern was to document and analyse traditional Aboriginal languages, and many scholars regarded any non-standard varieties of English as simply 'bad English'. Further, many regarded the non-standard English spoken by Aboriginal people as a particularly bad kind of 'bad English', namely 'pidgin' English, which was not worthy of linguistic study. In linguistics the earliest widely known work that legitimised non-Standard dialects of English was Labov's 1972 work on (American) Black English Vernacular.

Secondly, at the time of Strehlow's work on this case academia was concerned mainly with pure research, and it is likely that the applied nature of the legal work would have not interested many academics. And thirdly, it appears that personality clashes and factionalisation led to a situation in which Strehlow was somewhat ostracised from other Australian linguists. (However, his work on the Aranda language and people was widely known, e.g. Strehlow 1947.)

Thirty years later, studies of Aboriginal English are within the mainstream of Australian linguistics, particularly sociolinguistics, and studies of non-traditionally oriented Aborigines are much more widely accepted in all of the social sciences (see Keen 1988). As well, there is a strong interest in Australia, as elsewhere, in the application of linguistics to social concerns, as evidenced by the large membership of the Applied Linguistics Association of Australia. While this interest has been manifested primarily in terms of education, there is a newly developing interest in the application of linguistics to the law.

Turning to the linguistic work on AE in the Condren case, it has been shown elsewhere (Eades 1993) that work on this case provided important evidence in the description of AE. Most descriptions of AE have focused on aspects of the sound system (phonology), grammar (morpho-syntax), and words and their meaning (semantics). If only these aspects of AE are examined in Condren's case, linguistic analysis can make very little contribution to questions about the 'confession'. However, modern sociolinguistics demonstrates (e.g. Gumperz 1982a) that the sociocultural context of language use (pragmatics) must be involved in any language analysis. The inclusion of pragmatic analysis led to important findings in Condren's case. Thus linguistic work on this case contributed to the recognition and description of AE.

8.9 The future

The similarities between the Stuart case and the Condren case are remarkable. In both cases an Aboriginal man was convicted of murder on the basis of a signed 'confession', which he alleged had been fabricated by the police. In both cases the man alleged that assault and harassment by the police induced him to sign this 'confession'. In both cases the police officers concerned swore several times under oath that the words in the 'confession' were the exact words of the accused. In both cases expert linguistic evidence was presented in the accused's defence to show that the language patterns of the answers attributed to him were not consistent with the way he spoke English. In both cases this linguistic evidence was complex, because of the fact that the accused spoke a dialect of English related to Standard English. And in both cases the judicial opinion was that this linguistic evidence was not relevant.[9]

It appears that some things have not changed in the last thirty years in relation to the legal issue of 'verballing'. This chapter has shown that the law still appears to hold the belief that linguistic expertise on dialectal differences between SE and AE either can be countered by non-experts or is otherwise not relevant to the law.[10] But there has been an important development on the issue of confessional evidence since the time when the then South Australian premier, Sir Thomas Playford, said in relation to the Stuart case, that the 'police would never extort a confession out of an innocent man' (Inglis 1961, p. 321). Evidence presented by several witnesses to the 1988 Fitzgerald Inquiry into Police Corruption in Queensland (Fitzgerald 1989) confirmed widely expressed suspicion that police regularly made up confessions to gain convictions against defendants they thought were guilty. (These witnesses included some of the most senior Queensland police officers.) And it is not only in Queensland that concern has been growing over apparent instances of the practice of verballing (see for example Masters 1992, p. 218).

This concern was acted on by the High Court when it ruled in March 1991 that uncorroborated police evidence must be accompanied by a warning to the jury of the danger of convicting people solely or mainly on the basis of their signed confessions to police (*McKinney v The Queen*). This ruling was unprecedented and created considerable controversy, particularly from some police officers. The decision was described by the New South Wales Police Association as 'yet another attack on the credibility of police' (*Sydney Morning Herald*, 23 September 1991).

It is expected that this High Court ruling will do much to change the nature of prosecutions. It appears that in both the Stuart case and the Condren case the confession was uncorroborated police evidence, and, following the High Court ruling, it is unlikely that a prosecution such as either of these would proceed in the future.

The new ruling on uncorroborated police evidence has confirmed the need for the video-recording or audio-recording of confessions that has already been introduced in most states. The strongest position is in Victoria, where it has been compulsory since 1989 for police to tape-record interviews that relate to charges on indictable matters. (Confessions not recorded are inadmissible in such cases.) This taping of confessions made to police should help prevent both perpetrations and allegations of police verballing (or fabricated confessions). And it seems that eventually no confession will be admissible in Australian courts unless it has been electronically recorded. When that development is finally established the type of forensic linguistics reported in this chapter should become unnecessary. However, as Jensen (1995), and Bowe and Storey (1995) have shown, forensic linguists still have a vital role to play in presenting expert evidence. The matter of interpretation, such as examining whether the accused understood their rights, will become increasingly important, as long as there is a concern for equity for all people in multicultural Australia (see ALRC 1992).

See the final paragraph in Section 7.2.2 for a recent update. Also, note that linguists are sometimes asked to analyse recorded police interviews in order to present expert evidence on questions relating to the suspects' understanding of their rights and/or of interview questions.

And on this point the position of Aboriginal people is particularly significant. While Aboriginal people are so seriously overrepresented in the police custodial and prison populations[11] the issue of their language and communication needs must be addressed. Leaving aside questions of alleged verballing, such as in the Stuart and Condren cases, it has been shown that the dialectal differences between AE and SE are a central concern in regard to the participation of Aboriginal people in all stages of the legal system (Eades 1992, 1993, 1994a). In addressing this issue linguistics unarguably has a role to play in the legal system. But, before this can happen in any significant way, linguistics has to be made accessible to legal professionals. It is clear from the examination of the Stuart case and the Condren case that linguistics still has to demonstrate to the law that there are subtle and patterned differences between AE and SE, and that linguistic analysis is the appropriate tool for examining these differences.

NOTES

1. This chapter is based in part on previously published studies of the Condren case (Eades 1988a, 1993). For comments on drafts of this chapter I am grateful to Terry Crowley, Cliff Goddard, Mee Wun Lee and Jeff Siegel. I am also indebted to Terry O'Gorman of Robertson O'Gorman Solicitors for legal advice. All errors are entirely my responsibility.
2. When asked at the Royal Commission 'What special facilities do you think you have for reproducing verbatim a conversation some 18 hours later...?', one of the police officers concerned replied: 'Memory gets training through practice'. But he did concede that 'in an odd case or two they probably would not be [the very words used]' (Inglis 1961, p. 234).

3. A Voir Dire, or 'trial with a trial', is a separate hearing in the absence of the jury, often at the beginning of a trial. In the Voir Dire the judge hears evidence which one of the parties (or 'sides' in the trial) wants to use in the trial proper (or main part of the trial) but which the other party objects to being used. After hearing this Voir Dire evidence, the judge decides if there is any legal basis for excluding this evidence from the jury trial. (I am grateful to John Nicholson, SC, for assistance with this 2013 version of the original footnote.)
4. Note that Strehlow was using a more phonetically accurate version of English spelling, to indicate that the 'h' sound at the beginning of words in Standard English is often not pronounced in the NTE translation of the word. However, this detail is not directly relevant to the point he was making here, namely that Stuart uses the masculine form *'e (or he) for both masculine and feminine reference*, i.e. to translate both 'he' and 'she' from Standard English. Also note that Dixon appears to use three dots to indicate a pause, not the omission of material.
5. On a standard diagnostic mathematical test, which I administered to Condren in May 1986, he was placed in the lowest 4 per cent of Australian Grade 6 primary school students.
6. However, this view of pidgin languages was being debated by linguists in other countries, and 'unprejudiced investigators' using 'modern techniques of linguistic investigation and analysis' were demonstrating that pidgin languages 'are as amenable to description and formulation as are any other languages' (Hall 1966, p. 107).
7. These rules are about to change considerably, making it much less difficult for expert evidence to be admitted, following the passage early in 1995 of the new Evidence Bill in Federal Parliament. But this will mean changes initially only at Federal level. They will not necessarily be implemented at State level, which is where most criminal trials are held.
8. This lack of understanding of dialectal variation in English may be similar to the situation described by Sato (1991) in which she gave evidence about Hawaiian Creole English (HCE) in a federal lawsuit filed by two National Weather Service employees. These men had brought a case of discrimination against their employer on the basis of race and national origin, specifically as reflected in their HCE accents. Following (and despite!) Sato's evidence about the nature of HCE as a dialect of English, the judge, in handing down his ruling that they had not been discriminated against, 'even suggested that these men put more effort into improving their speech' (p. 656).
9. A striking difference between the cases was the time over which the various appeals were conducted. Stuart's case in 1959 took less than eight months from his initial committal in the Police Court at Ceduna to his final appeal to the Privy Council in London. Before the year was over a Royal Commission into the case had been announced, had taken evidence, and had released its conclusions. Decades later, Condren's case took nearly seven years from his initial committal in the Magistrate's Court in Mt Isa in 1983 to the conclusion of his final appeal in 1990.
10. However, there is a promising development in the acceptance at the end of 1993 of linguistic expertise on dialectical differences between SE and AE by the Queensland Court of Criminal Appeal (the same court that had some six years earlier rejected linguistic evidence in Condren's case) in the case of Robyn Kina. The evidence, in *R v Kina*, which was also presented by this writer, related not to any question of the veracity of a confession but to the role played by dialectal differences in ways of seeking and giving information in the serious miscommunication that occurred between Kina and her lawyers in the leadup to her trial (see Chapter 7, Eades 1994c).
11. Aborigines make up about 1.5 per cent of the population of Australia, but 14 per cent of the country's prison population, and 28 per cent of the police custodial population. (RCIADC 1991, vol. 1, p. 227–228.)

Chapter 9

A case of mistaken assumptions

Although this short invited column for a Queensland newspaper in 1995 was a response to a particular case ('the Pinkenba case'), it provides a brief statement of central sociolinguistic issues impacting the participation of many Aboriginal speakers of English in the criminal justice process. Section 7.4.2 introduced the facts of this case and some of the linguistic issues. For further discussion and examples see Chapters 10 and 11. A detailed analysis of this case can be found in Eades (2008), in which I also explain how I was asked to write an expert report for the court (which was never used).

'Facts', assumptions and conclusions — consider the following:

1. Silence in answer to a question indicates ignorance, shyness, or unwillingness to cooperate. And silence in answer to an accusation (possibly masquerading as a question) indicates guilt.
2. If a person being interviewed can't look the interviewer in the eye, then they are trying to hide something.
3. Conflicting answers in an interview are a sure clue to a speaker's dishonest and untrustworthy character.
4. The most effective way to find something out is to ask a question.
5. The most effective way to find out lots of things is to ask lots of questions.
6. The best way to test a person's truthfulness is to put conflicting propositions to them and see what they agree to.
7. Someone who answers *I don't know* to lots of questions in a long interview is pretty ignorant of the interview topic.

First published as Eades, D 1995, 'A case of mistaken assumptions', *The Weekend Independent*, Indepth, March 10, p. 13.

Seven quite straightforward facts about the way we communicate, you may think. But no, these are not facts: they are cultural assumptions. And these cultural assumptions underpin the use of interviews in many contexts in Australia. In fact they are central to the culture of schooling, the culture of the media, and the culture of the legal system in western societies.

And if you are a Queenslander whose culture does not share these assumptions, then you can be greatly disadvantaged in the legal system (as well as in schooling, the media, etc.). This is what happened in the well-known case of Robyn Kina, whose murder conviction was quashed by the Court of Criminal Appeal in November 1993.

Let's put the shoe on the other foot and look at some important cultural assumptions which [many] Aboriginal people all over Australia learn as they grow up:

8. People who use silence should be respected for their thoughtfulness and their recognition of the value of time.
9. It's rude to make direct eye contact with a person you should respect, especially an older person.
10. If you want to find out whether a person is honest and trustworthy you need to take time to get to know them, don't rush them, and don't talk all the time when you are with them.
11. Interrupting a person's story with questions makes it harder for them to be accurate and consistent.
12. Asking lots of questions is rude, and it is a very ineffective way of finding things out.
13. If a White person in authority asks you lots of questions, especially in a pressured situation, the best thing is to say *yes*, and keep them happy. (If it's a negative question, say *no*.)
14. Answering *I don't know* is one way of handling excessive questioning from White people.

Separating 'fact' from cultural assumption is a prerequisite for giving Aboriginal people a 'fair go' in the legal system. Nowhere could this be seen in a more startling way than in the handling of the evidence of the three teenage Aboriginal boys in the 'Pinkenba case' in the Brisbane Magistrates Court a few weeks ago.

Cultural assumptions, such as 1–7 above, were wrongly presumed to be facts and were used as the basis for conclusions about the character and credibility of the boys.

Is our justice system interested in a 'fair go' for Aboriginal Australians? Or is it a one-sided game where the cultural assumptions of the dominant group are taken as facts, and where verbal trickery can be used to mangle and distort the evidence of witnesses, and 'prove' them to be liars?

Chapter 10

Telling and retelling your story in court: questions, assumptions and intercultural implications

First published in 2008 in a criminology journal, this chapter uses sociolinguistic findings about how stories are told and retold, to raise issues about the participation of Aboriginal people in court. It does not assume any knowledge of linguistics, and the abstract provides a summary of the chapter. The chapter shows the importance of considering not just how Aboriginal people speak English, but how their evidence is summarised, responded to and evaluated. Section 10.3.5 examines an example from the Pinkenba case, which was introduced in Section 7.4.2, and was the catalyst for the two-page newspaper column in Chapter 9. In the current chapter, this case provides an example of how lawyer manipulation of witnesses' stories can perpetuate negative stereotypes about Aboriginal people.

Abstract

This chapter presents a sociolinguistic examination of the ways in which stories are told and retold in the criminal justice process, particularly in court. The main argument concerns the fundamental contradictions between everyday storytelling and retelling on the one hand, and the expectations and interpretations of storytelling and retelling in court on the other. Drawing on research on police interviews, lawyer interviews and courtroom talk, the chapter examines issues such as consistency and inconsistency, and the role of questions in shaping a person's story. While there are a number of distinctive assumptions and practices in the culture of the law that are not shared in the wider Australian community, there are particular implications for Aboriginal people, who are still twenty times more likely to come into contact with the criminal justice system

First published as Eades, D 2008, 'Telling and retelling your story in court: questions, assumptions, and intercultural implications', *Current Issues in Criminal Justice,* vol. 20, no. 2, pp. 209–230.

than non-Aboriginal people. These implications are introduced and exemplified, and the chapter concludes by raising questions about alternative approaches to storytelling and retelling in court.

10.1 Introduction[1]

Culture can be defined as the ways of thinking, believing and acting which are shared within a social group, and passed on from generation to generation. We typically think of the social group that shares culture to be an ethnic group, such as Aboriginal people, or Vietnamese people. But there are other kinds of cultural (or sub-cultural) groups, for example in particular religious organisations or professions, such as the legal profession. In legal culture, there are many assumptions about ways of thinking, believing and acting which are at odds with those in other Australian societies. The ways of acting, which are the focus of this chapter, are the ways in which stories are told and retold in court in the criminal justice process. And the related ways of thinking and believing to be discussed here are the assumptions about how language works which underlie these courtroom linguistic practices.

While there are a number of distinctive assumptions and practices which are not shared in the wider Australian community, there are particular implications for Aboriginal people, who are still twenty times more likely to come into contact with the criminal justice system than non-Aboriginal people (Findlay et al. 2005, p. 326). The main focus in this chapter is on courtroom hearings, but before a witness gets to the courtroom they tell their story in interviews with police and lawyers, and these occasions of storytelling cannot be ignored.

The main argument to be developed in this chapter concerns the fundamental contradictions between everyday storytelling and retelling on the one hand, and the expectations and interpretations of storytelling and retelling in court on the other. Section 10.2 will draw on sociolinguistic research to examine characteristics of storytelling in court and the related cultural assumptions about how language works. Section 10.3 will highlight some aspects of Aboriginal language use which give rise to particular implications of courtroom storytelling practices for Aboriginal people. Section 10.4 will ask about alternative approaches to storytelling in court.

The approach in this chapter is a sociolinguistic one, examining the ways in which language is used in social contexts. There is no assumption that readers have any knowledge of sociolinguistics, but those who would like an introduction to the field are recommended to read Holmes (2008). Throughout the chapter the term 'witness' is used to refer to any person giving evidence, including defendants. Informal expressions such as 'telling your story' are also used in places, to make this chapter more readable than it would be with repeated use of the more formal 'telling one's story' or the more cumbersome 'the witness's telling of his or her story'. The term 'storytelling' is also used in places to include 'story-retelling'.

10.2 Sociolinguistic research on storytelling

Courtroom hearings revolve around competing stories: to a considerable extent the aim of legal representation is to present the winning story. As Mauet's (2000, p. 26) trial textbook instructs law students: 'Effective storytelling is the basis for much of what occurs during a trial.' Although it is the witnesses whose stories are told, this storytelling is organised and managed by their legal representatives, and Mauet believes that 'good trial lawyers are inevitably good storytellers'. While storytelling is central to the legal process, it is more generally a common social activity which probably occurs in all sociocultural groups. But the ways in which you tell your story in the legal process are very strange, and are subject to a number of restrictions that do not occur in other storytelling contexts to anything like the same degree, if at all.

10.2.1 STORIES STRUCTURED BY QUESTIONS

The most striking of these restrictions is that the story has to be told in very short bits, segmented by lawyer questions (see e.g. Heerey 2000; Tiersma 1999). Similarly, in police interviews the interviewee's story is segmented by the interviewing officers' questions. It is not just that the questions effectively interrupt any natural storytelling flow that we might expect on the basis of other storytelling situations. More than this, the interviewer questions organise the story, deciding what parts can be told, and in what order, as well as what parts can't be told.

This structuring of a person's story by interview questions often begins in the police interview. Cooke (1996) discusses a Western Australian case of an Aboriginal woman – referred to with the pseudonym 'Daphne' – who was charged with the stabbing murder of her partner. In her police interview,

Daphne had no opportunity to present details of the violence and torture her partner had subjected her to. It was only when she wrote an account for her lawyer, while she was in prison awaiting trial, that crucial details emerged that presented the stabbing in a rather different light. Cooke explains that the way in which the police interview had been conducted had resulted in 'disrupting or prematurely closing' Daphne's story (p. 283), although there is no suggestion that this was the intention of the officers involved. In contrast, in her examination-in-chief, her lawyer allowed her to give her own narrative account of her story, interspersed by very few questions. Being able to present her own story in this way, and not structured by questions, enabled Daphne to present a rather different account from the one which had been structured and limited by questions in the police interview. The person whose identity in the police interview was that of a killer, emerged during her courtroom evidence as a 'courageous victim' (p. 279).[2] Hearing her tell her own story, the prosecutor dropped the wilful murder charge, substituting it with manslaughter, to which Daphne pleaded guilty.

Examination-in-chief (called 'direct examination' in some countries) is the courtroom questioning of a witness by the lawyer who has called them to give evidence. It is usually cooperative in nature and tone, as both lawyer and witness are 'on the same side'. In cross-examination, the witness is questioned by the lawyer for 'the other side' in the courtroom adversarial struggle (see Eades 2010, p. 42).

While Daphne did have the opportunity to tell her story in her own words to the jury, a rather different situation occurred in the Kina case [*R v Kina*] in Queensland. Robyn Kina is an Aboriginal woman who was also accused of murder in the stabbing death of her partner. In Kina's case, her own lawyers' questions in preparation of her defence were unable to elicit crucial factors involved in the fatal stabbing of her abusive partner. Elsewhere (Eades 1996a, 2003b) I have discussed the problems which arose from her lawyers being unaware of cultural differences in how to find out information [see also Section 7.3.1]. These cultural differences — in the use and interpretation of silence for example (see below) — mitigated against her lawyers finding out Kina's story, in interviews structured by lawyer questions. Kina's case shows how the preference in the legal system for structuring witness's stories as short answers to interviewer's questions can prevent the most important parts of a witness's or defendant's story from ever being heard by the jury.

But more typically, in examination-in-chief a witness's story is managed by their lawyer's questions, and at times also by the questions of the judge or magistrate. Eades (2000, pp. 181–189) shows how the story of an Aboriginal defendant in a sentencing hearing was 'hijacked' by her lawyer and the judge, who were unwilling to allow her to tell her story in her own words. The judge asked this defendant 'How did you set up a legal service?' (in response to her evidence that she had done this, as evidence of her important community work). But despite this interest in her story, he was unwilling to allow her to explain this in her own words, and he happily accepted her lawyers' suggestion that he might be 'able to cut through some of this' (that is, the defendant's story). Accepting this suggestion, the judge asked her lawyer to put the defendant's words 'in legal terms for [him]'. Interestingly, these 'legal terms' did not involve any specialised legal terminology. The lawyer simply took control of the story, presenting his own summary of the story in propositions to which the defendant could only answer *yes* or *no*. When she tried to elaborate on an answer, the lawyer ignored this contribution, interrupting her with his next question.

There are good *legal* reasons why witnesses' stories are filtered, organised and restricted in the courtroom, as in the example above (such as the prohibition on hearsay evidence, or the strategy of a lawyer in examination-in-chief preventing a witness from introducing any matters which may damage their case). Similarly, there are good legal reasons for constraints on a suspect's story in police interviews (such as a police officer bolstering the prosecution case by gaining evidence from a suspect in a certain light). But, the way in which a witness's story has to be filtered through lawyer questions is a fundamental problem for the ability of witnesses to tell their own story in their own way. It is also a fundamental sociolinguistic problem for the ability of a court to hear, understand and assess the competing stories which form the basis of a courtroom hearing.

The rule about hearsay evidence generally prohibits a witness from reporting in court anything which another person has said (but note that there are complex exceptions to the general rule).

In addition to the problems caused by the structuring of stories in court through questions, it can be argued that it is typical for much of a witness's story to be actually told in the words of lawyers rather than witnesses. Indeed, sociolinguistic studies of courtroom talk have found that witnesses are typically asked a large number of questions requiring a minimal response, and they say very little compared to the verbosity of those who are questioning them (e.g. Danet et al. 1980; Sandra Harris 1984; Luchjenbroers 1997). Studies also find that the majority of questions put to witnesses contain already completed propositions (Sandra Harris 1984), and that 'witnesses can hardly be thought to tell their stories in their own words' (Luchjenbroers 1997, p. 501). While these findings apply to both examination-in-chief and cross-examination, the important differences in terms of legal strategy and allowable questions mean that there are different emphases in questioning types. Thus, a number of studies have found that there are more Yes–No (or closed) questions in cross-examination, and more WH (or open questions) in examination-in-chief.[3]

Not only is it the lawyers' versions of the witnesses' stories that are told in court, but there are also serious restrictions preventing witnesses from negotiating particular points of the storytelling. The rules of evidence which constrain witnesses to speak only in direct answer to the specific question which has most recently been asked, effectively prevent them from participating in meaningful negotiation on anything but the smallest point of clarification on this most immediate question.[4] This makes courtroom interaction the most highly restricted type of interaction, and is another factor which compromises the ability of witnesses to present their own story.

This subsection has identified major problems for witnesses in telling their own stories, which relate to the ways in which courtroom talk is controlled by lawyer questions. The next subsection focuses in more detail on sociolinguistic research about storytelling and retelling and its relevance for courtroom practices and assumptions.

10.2.2 TELLING AND RETELLING YOUR STORY

When a witness tells their story in court, this is by no means the first time they have told it — in effect, it is a retelling of their story, and the similarities and differences between telling and retelling their story are frequently central to cross-examination. Indeed the comparison of different tellings of the witness's story is at the core of the assessment of the witness's credibility, reliability and truthfulness. So the process of retelling one's own story is of central interest to the ways in which courtroom talk works and is evaluated. Practices involved in storytelling and retelling have recently been receiving attention from sociolinguists and linguistic anthropologists, both in terms of everyday conversations (e.g. Norrick 1998; Schiffrin 2006), and in some institutional contexts (see below).

The social context

Stories cannot be understood or investigated without the context of their telling, this includes such concerns as:

- Who is the story being told to?
- What is the relationship between the teller and the listener(s)?
- Why is the story being told?
- How is the listener(s) reacting to the story as it is being told?
- How do these reactions help to shape the ways in which the story is being told?

Such features of the social context of storytelling relate to both the functions of storytelling (why the story is being told, and what the storyteller is hoping to achieve in telling the story) and to the details of form (what people actually say).

Co-construction of stories

Further, sociolinguistic research shows that in everyday conversations in diverse societies, storytelling is often a collaborative practice. That is, even if I am telling friends about an event at which they were not present, I develop my story of that event partially in response to the ways in which they respond to my story. This may be for example in the details which I emphasise, or how I emphasise them, which may be shaped by my unconscious response to their reactions – for example, of surprise, or shock, or disbelief. Or it may be more linguistically overt, for example I may remember details of the event in response to specific questions asked by others. The ways in which conversational interaction contributes to the telling of a story is sometimes referred to as the co-production or co-construction of narrative (e.g. Trinch 2003).

Variations

Often related to the co-constructed nature of many stories, it is common for the same story to be retold in different ways, especially when the participants in the retelling are not the same people as in the original telling. When a story is retold in a different context to different listeners, it is effectively recontextualised.[5] For example, these new listeners may need more background explanation, or this new telling may be fulfilling some different functions. The recontextualisation involved in story-retelling may involve different emphases for different audiences, and it may result in some important changes. For example, it may involve the omission of details from the original telling of the story, or inclusion of details not found in its original telling, or a different choice of some of the words and expressions used. These variations in the way in which individuals tell the same story can be quite subtle, as Norrick's (1998) and Schiffrin's (2006) research found. Because it is not common conversational practice to keep a written record of everyday stories with which to compare later retellings, we may often be unaware of the extent to which variation is involved in everyday story-retelling.

Studies of story-retelling in the legal process

Of particular interest to the concerns of this chapter is the sociolinguistic research in four domains of the legal process:

1. Trinch (2003) examines the ways in which stories told by domestic abuse survivors are rewritten in affidavit form by the lawyers and paralegals who help them to apply for protective orders. The emphasis in this work is on retelling of the women's stories by their legal advisers. One of the most interesting findings of this study is that elements of the original stories in which the women present themselves as agents who try to stand up to abusive spouses are omitted from the versions of their stories presented in the affidavits written by their legal advisers. Thus in their retold stories, these women appear only as victims.
2. Work by Rock (2001) in England, Jönsson and Linell (1991) in Sweden, and Komter (2006) in the Netherlands investigates the ways in which police prepare written reports (sometimes in summary form) of police interviews. These studies all show that while the police statement is produced interactionally — as a result of talk between interviewer and interviewee — it is presented in court as the product of a single person, namely the witness or the suspect interviewed.
3. Maryns (2006) looks at the ways in which the stories of asylum seekers are repackaged and retold as they go through

the bureaucratic, and sometimes also legal, steps in verifying their claims to refugee status. She demonstrates the 'filtering process' by which significant elements of asylum seekers' stories are sometimes transformed or deleted.

4. The ways in which lawyers' questions in cross-examination can retell aspects of witnesses' stories has been examined by Matoesian (1993), Ehrlich (2001, 2007), Cotterill (2004) and Eades (2008).

All of these studies demonstrate that it is problematic to view the stories which emerge in these contexts as the sole product of the storyteller. As with everyday storytelling, these stories are co-produced or co-constructed. For example, Jönsson and Linell (1991, p. 434) talk about the problem of 'the blurring of source distinctions'. They explain that 'one cannot know from reading [the written reports of Swedish police interviews] under what conditions a given piece of information has been introduced'. Has it been introduced 'more or less spontaneously by the suspect in a narrative turn', or is it introduced in the proposition of the interviewer's question and only then 'confirmed (or sometimes, modified or denied) by the suspect'? This 'blurring of source distinctions' has also been investigated by Shuy in his work on undercover FBI recordings (e.g. 2005).

It might be thought that this cannot happen in the Australian legal system, because suspect interviews with police are presented as verbatim interviews, not in summary form (unlike the Swedish examples discussed by Jönsson & Linell 1991). However, the decontextualised way in which extracts from police interviews are read in cross-examination (to be discussed below), arguably can also result in the blurring of source distinctions, making it impossible to understand crucial contextual factors involved in the original co-construction of the story.

This sociolinguistic research on story-retelling in the first three of the above four legal contexts concerns the retelling of an interviewee's original oral story by the interviewer in written form. In the courtroom, however, the retold story is oral, and it appears to be retold by the original teller. That is, in examination-in-chief the witness retells the story they have earlier told in police interviews, and aspects of this retelling are further retold during cross-examination.

But in the courtroom it is not as simple as a witness retelling their own story. Here too the story is co-constructed, with the interviewer actively contributing to the telling of the witness's story. This active contribution is seen in the choice of words in the propositions of questions, the order in which topics are introduced, the ways in which topics are linked, and the topics which are omitted or which the witness is prevented from talking about.

10.2.3 THE IDEOLOGY OF INCONSISTENCY

While sociolinguistic research has established that there are inevitable variations in the ways in which stories are retold, such variations attract a special significance in the legal process. This is particularly the case in cross-examination, where such variations are more negatively perceived as inconsistencies. For example, Mauet (2000, p. 280) recommends 'raising prior inconsistent statements' as the central strategy in discrediting a witness. Skilful cross-examination often involves tripping up a witness on inconsistencies between different earlier tellings of their story (for example comparing two police interviews, or comparing a police interview with examination-in-chief), or between one or more earlier tellings on the one hand, and answers about the story in cross-examination on the other.

These variations or inconsistencies between the ways in which a witness tells a story on different occasions can be interpreted in court as lies, and can enable participants in a trial process to decide that a witness is unreliable or untruthful. But not all inconsistencies are lies. In addition to the sociolinguistic research on variations in storytelling, discussed above, there is a wealth of relevant psychological research on memory (some of which is discussed by McClellan 2006). This psychological research tells us that the memory process involves three stages: acquisition, retention and retrieval, and that recollection is a 'reconstructive process' (Parkin 1999, p. 17). Accuracy in recollection involves many complexities at all three stages of the memory process.

Courts may take account of such findings, as for example in the Californian standard (pattern) jury instructions given to jurors in the OJ Simpson case: 'Failure of recollection is a common experience, and innocent misrecollection is not uncommon' (Tiersma 1999, p. 253).[6] But such examples of the legal system appearing to recognise that events are not always remembered in the same way are somewhat undermined by the central legal activity of exploiting variations in witnesses' stories. And the ways in which witnesses' stories in the legal process are structured by lawyer questions appear to ignore psychological experiments which demonstrate that free reports, not interrupted by questions, produce the most accurate recollections (Loftus 1979). Similarly, there appears to be little regard in the legal process for experimental findings on the power of word choice in questions in affecting a person's recollection (see also Loftus 1979).[7]

So, there are two major issues to be taken into account in the consideration of 'inconsistencies' or variations between a witness's different tellings of their story: perceptual and social. The perceptual issues relate to how the mind processes the past, including what Gray (2007, p. 6) summarises as 'the innate inaccuracy of human recollection'. The social dimensions include the way in which stories are often co-constructed, and are always told in specific social contexts for specific reasons — that is, contextualised, as well as the fact that there are often variations in the ways in which stories are retold in different contexts — that is, recontextualised.

But the perceptual and social dimensions of inconsistency in storytelling are often ignored by the legal system, which, as Matoesian (2001, pp. 37–38) points out, conceives of inconsistency as 'logical' incongruity. Matoesian argues, on the contrary, that inconsistency is not necessarily an attribute or failing of an individual, it can be interactively constituted and sustained. That is, inconsistency can be *achieved* through the interactional work which is done during the hearing. And in this interactional work, witnesses are greatly limited by the rules of evidence. They can only speak in answer to a question, and attempts to raise issues not addressed by a specific question generally result in commands such as 'just answer the questions asked'. Further, the questioner (lawyer or judicial officer) has the linguistic power to introduce into questions presuppositions which many witnesses may not be able to dispute, as we will see in Extract 2 below.

This interactionally achieved inconsistency between two or more tellings of a story, whether by different witnesses, or the same witnesses in different contexts or on different occasions, is used by lawyers to guide decision makers in making 'findings of fact'. As Gray (2007, p. 1) explains, this is typically based on determinations about the truthfulness of witnesses. This is not the place to enter into the problematic arena of 'truth' in the law.[8] But leaving aside problems in conceptualising 'the truth', in the way in which the truthfulness of witnesses is determined there is an underlying 'linguistic ideology of inconsistency' (Matoesian 2001, p. 68). The interactional work involved in achieving inconsistency is not considered. It is perceived as the failing of individual witnesses, who can be therefore deemed to be lacking reliability and truthfulness.

10.2.4 DECONTEXTUALISING THE WITNESS'S STORY

In addition to the witness's story being recontextualised (or retold) in courtroom hearings, it is often also decontextualised in cross-examination questions. That is, when a witness answers questions about an earlier telling of their story (for example from a police interview), parts of the story are often excerpted and questioned in isolation from the rest of the previous telling. To apply the words of linguistic anthropologists Bauman and Briggs (1990, p. 73) to the courtroom situation, the story which the witness has told on an earlier occasion is 'lifted out of its interactional setting' or decontextualised. There are several notable features of such decontextualised fragments of a witness's story. I have mentioned above that such decontextualisation can omit key aspects of earlier questions and answers, which are thus not provided to hearers on the new occasion. This can result in the 'blurring of source distinctions', in that it can be difficult to discern the particular conditions in which particular parts of the story have been told.

But there are more serious concerns about how the decontextualised fragments of an earlier telling are read by the cross-examining lawyer from the interview or hearing transcript. Transcripts present propositional content, and do not record many important elements of the talk, such as emphasis, intonation, volume, and pauses (see Eades 1996b). But no-one can read out a transcript without making (often subconscious) choices about these aspects of speech. And they can make a fundamental difference in meaning. For example, a question such as 'You were there, weren't you?' can be uttered with different word stress (or emphasis), intonation, volume and pauses to convey a range of meanings and attitudes, from bullying coercion, to uncertainty, to supportive reassurance. And the simplest monosyllabic answer 'yes' can be read from a transcript to convey confident agreement, when it may have been uttered after a lengthy pause in a tentative and barely audible voice.[9] Thus the decontextualised fragment of a witness's earlier telling of their story can be presented by a lawyer in cross-examination in such a way as to convey a rather different version of the story or part(s) of it. And the rules of evidence which control courtroom talk make it difficult for even the most analytical of witnesses to present a meta-commentary on such a transformation of their story.

A particularly problematic use of the decontextualisation of fragments of an earlier telling of a witness's story can occur in interpreted proceedings. No matter how accurate an interpreted version of an original utterance may be, there can be minor differences when this interpreted version is re-interpreted into the speaker's language (this is known as backtranslation). Variations between an original text and its backtranslated version do not necessarily reflect inaccuracy, but rather the reality that there can be more than one way of expressing the same meaning in any language. But asking a witness to recognise the backtranslated version as their own words can be problematic.

And Cooke (1995a) discusses the difficulties which can be experienced by traditionally oriented Aboriginal witnesses who find it hard to understand why a lawyer is claiming that a written document is the story that they told some time earlier to a different person, namely the police officer. Cooke (p. 71) cites the example of a witness who expressed his confusion in such a situation, saying *My story is a short story, this paper is many pages. I don't understand why this is supposed to be my story.*

10.3 Implications for Aboriginal witnesses

We have seen in the previous section that there are fundamental contradictions between everyday storytelling on the one hand, and the expectations and interpretations of storytelling in court on the other. There can be no doubt that these contradictions exist for a variety of complex legal reasons. And there can also be no doubt that they create difficulties for many witnesses, particularly for witnesses with little or no understanding of the intricacies of legal culture. For example, witnesses may be unable to explain that some inconsistencies are memory lapses or failures. They may also be unaware of, and/or unable to explain, the complex ways in which a story may be told in a slightly different way on different occasions and/or to different audiences.

In the remainder of this chapter, I turn to some implications of these contradictions for intercultural communication in court with Aboriginal witnesses. Despite superficial lifestyle similarities between Aboriginal and non-Aboriginal people in many parts of Australia, Aboriginal culture remains strong. While it is important not to overgeneralise, and there are indeed many different Aboriginal cultures, we can see some subtle but important ways in which Aboriginal ways of thinking, acting and believing differ from those of other cultures in Australia. Of particular relevance here are differences in ways of using and interpreting language between Aboriginal cultures and the culture of the law. There may well be greater similarities between Aboriginal cultures and those of some immigrant groups, than between Aboriginal cultures and the culture of the law, but this possibility is outside of the scope of this chapter and of my expertise. It is also important to point out that bicultural Aboriginal people can switch between Aboriginal ways of thinking, acting and believing, and those of the mainstream society. It is Aboriginal people who do not have such bicultural skills who are the focus of the discussion in this section.[10]

There are a number of aspects of Aboriginal ways of communicating which are particularly relevant to the consideration of telling your story in court. Some of these will be discussed below in relation to the assumptions about how language works that are central to the legal culture of the courtroom (see also Cooke 1996; Eades 1992; Gray 2000; Mildren 1997; Neate 2003; Walsh 1994).

10.3.1 ASSUMPTIONS ABOUT REPEATED QUESTIONING

We have already discussed the central role of questions in structuring, organising and limiting the ways in which a witness can tell their story in court. But more than this, underlying any adversarial courtroom hearing is the assumption that repeated questioning allows a witness's truthfulness to be assessed. While repeated questioning undoubtedly puts a cognitive and emotional strain on many witnesses, it is nevertheless consistent with the mainstream western cultural assumption that information is generally sought and verified by questions. And repeated questioning effectively forms the basis of other common speech events in mainstream western societies, such as interviews, questionnaires, quizzes, and so on. But the interview is not a speech event found in traditional Aboriginal societies, and nor is it typical in non-traditional twenty-first century Aboriginal societies. Important information is often sought and verified in much less direct ways than by repeated questioning. This means that many Aboriginal people are less practised in handling repeated questioning than mainstream non-Aboriginal Australians who have been socialised to deal with this from an early age. Further, the common courtroom questioning strategy of lawyers only asking questions for which the interviewer already knows the answer is one that Aboriginal people may be much less familiar with than other Australians.

The next two subsections will briefly consider ways in which Aboriginal people respond to repeated questioning.

10.3.2 ASSUMPTIONS ABOUT YES ANSWERS

It has been documented for many decades that Aboriginal people often answer *yes* to a question (or *no* to a negative question) regardless of whether they actually agree with the proposition being questioned, or even understand the question (e.g. Strehlow 1936, p. 334; Elkin 1947, p. 176). In 1959, Justice Kriewaldt of the Northern Territory Supreme Court explained:

> ...the very process of question and answer which is the basis of the extraction of evidence, might not fully extract what he [the Aboriginal witness] knows, what he tried to say, nor what his intent was. An answer in the affirmative could indicate that the Aboriginal witness is trying to understand the question, that he has understood it, that he has understood part of it, that he may not have understood it at all, or that he does not want the question to go unanswered, or that he thinks that an affirmative answer is more likely to be acceptable to the questioner than a negative answer. (*R v Aboriginal Dulcie Dumaia* (1959) NT 274, quoted in McCorquordale 1987, p. 33)

This conversational strategy is known as 'gratuitous concurrence' (Liberman 1980, 1981), and it has been found to typify many interviews with Aboriginal people (although it is not limited to this sociocultural group). This causes particular problems in legal contexts, where saying *yes* in answer to a question is taken as a binding agreement. This widespread Aboriginal tendency to use gratuitous concurrence is a particular problem for the ways in which witnesses' story-retelling is restricted in cross-examination. To express this cultural difference in legal terms, it seems reasonable to assume that many, if not most, Aboriginal witnesses who are not bicultural are highly suggestible, and that this cultural issue compromises the role of cross-examination in the delivery of justice. In Eades (2008), I examine this issue in a particularly disturbing case, widely known as the Pinkenba case (*Crawford v Venardos & Ors*; see also Eades 2002, 2003a, 2004a).

There can be no doubt that cultural factors (sometimes combined with other factors, such as feelings of intimidation) play an important part in the elicitation of gratuitous concurrence by the use of leading questions in the cross-examination of Aboriginal witnesses. Justice Mildren of the Northern Territory Supreme Court points out (1997, p. 15) that while it 'is generally thought that counsel has the right, in cross-examination to put leading questions to any witness', this is 'not the case'. Citing Justice Barry in *Mooney v James*, Mildren says that

Recent discussions with Justice Mildren and other judicial officers and lawyers in the Northern Territory and Western Australia suggest that this power is now being used more than previously with Aboriginal witnesses in these jurisdictions.

> more use should be made of [the] power to prevent questions being put unfairly to Aboriginal witnesses in leading form in cross-examination whenever it appears or it is made to appear to the trial judge that the witness is likely not to be protected from suggestibility..."[11]

One of the problematic factors involved in the Aboriginal tendency to use gratuitous concurrence is that this difference in language use is not apparent to many people. The word *yes* and its variants, such as *yeah* and *mm*, are English words. Many people appear to be unaware of dialectal differences in the use of English, and they mistakenly think they can understand any *yes* answer.

10.3.3 ASSUMPTIONS ABOUT SILENCE IN ANSWER TO QUESTIONS

A related assumption also affects the interpretation of Aboriginal silence following a question. Silence sounds the same in any dialect (or language), but it does not always carry the same meaning. Research with Aboriginal English speakers has found that silence is an important and positively valued part of many Aboriginal conversations (see e.g. Eades 1991a, chapter 4, 2007; Ngarritjian-Kessaris 1997). Silence often indicates a participant's desire to think, or simply to enjoy the presence of others in a non-verbal way.[12] This is a difficult matter for most non-Aboriginal people to recognise and learn, because in western societies silence is so often negatively evaluated in conversations. For example, between people who are not close friends or family, silence in conversations, or interviews, is frequently an indication of some kind of communication breakdown.

This difference has serious implications for police, lawyer, and courtroom interviews of Aboriginal people. Aboriginal silence in these settings can easily be interpreted as evasion, ignorance, confusion, insolence, or even guilt. According to law, silence should not be taken as admission of guilt, but it is difficult for police officers, legal professionals or jurors to set aside strong cultural intuitions about the meaning of silence, especially when they are not aware of cultural differences in the use and interpretation of silence. Further, a misunderstanding of Aboriginal ways of using silence can lead to lawyers interrupting an Aboriginal person's answer. Of course, we customarily define interruption as involving a second person starting to talk before the first speaker has finished talking. But if we accept that the first part of an Aboriginal answer often starts with silence, then to start the next question before the Aboriginal interviewee has had the time to speak is in effect to interrupt the first part of the answer. Similarly, Aboriginal witnesses' silences in the middle of an answer may also be interrupted.

This important cultural difference in assumptions about silence in answer to questions compounds for Aboriginal people the problems that all witnesses face in being required to present their story in court in the form of answers to questions.

10.3.4 ASSUMPTIONS ABOUT WORD MEANING

At the heart of cross-examination strategy there are often subtle but key differences in meaning. But in contrast to ordinary conversation, there are strong restrictions on the negotiation of word choice and meaning. And, as we have seen, any negotiation has to be framed in terms of an answer to the immediately preceding question. Witnesses with experience in professional cultures which place a high priority on language manipulation (e.g. lawyers and academics) may have the greatest advantage in defending their earlier storytelling in the face of such questioning. Subtle dialectal differences in word meaning can place Aboriginal witnesses at an even greater disadvantage than other witnesses.

A powerful example comes from Cooke's (1995a, p. 91) analysis of the cross-examination of an Aboriginal witness in a Northern Territory coronial inquiry. This witness gave evidence that on a particular night there was a *half moon* shining, and 'that he knew this because he remembered looking at the moon that night'. One of the cross-examining counsel who was 'confident that there was no half moon on that night' saw a chance to present the witness as unreliable, saying to him 'you're sure you're not just making this up now?'. In this situation, the manipulation of dialectal difference — which was likely to be unwitting — was averted by the interpreter's interjection. As a result, the witness was asked to draw the moon that night, and 'it became evident that he was using the [Aboriginal English] expression *half moon* to mean what is referred to in Standard English as a crescent moon'. On most occasions on which Aboriginal speakers of varieties of English give evidence, there is no interpreter and thus no mechanism for dialectal differences to be drawn to the attention of the court. But this was an unusual case because an interpreter was present in the court for witnesses who did not speak enough English. His initiative and skill in drawing the attention of the court to possible dialectal difference in the meaning of the expression *half moon* was complemented by the court's openness to receiving such communication facilitation.[13]

10.3.5 BEYOND CULTURE

We have seen some particular features of language use which are linguistically significant for Aboriginal people in court. The culture of the courtroom is based on ways of thinking about how language works, and ways of using language which can be quite different from those in Aboriginal cultures. There can be no doubt that these cultural differences have important implications for the delivery of justice to Aboriginal people. But wider societal power relationships are also relevant to intercultural communication. And the difficulties which Aboriginal people experience in telling their stories in court may at times have more to do with race relations, as well as the historical and political dimensions of their Aboriginality, than the cultural ones.

In Eades (2008) I examine in considerable detail the cross-examinations of three Aboriginal boys in the Pinkenba case, which involved a 1995 committal hearing in the Brisbane Magistrates Court (*Crawford v Venardos & Ors*). The boys were prosecution witnesses in a case in which six police officers had been charged with unlawfully depriving them of their liberty by taking them in the middle of the night to an industrial wasteland (in the Pinkenba area) in three police cars. The Pinkenba hearing highlighted the extremes that are allowable in cross-examination, with the harassment, haranguing and linguistic manipulation of the child witnesses being the worst that many lawyers have seen. In this hearing, there were many disturbing examples of cultural differences in language use, such as the apparent exploitation of the Aboriginal tendency to use gratuitous concurrence. But a number of courtroom linguistic strategies that impacted on the three Aboriginal witnesses were not related to cultural differences in communication. Space limitations permit just one brief example.

The boys all said in their examination-in-chief that they were *walking around* the Valley (Fortitude Valley near the Brisbane City Centre), before the police officers approached them and told them to get in the police cars. *Walking around* is a commonly used general Australian English, as well as Aboriginal English, description for a frequent and widespread youth activity in many cities throughout the world. In cross-examination, the first defence counsel (DC1) did not accept David's term *walking around* from his evidence-in-chief, and instead substituted his own term 'wander around' [the name David is a pseudonym]. David did not directly dispute this term, although he did not use it, as we see in the extract below:

Extract 1[14]

1. DC1: You wandered around the streets of Brisbane- we know that you were in the mall up in the heart of the town we know you walked down towards North Quay- we can see you on- tapes- we know you were in the Valley.
2. David: (2.7) Mm.
3. DC1: And you were just wandering around (2.0) [weren't you?
4. David: [Yes.
5. DC1: For [what?
6. David: [Yes.
7. DC1: For what?
8. David: (2.3) Looking.
9. DC1: Looking (1.5) At what?
10. David: (2.3) We was just walking around for nothing.

Despite David persisting with his expression *walking around* to describe what the boys were doing that night, DC1 persists with his alternative 'wandering around' in later questions. This might seem to be a subtle difference, but it is not a trivial one: while *walk around* does not imply a destination, it does imply a purpose (e.g. 'walking around window-shopping' or 'walking around and looking at the people'). 'Wander around' on the other hand seems to connote neither destination nor purpose, and it collocates easily with the adverb 'aimlessly'.[15]

David's answer in Turn 8 to the 'for what?' question is interesting: *looking* or 'observing the comings and goings of others around them' (see Section 4.5.1) is indeed an important Aboriginal social activity. As *walking around looking* is not an activity commonly practised by middle-class adults, it is possible that DC1 did not understand David's answers. And as DC1 persisted with his 'wandering around' in later questions, the thirteen-year-old Aboriginal witness was not able to counter the linguistic skills with which the defence counsel recontextualised his story of what he had been doing that night in the Valley. The difference between these two verbs may seem like a minor matter in terms of the witness's allegation of being unlawfully deprived of his liberty. But it played an important role in the construction of him and his two mates as a threat to public safety, particularly in combination with evidence about their criminal records – in effect, it was a linguistic tool used to construct these boys as vagrants.

A similar, but more powerful, recontextualisation of the witness's story by the lawyer took place with the oldest witness, who was fifteen years old at the time of the hearing. He also told the court that what he and his two mates were doing that night in the Valley was *walking around*. This was substituted by DC1, not with 'wandering around', as we saw with the youngest witness, but with 'prowling around', as we see in the extract below.

Extract 2

1. DC1: (3.2) And just prowling around <u>look</u>ing for <u>mis</u>chief weren't you?
2. Barry: (3.2) No- just walking around.

Central to the meaning of 'prowl' is that the agent is in search of something that is not legitimately theirs: 'prey or plunder', as the Macquarie Dictionary expresses it. Thus, this word 'prowl' is a clever tool in the implication that the boys were intending to engage in criminal activity, and thus were 'fair game' for law enforcement activity. Although no evidence was produced to indicate that the boys were engaged in criminal activity that night, their story about what they were doing was taken over by the lawyers in cross-examination, using such linguistic strategies as we have seen in these two extracts.

Although Barry was able to counter the accusation that he and his mates were 'prowling around looking for mischief' (in the form of criminal activity), DC1 exercised his greater control over Barry's story to use this loaded verb 'prowl' in the presupposition of a later question, asking of Barry's previous activities (for which he had already been dealt with by the courts): 'What sort of things did you steal- when you were wan- prowling around the streets?' DC1 started to say the word 'wandering' and changed it to 'prowling', suggesting the deliberateness of this lexical substitution strategy here.[16]

Although this is just one small example (with two parts), it indicates the ways in which lawyers' power to decontextualise and recontextualise parts of witnesses' stories can invoke and perpetuate cultural stereotypes. In the Australian media, Aboriginal people are constantly linked with crime (e.g. Jakubowicz et al. 1994, pp. 38–39). Using linguistic strategies such as we have seen in this example, the two defence counsel in this case succeeded in connecting to and contributing to this widespread view of Aboriginal people as a criminal threat to public safety. In dropping the charges against the six police officers, the magistrate devoted one-third of his decision to a criticism of the three Aboriginal boys. In taking up their criminal identity that had been the theme of their cross-examination, he said that the boys 'have no regard for members of the community, their property or even the justice system'.

In my view, there was more going on in the Pinkenba case than simply the reliance on and reproduction of negative stereotypes about Aboriginal people: this case was an important part of the struggle over the rights of police officers to remove Aboriginal people from public places. It is not possible to develop and justify this argument here, but it is the theme of Eades (2008), in which this case is situated in the ongoing societal struggle, which began in the colonial period [see also Chapter 11]. Today, the struggle is over neocolonial control over the lives of Aboriginal people, as exemplified in the actions of the police in taking the boys to the Pinkenba area that night and abandoning them there (without ever taking them to a police station, or charging them with any offence, or contacting any of their relatives or friends). In the committal hearing in this case, the struggle moved to the courtroom, and courtroom talk played a central role. I show in Eades (2008) how this case reveals the extremes of language use which are allowable in the 'proper' functioning of the criminal process. Central to these extremes of cross-examination are the ways of communicating and assumptions about language which have been discussed in this chapter.

10.3.6 SUMMARY OF IMPLICATIONS FOR ABORIGINAL WITNESSES

We have seen that the ways that a witness is allowed to tell and defend their story in court, as well as the ways in which their story is evaluated, are based on a number of cultural assumptions about how language works. These assumptions are part of legal culture, and they are somewhat at odds with the ways that storytelling works in everyday conversations. This can cause problems for any witness who is not familiar with the ways of thinking, believing and acting that are part of legal culture. An example is the way in which evidence in court is structured and controlled by lawyer questions, yet taken as the story of the witness, who may actually say very little in the co-construction of the story. But there are other assumptions about how language works which are found more widely in mainstream Australian culture, but are at odds with the ways that language works in Aboriginal cultures. An example is the assumption that repeated questioning allows a person's truthfulness to be assessed.

These cultural differences in the ways in which language is used in the courtroom are compounded by a number of other cultural differences. Space permits only a brief mention of these. There are important cultural differences in the ways in which people's actions outside the courtroom are understood and evaluated. For example, Cooke (1995a, pp. 89–91) contrasts the Yolngu[17] evaluation of an individual's habit of going for a very long walk by himself as a sign of ill-health (particularly of mental health problems), with an Anglo barrister's evaluation that it is a sign of good health. Cooke explains that this involves profound cultural differences about illness, health, and the ways in which mind and body are connected. And in Eades (2008) I contrast Aboriginal evaluations of the use of 'four-letter words' with those found in legal culture.

Also, this chapter has not dealt with intercultural differences in demeanour, which can be very important in assessing the credibility of a witness. One example is that while avoiding eye contact with your interlocutor can be a sign of respect in many Aboriginal societies, in the culture of the courtroom, it can be interpreted as evasion and/or dishonesty (see also Gray 2007). Justice Gray calls into question the judicial tendency to assess the truthfulness and credibility of a witness on the basis of such features of demeanour as a wide range of body movements including foot shuffling, nose-scratching, as well as eye contact or avoidance.

Another area which is not dealt with in this chapter concerns the implications of cultural differences in language use for Aboriginal people who require interpreting assistance in giving evidence in court (see Cooke 2002, 2004).[18]

10.4 Alternative approaches to storytelling in court?

The previous two sections have highlighted some of the problems involved in the ways in which stories are told and retold in the courtroom, and the underlying cultural assumptions. We have seen some fundamental problems in *telling* your story in court, compounded by other problems involved in the *assessment* of this storytelling. We have also seen some particular significance of these issues for Aboriginal Australians. It has been beyond the scope of this chapter to consider issues related to Australians from other cultural groups. But given the well-documented difficulty which the criminal justice system has in delivering justice to Aboriginal people, we should ask: How can the criminal justice system respond to these issues?

In September 2012 the Queensland government announced the abolition of the Murri Court, as a cost-saving measure.

The most important legal response to Aboriginal needs to date has been the introduction of Indigenous sentencing courts, such as the Nunga Court in South Australia, the Koori Court in Victoria, the Murri Court in Queensland, and Circle Sentencing Courts in New South Wales. The major focus of these initiatives has been bringing Indigenous community members, particularly Elders and other respected persons, together with legal professionals to deliver justice. These courts are being credited with considerable effectiveness in addressing law and order breakdown in communities, in restoring balance to communities, in giving victims a voice, in rehabilitating offenders, and in assisting them to take responsibility for their actions.

A number of features of the way in which Indigenous courts operate are seen as central to this effectiveness, and one of these relates to language use. A review of circle sentencing in New South Wales found that the 'use of colloquial language in place of complicated terms and legal jargon was striking' and that this colloquial language 'facilitated communication' (Potas et al. 2003, p. 10). Aboriginal participants commented favourably on the fact that they can use 'Aboriginal English, rather than the language used in other courts' (Potas et al. 2003, p. 20), and that 'you can use your own language and [the other circle members] know what you mean or understand, and most importantly you are respected for who you are at the same level' (p. 43). It is quite likely that using Aboriginal English implies not just accent, grammar and vocabulary, but also ways of communicating, such as the use of silence discussed above.

To date, there is little research on the workings of Indigenous courts (but see Stroud 2006 for a sociolinguistic overview of the Koori Court in Victoria). But initial investigations from a sociolinguistic perspective indicate that there are important differences in discourse structure between circle sentencing and traditional courts. These differences are likely to be of far greater consequence than the avoidance of 'complicated legal terms' (which in my observations in courts do not actually occur very frequently in talk addressed to witnesses, but much more frequently in talk between legal professionals, often about a witness, see also Heffer 2005). In circle sentencing, defendants' stories are not structured by questions. While the magistrate convenes the circle, and acts as the facilitator, the aim is to encourage participants to talk, not to control their contributions. Most importantly for the discussion in this chapter, it appears that questions do not play a central role. The talk is free flowing, and typically participants often take long turns. Repetition is not a problem, and relevance is not an issue – there is a widespread recognition that the issues facing the circle are complex, and interrelated, and that many factors need to be considered.

The fact that these Indigenous courts operate with everyday ways of using language is an encouraging sign. The emphasis is on communication and community, rather than propositional content and a rigid discourse structure, in which witnesses are limited in what they can say by the questions they are asked. But these innovative courts deal only with sentencing in cases where the defendant has pleaded guilty, and where there would already be a greatly reduced, if any, role for cross-examination. They do not take the place of trials, and it is hard to see how that could ever happen. The rights of an accused person to remain innocent until proven guilty are protected to a considerable extent by the rules of evidence which have the consequences for cross-examination discussed above.

Moving away from criminal courts and away from Aboriginal witnesses specifically, we can also look to civil courts and tribunals for alternative approaches to storytelling in court. For example, it is now common in commercial courts for witnesses to be allowed, or even required, to give their evidence-in-chief in the form of affidavits or witness (written) statements. But this practice means that witnesses do not have any chance to tell their story in evidence-in-chief: what is presented is a carefully crafted written document, co-produced by witness and lawyer. While this approach removes the opportunity for evidence-in-chief to be interrupted by lawyer questions, it also removes the opportunity for the witness to tell their own story in court. And variations between the lawyer language of the statement and the witness's own words in cross-examination can then lead to extensive questioning over inconsistency. Some judges have become disenchanted with this practice, and have reverted to the previous method of examination-in-chief. But, while practices vary between judges, some other judges invite witnesses to tell their stories in their own words, minimising interruptions and objections by counsel.[19] This approach also minimises some of the problems discussed in this chapter with decontextualisation and recontextualisation of witnesses' stories. But, in common with the Indigenous sentencing courts, this alternative approach cannot address the sociolinguistic problems with cross-examination which have been discussed in this paper.

My sociolinguistic perspective has pointed to some problems with legal cultural ways of limiting and interpreting story-retelling in cross-examination, as well as storytelling in examination-in-chief. But this perspective is inevitably legally naïve. The adversarial common law system has a long history and is very complex. There are many legal reasons why language is used in courtroom hearings in the ways outlined in this chapter. I have not made any suggestions about how to address the incompatibility between language practices and assumptions in the courtroom on the one hand, and in everyday language use on the other. Nor have I made suggestions about how to address the particular implications which have been raised for the participation of Aboriginal witnesses in the legal process. Such suggestions need careful consideration and input from legal professionals and scholars. I hope that this chapter can provide some stimulus for fruitful interdisciplinary dialogue on this topic.

NOTES

1. This chapter is based on a talk I first presented at the annual conference of the Australasian Institute of Judicial Administration in October 2007. Since then, I have drawn on this talk for presentations to the Migration and Refugee Review Tribunals Annual Members conference, the Queensland Magistrates Annual conference, and the Law School at the University of New England. I am grateful to audiences at these talks for questions and comments. I also acknowledge Michael Cooke, Justice Peter Gray, Jeff Siegel, and two anonymous reviewers who made valuable comments on the draft. All remaining errors are my responsibility.
2. Another important factor which enabled Daphne to tell her own story in court was the linguistic assistance provided by an interpreter. The court allowed Daphne to use her first language as required, and although she gave most of her evidence in English, she switched to her first language for complex matters such as her mental state at the time of the stabbing (see Cooke 1996).
3. Yes–No questions are those which can be answered by either 'Yes' or 'No' (although they are not restricted to these answers), e.g. 'Was Aunty Mabel at the house?' WH-questions are those that ask who, where what, how and why, e.g. 'Who was at the house?' 'Where was Aunty Mabel?' 'How did that happen?'

4. A reviewer has questioned whether re-examination by the witness's lawyer can provide opportunities to 'rectify interferences with the witness's own story which have occurred in cross-examination'. However, my observations and studies (e.g. Eades 2008) suggest that such a safeguard can only address some of these 'interferences', and cannot address the major problems caused by the structuring of stories through questions which occur in both examination-in-chief and cross-examination.
5. Note that in this section we are considering recontextualisation of a story by its original teller. But stories can be recontextualised by another storyteller, as when lawyers in cross-examination present in their assertions and questions a different version of the witness's story. We will see an example of this in Section 10.3.5 below.
6. Tiersma (2006, p. 10) recommends that this example of a triple-negative legalese statement be revised to 'People often forget things or they may honestly believe that something happened even though it turns out later that they were wrong'.
7. For example Loftus (1979, pp. 77–78) reports an experiment in which subjects were asked questions about a car accident they had seen on film. Asked to estimate how fast the cars were going, those who were asked '... when they smashed into each other' gave higher estimates of speed than those were were asked '... when they hit each other'.
8. For four rather different approaches see Gray (2007), Heerey (2000), McClellan (2006) and McKillop (2002).
9. See Hale (2004, pp. 96–104) for a study of interpreted courtroom talk in which she shows how interpreters' omissions of pauses and hesitations from witnesses' Spanish testimony result in a rather different speaking style. Hale (pp. 144–157) also conducted an experimental study, which combined pauses and hesitations with other features of witnesses' speech which are not relevant to this chapter, such as grammatical errors and problems of pronunication. This experimental study found that such seemingly small aspects of the speech style of testimony can have a significant effect on the ways in which witnesses are evaluated (consistent with earlier American work by Conley & O'Barr and colleagues, e.g. Conley et al. 1978; Berk-Seligson 1990).
10. It is beyond the scope of this chapter and my expertise to consider Torres Strait Islander cultures.
11. Justice Mildren used this power in *R v Kenny Charlie* 28 September 1995, unreported (see CJC 1996, pp. 51–52).
12. Some similarities can be noted with the use of silence in Native American societies (Basso 1970; Philips 1976).
13. Other examples are found in Cooke 1995b.
14. See the appendix for transcription conventions.
15. The relevant definitions from the Macquarie Dictionary of Australian English give 'walk' as '1) to go or travel on foot at a moderate pace', and 'wander' as '1) to ramble without any certain course or object in view, roam, rove, or stray; 2) to go aimlessly or casually'.
16. Elsewhere (Eades 2006, 2008) I have discussed this strategy in more depth, using the term 'lexical perversion' to describe the substitution of words and phrases such as this, where this substitution distorts (or perverts) the way in which a person reports their own experiences.
17. 'Yolngu' refers to Aboriginal people and culture in Northeast Arnhem Land.
18. Another area which may prove fruitful for future research would involve extending the work by Malcolm and his colleagues (e.g. Malcolm & Rochecouste 2000; Malcolm & Sharifian 2002) on the stories which Aboriginal children tell in varieties of English about their own experiences (i.e. first person narratives). These stories involve a small number of recurring schemas, of which the most frequent involves travel. The cyclical nature of the stories contrasts with the widespread linear nature of Anglo stories.
19. I am indebted to Justice Peter Gray (2007, pers. comm., 19 September) for this information.

Chapter 11

The social consequences of language ideologies in courtroom cross-examination

First published in 2012, this chapter expands on some of the issues raised in Chapter 10, and considers aspects of the ways that English is used by, to and about Aboriginal people in the criminal justice process. Written for an international sociolinguistic audience, this chapter shows that there is more to courtroom talk than the issues most frequently researched, namely the power struggle over questions and answers and rights to speak. The argument in this chapter is that we need to examine language ideologies, which I refer to in writing for a wider audience (as in Chapters 9 and 10) as 'assumptions about language'.

Understanding the concept of language ideologies enables us to see how problematic courtroom practices are accepted as necessary for the operation of the law. We will also see the central role of language ideologies in the evaluation of witnesses' stories. The Pinkenba case (which has also provided examples and discussion in Chapters 7, 9 and 10) shows how this all works, and leads to my argument about societal inequality, specifically about the role of courtroom talk in the perpetuation of neocolonial control. Where most (but not all) sociolinguistic courtroom research treats inequality as something that happens in the courtroom, this case study shows how courtroom talk can have much wider social consequences.

Abstract

Investigations of inequality within the courtroom have mostly examined ways in which discourse structure and rules of use constrain witnesses. This chapter

First published as Eades, D 2012, 'The social consequences of language ideologies in courtroom cross-examination', *Language in Society*, vol. 41, no. 4, pp. 471–497.

goes beyond interactional practices to deal with four central language ideologies, which both facilitate these practices and impact on the interpretation and understanding of what people say in evidence. The chapter further shows that language ideologies can have much wider consequences beyond the courtroom. Focusing on language ideologies involved in storytelling and retelling in cross-examination, and using an Australian example, the chapter traces the recontextualisation of part of a witness's story from an initial investigative interview to cross-examination, then to its evaluation in closing arguments and the judicial decision, as well as its (mis)representation in the print media. The analysis reveals the role of these language ideologies in the perpetuation of neocolonial control over Australian Aboriginal people.

11.1 Introduction[1]

In the first three decades of research on courtroom talk, sociolinguists have documented a number of specific ways in which defendants and witnesses are controlled, coerced and manipulated through the rigid and asymmetrical discourse structure of courtroom hearings, which restricts the interactional rights of witnesses to providing answers to specific questions (see, for example, Woodbury 1984, Cotterill 2003, Gibbons 2003).

In contrast to the focus in much of this research on investigating inequality and imbalance <u>within</u> the courtroom, some recent studies have been asking about consequences beyond the courtroom, within an approach which integrates structure and agency. This approach examines courtroom talk not just in its immediate context, but also in its social, cultural and historical contexts. For example, Matoesian (e.g. 1993, 2001) and Ehrlich (e.g. 2001) show how the patriarchal social order is reproduced through talk in rape trials in their analyses of how victims are questioned in court, and how their accounts of their experiences are transformed by lawyers' questions and summaries. Like most of the sociolinguistic research on courtroom talk to date, this chapter focuses on the common law legal system, as found in Australia, the UK, most of the US, and most of Britain's other former colonies.

This chapter draws on my recent Australian work (e.g. Eades 2008) which examines the social consequences of courtroom talk in ongoing neocolonial control of the state over Aboriginal people, and which has shown, for example, how lawyer questions and summaries can define Aboriginal people as a threat to public safety on the streets (Eades 2006). In this chapter I focus on language ideologies, and their role in facilitating problematic interactional practices in court, as well as their impact on the interpretation and understanding of what witnesses say, as part of my response to the call by Conley and O'Barr (2005) for analysis of the actual mechanisms through which the legal system fails to deliver justice.

Section 11.2 sets the background for understanding the particular context of inequality dealt with in this chapter, namely the neocolonial situation of Australian Aboriginal people. Section 11.3 then introduces the concept of language ideologies, and in Section 11.4, I narrow the focus to four language ideologies centrally involved in storytelling and retelling in the legal process. In Section 11.5, I move to examine a case study, from Brisbane (Queensland), which exemplifies the workings of these language ideologies. Known as the Pinkenba case, it involved three teenage Aboriginal boys giving evidence in court in the committal hearing against six police officers charged with their abduction. Section 11.6 considers how and why these language ideologies were privileged in this hearing, used to normalise bullying and harassment of the child witnesses by the two defence counsel. This involves an understanding of both the function and practice of cross-examination, and the role of this case in the struggle between Aboriginal people and the state, connected as it is to ongoing moral panic. Section 11.7 then glimpses a crucial step in the perpetuation of moral panic, with the focal language ideologies from cross-examination operating beyond the courtroom, in the print media. Section 11.8 concludes with the wider sociopolitical consequences of this hearing, particularly highlighting the role of courtroom language ideologies in connecting the questions and answers in court with ongoing naturalisation of the neocolonial control of police over the movements of Aboriginal people.

11.2 Understanding neocolonial control

Following colonisation by the British in the late eighteenth century, Indigenous Australians[2] were under colonial domination until the second half of the twentieth century, when they were granted formal equality with other Australians. However, there are many ways in which this apparent equality is a mere fiction. As with other Indigenous minorities around the world, Australian Aboriginal people experience the legacies of colonial dispossession, with living conditions typical of people in third world countries. Several recent reports have drawn attention to 'wide gaps' between Indigenous and non-

Indigenous Australians. The most recently published report of 'Indigenous disadvantage' in Australia states that many indicators show that these gaps 'are not improving, or are even deteriorating' (SCRGSP 2011, p. 4).

Table 1. Summary of key indicators of 'Indigenous disadvantage' (drawn from SCRGSP 2011)

INDICATOR	*RATE* (Indigenous to non-Indigenous)	*COMMENT*
imprisonment	14 times	age-adjusted
juvenile detention	22 times	
long term unemployment	6 times	
weekly household income	$300 less per week	median gross
not completed high school	almost twice	
infant mortality	1.6 to 3.1 times	
child mortality	1.8 to 3.8 times	
all causes mortality rate	twice	age-adjusted
life expectancy male	11.5 years less	
life expectancy female	nearly 10 years less	

The summary presented in Table 1 gives substance to the claim that the end of colonialism between the 1960s and the 1980s has not resulted in equality. More specifically, the work of criminologists such as Cunneen (e.g. 2001) highlights the way in which government power, through the criminal justice system, systematically oppresses Indigenous Australians, for example through overpolicing and overimprisonment (discussed in Section 11.6.2 below). Cunneen (2001, p. 232) argues that the term 'neocolonial' is particularly apt here, as it 'recognises the fact that the relationship between Indigenous people and the dominant society is still manifestly colonial, although the modality of colonial power may have changed with the formal emphasis on equality and citizenship'.[3]

The aim of this chapter is to contribute a new dimension to the understanding of how neocolonial control is perpetuated, by examining the work being done by courtroom talk. An important aspect of the critical sociolinguistics approach in my work is the notion of the integrated nature of micro-practices with macro-structure (Eades 2008, e.g. pp. 47–49, pp. 334–336), as found in the work of sociolinguists such as Cicourel (e.g. 1981), Collins (e.g. 1988), Matoesian (1993), and Heller (e.g. 2001). Studies such as these show that the sociolinguistic investigation of language and inequality has much to learn from the social theoretical study of power relations and power struggles, and the complex relationships between structures, such as the legal system, and the agency of individuals and groups – what particular people do. In this case, we find that outrageous actions by individual police officers – taking young teenage Aboriginal boys out of town late at night and abandoning them – are only one part of the story of ongoing neocolonial control. The regular functioning of the legal process, particularly the practices and interpretations in cross-examination, provides an essential ingredient in the legitimisation of this control. Sociolinguistic analysis provides a key to understanding how this neocolonial control works.

11.3 Language ideologies

In exploring the link between individual moments of agency, and the perpetuation of structural inequalities, sociolinguists and linguistic anthropologists are turning attention to the taken-for-granted assumptions about how language works, which are termed 'language ideologies' (sometimes also 'linguistic ideologies', 'folk views' or 'folk linguistics'). Blommaert (2005, p. 253) defines language ideologies as 'socially, culturally and historically conditioned ideas, images and perceptions about language and communication' (see also Woolard & Schieffelin 1994; Kroskrity 2004).

Central to work on language ideologies is the understanding that 'ideologies of language are not about language alone' (Woolard 1998, p. 3). In fact, they often serve the interests of a specific social or cultural group, and in this way they can play an important role in the reproduction of inequality. One of the major contributions that sociolinguistics can make to the study of social life is to uncover the ways in which language ideologies can 'often serve to rationalise existing social structures, relationships and dominant linguistic habits' (Swann et al. 2004, p. 171). Thus, for example, Angermeyer's (2008) work in New York courts shows how the powerlessness of immigrants in the legal process is perpetuated through the monolingual language ideology. This assumption that monolingualism is the norm in society and the best way for the operation of society generally and the legal system specifically, was found by Angermeyer to be intrinsically bound up with the court's inability to recognise the complexities of bilingualism. Thus, the courts in New York, as in many other jurisdictions around the world, appear unable to understand that many people require an interpreter some of the time, but also have both the ability and the desire to communicate some of the time in the language of the court (here, English), for example in answering fairly straightforward questions. So, as Angermeyer found, the monolingual language ideology results in a situation in which people with degrees of bilingual fluency are forced to act as monolinguals. People who do not hide the fact that they have some bilingual fluency run the risk of being seen as misrepresenting their need for an interpreter.

It is language ideologies involved in the discursive testing of witnesses' stories in court that are the focus of this chapter. Given that the work of sociolinguists revolves around studying how people use language, how people talk about language use, and what happens when people use language in particular ways, we are in a good position to uncover and reflect on disjunctions or contradictions between these three aspects of language use. In this chapter these three aspects of language use are examined in relation to the evaluation of witnesses telling their stories in court in common law legal systems. Drawing on the detailed study of an Australian case provides the opportunity to see both the operation and the impact of these language ideologies, which lie beyond interactional practices, such as the ways in which witnesses' talk is constrained. While some of the issues to be dealt with in this chapter are relevant also to the continental legal system, my discussion of what happens in 'the legal process' should be understood to be specifically about the legal process in common law jurisdictions.

The analysis in this chapter will show how language ideologies facilitate certain interactional practices, and further, how they impact on the interpretation and understanding of what people say. But I will argue that more is involved in the case study examined here than these beliefs about how language works, and the constraints on language use that are built into and accepted in the common law system. An understanding of the sociopolitical work being done through the case is also required in order to make sense of the courtroom talk. I will show that this sociopolitical work is enabled through discursive practices which are naturalised by the language ideologies to be introduced in the next section.

11.4 Storytelling and retelling in the legal process

Perhaps the most important and pervasive assumptions about how language works in the legal process are those related to storytelling and retelling, and here the work on entextualisation which began in linguistic anthropology is particularly relevant. 'Entextualisation' is defined by Bauman and Briggs (1990, p. 73) as 'the process of rendering discourse extractable, of making a stretch of linguistic production into a unit — a *text* — that can be lifted out of its interactional setting' (emphasis in original, see also Blommaert 2005). This process involves decontextualisation — taking a story (or part of it) out of its context, and recontextualisation — retelling the story (or part of it) in a new context. These processes of entextualisation, decontextualisation and recontextualisation occur in all social contexts. It is both the practices and the assumptions involved that make them of interest to the investigation of how language works in the legal process.

In lawyer interviews, police interviews, courtroom hearings, and informal and alternative legal processes, laypeople are required to tell their side of the story. Often these stories have to be retold at a later stage in the legal process. Sometimes the story has to be retold by the original teller, as, for example, when a witness in court has to retell the story they had earlier told in a police interview. At other times the story is retold by an officer within the legal process. For example, police officers and lawyers summarise the stories of their interviewees, and lawyers summarise witnesses' stories in the propositions of cross-examination questions. This process of decontextualisation and recontextualisation can involve significant transformations (e.g. Trinch 2003). Further, many legal decisions involve the evaluation of individuals' stories, in terms of such features as consistency, accuracy, reliability and honesty. I now turn to four recurring language ideologies that are central to the evaluation and assessment of people's stories and their recontextualisations in the legal process.

11.4.1 THE IDEOLOGY OF INCONSISTENCY: THE ASSUMPTION THAT INCONSISTENCY BETWEEN DIFFERENT TELLINGS OF A STORY INDICATES LACK OF TRUTHFULNESS[4]

Exposing inconsistencies between different tellings of a story in different legal contexts forms a central strategy in challenging the credibility of a witness in cross-examination (provided for in rules of evidence in terms of the legal strategy known as 'raising prior (or previous) inconsistent statements', see Eades 2011). While it may appear that inconsistency can be a reliable symptom of untruthfulness, jurors are often reminded that not all inconsistencies are lies. For example, in a striking example of a triple-negative construction, the jurors in the OJ Simpson case were reminded that 'Failure of recollection is a common experience, and innocent misrecollection is not uncommon' (Tiersma 1999, p. 253). In fact, there are a number of other factors that may give rise to inconsistency in aspects of a witness's account, only one of which is untruthfulness; others are memory problems, variations in different tellings of the same story (Schiffrin 2006; Norrick 1998), and the different effect of different interviewer questions. However, the evaluation of inconsistencies in story-retelling in order to determine witness credibility relies on a number of problematic assumptions. One of these is the assumption that people always tell the same story in the same way. Recent sociolinguistic work on narratives shows that this is a naïve assumption. For example, Schiffrin's (2006) analysis of individuals retelling a particular story over a period of time (not in a legal context) shows that no two tellings are the same: there are shifts in perspective and different details are included or omitted, highlighted or backgrounded.

But these social and perceptual dimensions of inconsistency in storytelling are often ignored by the legal system, which, as Matoesian (2001, pp. 37–38) points out, conceives of inconsistency as 'logical' incongruity. Matoesian argues, on the contrary, that inconsistency is not necessarily an attribute or failing of an individual, it can be interactively constituted and sustained. That is, inconsistency can be *achieved* through the interactional work which is done during the hearing. This interactionally achieved inconsistency between two or more tellings of a story, whether by different witnesses or the same witnesses in different contexts, is used by lawyers to guide the decision makers in their 'findings of fact'.[5] Thus, in the way in which 'the facts' are determined in a legal matter, there is an underlying 'linguistic ideology of inconsistency' (Matoesian 2001, p. 68), that is the assumption that inconsistency between different tellings of a story indicates lack of truthfulness. In this linguistic ideology underpinning the adversarial cross-examination process, the interactional nature of inconsistency is not considered: it is the failing of individual witnesses, who can be therefore deemed to be lacking reliability and truthfulness. We will see an illustration of this in Section 11.5 below.

11.4.2 THE IDEOLOGY OF DECONTEXTUALISED FRAGMENTS: THE ASSUMPTION THAT INDIVIDUAL WORDS OR FRAGMENTS TAKEN FROM A STORY CAN BE UNDERSTOOD WITHOUT THEIR CONTEXT

One of the ways in which recontextualisation often works is through the decontextualisation of very short extracts of earlier texts, sometimes as short as one word. Decontextualising words or phrases enables the questioner to change important aspects of the original text. This is particularly noticeable with an important strategy used to raise prior inconsistent statements, namely reading in cross-examination a quotation from the transcript of an earlier interview, and then asking questions about it. This decontextualisation of evidence from its interactional production is consistent with the attention in legal decision-making to 'what is said' rather than 'how it is said' (see Eades 1996b).

Transcripts present propositional content, and do not record many important elements of the talk which are part of their linguistic context, such as emphasis, intonation, volume, and pauses (Eades 1996b). But it is impossible to read aloud a transcript without making (often subconscious) choices about these aspects of speech. Such choices can make a fundamental difference in meaning. For example, the simplest monosyllabic answer 'yes' can be read from a transcript to convey confident agreement, when it may have been uttered after a lengthy pause in a tentative and barely audible voice. Thus the decontextualised fragment of a witness's earlier telling of their story can be presented by a lawyer in cross-examination in such a way as to convey a rather different version of the story or part(s) of it, as well as a rather different impression of the witness's demeanour in the earlier interview. And the rules of evidence that control courtroom talk make it difficult for even the most analytical of witnesses to present a metacommentary on such a transformation of their story. I use the term 'ideology of decontextualised fragments' to refer to this assumption that individual words or fragments taken from a story can be understood without their context.

11.4.3 THE IDEOLOGY OF NARRATOR AUTHORSHIP: THE ASSUMPTION THAT A WITNESS'S OR INTERVIEWEE'S STORY IS SOLELY THEIR OWN ACCOUNT (TRINCH 2003)

But it is not just that entextualisation in the criminal justice process takes utterances out of their original context and transforms them in this way.

This decontextualisation also conceals the *process* by which stories are generated, and the role of the interviewer in the ways in which stories are told, including what is left out, what is included, and what is emphasised. The ways in which such interactional processes involve collaboration between interlocutors in everyday storytelling have been studied by researchers such as Norrick (1998).

In the legal context, several scholars have found that while written witness or suspect statements result from an interactional process, namely an interview, they are presented as the product of a single person, that is the person being interviewed. (See e.g., for police interviews the work of Rock 2001; Komter 2002, 2006; and Jönsson & Linell 1991; for lawyer and paralegal interviews the work of Trinch 2003; and for investigative interviews with asylum seekers the work of Maryns 2006). An important consequence of the transformation of interviews into the product of the interviewee alone is what Jönsson and Linell (1991, p. 434) term 'the blurring of source distinctions'. They explain that 'one cannot know from reading the reports under what conditions a given piece of information has been introduced'. For example, has it been introduced 'more or less spontaneously by the suspect in a narrative turn', or is it introduced in the proposition of the interviewer's question and only then 'confirmed (or sometimes, modified or denied) by the suspect' (1991, p. 434)?

Trinch's (2003, pp. 49–50) work on lawyers and paralegals producing written statements on the basis of interviews with clients establishes the 'ideology of narrator authorship': the assumption that a witness's or interviewee's story is solely their own account. She points out that it is found not just in the culture of the law, but more generally in western culture. This ideology relies on the 'prevalent' and 'tenacious' cultural notion of the 'true story', but ignores the collaborative nature of storytelling. As Trinch points out, one of the problematic consequences of this ideology comes in the form of challenges to the credibility of the narrator, in ways that link this ideology of narrator authorship with the ideology of inconsistency. This linking plays an important role in cross-examination, and we will see it in the example below.

The studies referred to above demonstrate that it is problematic to view the stories that emerge from interviews as the sole product of the interviewee, although this is exactly the way in which such stories are typically received and assessed within the adversarial legal process.

11.4.4 THE IDEOLOGY OF REPEATED QUESTIONING: THE ASSUMPTION THAT REPEATED QUESTIONING PROVIDES THE OPPORTUNITY TO PROPERLY TEST A WITNESS'S TRUTHFULNESS

One of the most important language ideologies underpinning the cross-examination process is that repeated questioning provides the opportunity to properly test a witness's truthfulness. As with the ideology of narrator authorship, this ideology is found not just in the culture of the law, but also more generally in western culture. But this assumption about repeated questioning can be particularly problematic in providing clues about truthfulness in court, particularly with certain groups of witnesses. For example, research has documented a common tendency among children to change their answers when they are asked the same question more than once in the same interview (e.g. Ceci & Bruck 1993). Also relevant is the well-recognised tendency of Australian Aboriginal people to use 'gratuitous concurrence' that is, to say *yes* in answer to a question (or *no* to a negative question), regardless of actual agreement, or even understanding of the question. Gratuitous concurrence has long been recognised by people working with Aborigines (see e.g. Liberman 1981; Mildren 1999; and the references in Eades 2008, pp. 92–96). It is a common feature of the ways in which Aboriginal people respond to questions. In fact, this pragmatic feature is one of the most significant features of Aboriginal ways of communicating throughout Australia.

Within legal contexts, there is an awareness that some people are particularly suggestible, that is they are easily led into providing a required answer. In a much-quoted Australian case (*Mooney v. James* 1949, p. 22) which established that there 'is no absolute right to put leading questions in cross-examination', Justice Barry explained that:

> The basis of the rule that leading questions may be put in cross-examination is the assumption that the witness's partisanship, conscious or unconscious, in combination with the circumstance that he is being questioned by an adversary will produce a state of mind that will protect him against suggestibility. But if the Judge is satisfied that there is no ground for the assumption, the rule has no application, and the Judge may forbid cross-examination by questions which go to the length of putting into the witness's mouth the very words he is to echo back.

In Queensland, the Criminal Justice Commission (CJC 1996, p. 52) found that this 'discretion to disallow the use of leading questions is rarely exercised by the courts'. This discretion is generally seen as applicable in some instances to intellectually disabled people and children, who are taken as lacking the normal adult ability to resist suggestion. But a sociolinguistic approach would go further than this psychological approach, by recognising that the belief that repeated questioning can reveal the truth is based on strong cultural practices and norms. And for some sociocultural groups this belief does not hold, such as for Australian Aboriginal people. Morrow (1996) reports a similar communicative pattern among English speaking Yup'ik Eskimos, as does Berk-Seligson (2009) for US Hispanics. For sociocultural groups such as these, it is arguably problematic to assign any significant probative value to repeated questioning (that is, to see that repeated questioning enables proof or evidence to emerge). There is a serious challenge, therefore, for the justice system to allow cross-examination, which is the right of all defendants, while protecting 'suggestible' witnesses.

But while this fourth language ideology raises particular issues for Aboriginal people (and some other groups), the first three ideologies can be used in problematic ways in cross-examination against people of any sociocultural group.

11.5 The Pinkenba case

Having introduced four language ideologies that are central to cross-examination in the adversarial process, this section will show these language ideologies at work with an example from the Pinkenba case. This case resulted from six police officers approaching three young teenage Aboriginal boys in a Brisbane street late one night, and telling them to get into three separate police cars. Although never charged for any offence in relation to that night, the boys were then driven fourteen kilometres out of town to a dark industrial wasteland, where they were threatened and abandoned. The boys' complaints led to an independent investigation which resulted in charges of 'unlawful deprivation of liberty' being laid against the six police officers. Thus the boys became prosecution witnesses in a criminal hearing against the six accused police officers. This hearing provides an extreme example of the way that cross-examination works in the common law system. Not all cases operate in this way, but extreme cases are valuable because they bring to the surface assumptions and practices that may ordinarily be too subtle to be perceived or understood (and to analyse in a [book chapter or] journal-length article).

While my detailed analysis of this case has been the subject of a monograph-length study (Eades 2008), this is the first article [or chapter] to examine how inequality and neocolonial control over Aboriginal Australians is perpetuated by language ideologies that are taken for granted in cross-examination. The analysis here builds on twenty-five years of sociolinguistic research and applied practical work with Aboriginal people in the legal process. Much of my interactional sociolinguistic work has focused on intercultural communication in legal contexts: involving research, mainly in courtroom hearings (e.g. Eades 1994a, 2000), training workshops and publications for legal professionals (e.g. Eades 1992), and presentation of expert evidence in specific cases (e.g. Eades 1996a).

The prosecution against the police officers in the Pinkenba case relied almost completely on the evidence of the three young teenage boys. The repeated recontextualisations of their stories can be seen as a filtering process through which each of the boys' stories were 'heard' by the legal system. This filtering process included six stages, the first three of which took place within a few weeks of the incident. The last three stages took place some ten months after the incident, when the case went to court for a committal hearing, in which a magistrate (equivalent to a lower court judge in the United States) hears the case against the accused in order to make a decision about whether to send the case to a jury trial.[6] The stages in the filtering of the boys' stories were: (i) interview with lawyers from Aboriginal Legal Services (ALS); (ii) interview with investigators from the Criminal Justice Commission; (iii) interview with prosecutor; (iv) examination-in-chief (direct examination) questioning by prosecutor in the courtroom hearing; (v) cross-examination questioning by first defence counsel (representing three of the police officers) in the courtroom hearing; (vi) cross-examination questioning by second defence counsel (representing the other three police officers) in the courtroom hearing. In (v) and (vi) lawyers read excerpts from the transcripts of (ii) and (iv) in order to expose apparent inconsistencies by raising prior inconsistent statements.

It is important to point out that there was never any doubt that the six armed police officers had taken the boys, in three separate police vehicles, out of town in the middle of the night to Pinkenba and left them there to find their own way back. Although the boys were never charged with any offence that night, the police union president told the media that the boys were 'taken down to Pinkenba to reflect on their misdemeanours' (ABC 1996). The case centred on the issue of whether the boys knew they had the right not to get in the police cars when the police officers told them to. The defence case was that the boys 'gave up their liberty' and that 'there's no offence of allowing a person to give up his liberty',[7] and therefore that 'the deprivation of liberty was not unlawful' (as quoted by the magistrate in his decision, 24 February 1995).

In the courtroom recontextualisation (in stages iv–vi) of the boys' reports of being taken for a ride by police, beliefs about storytelling and truth (in particular the four language ideologies discussed above) combined with constraints on ways of talking in court and adversarial manipulation. This powerful combination of language ideologies and interactional practices enabled the two defence counsel to reverse the boys' allegation of police abuse, and instead to construct the boys as liars who were out to 'get even with the police'.

11.5.1 FROM INVESTIGATIVE INTERVIEW TO CROSS-EXAMINATION

The example below concerns the middle of the three witnesses, Albert, who was thirteen years old at the time of the event and the court hearing ten months later. (All personal names are pseudonyms.) The two defence counsel worked hard to establish that Albert was a liar (using the words 'lie', 'lies', 'lied' or 'lying' forty-three times while cross-examining him). Unsurprisingly, the main strategy in the defence construction of Albert as a liar involved the ideology of inconsistency. For example, the defence lawyers read excerpts from the transcripts of (ii) and (iv) in order to expose apparent inconsistencies between different occasions on which Albert had told the story of the boys' abduction. Then, whenever they found an inconsistency they overtly interpreted it as 'a lie', ignoring other well-recognised reasons for inconsistencies between different tellings of the same story.

An important issue in Albert's cross-examination came from part of his interview with lawyers and a field officer of ALS on the day after the incident occurred. In this interview, Albert had apparently used the verb *grab* in his account of what happened when the police first came up to them in the mall, saying *They grabbed the three of us- two grabbed Barry- two grabbed me*. Ten months later, he gave his evidence-in-chief in court, answering the prosecutor's questions about what had happened on that day that the police had taken them for the ride. Here Albert did not say that they were *grabbed*, but rather that they were *told to get in the police cars*, and that they did. Then in cross-examination, the first of the two defence counsel (DC1) seized on this inconsistency between what Albert had said in court earlier that day, and what he had said to investigators ten months earlier. Questioning Albert about this inconsistency, DC1 read out the section of the interview with ALS in which Albert had said they were *grabbed*, and then proceeded to make much of the inconsistency. Such recontextualising of a statement that a witness has made during the investigation is standard practice during cross-examinations generally. It is used to raise prior inconsistent statements, and it relies on both the ideology of inconsistency and the ideology of decontextualised fragments. But, we have seen that the assumption that honest witnesses should always tell their story in the same words is at odds with ways in which people often retell their stories.

Extract 1 DC1 to Albert (Eades 2008, p. 103)[8]

1. DC1:	Now LISTEN to me- that didn't happen at all- did it? (2.0) that you were grabbed- it DIDN'T HAPPEN- did it?
2. Albert:	°No°.
3. DC1:	Beg your pardon?
4. Mag:	He said no.
5. DC1:	Well WHY did you say that it did? (27.1) well- WHY?(12.2) I'll suggest this answer to you- that you were TRYING TO MAKE THINGS LOOK WORSE FOR THE POLICE- is that the correct answer? (27.8) is that the correct answer?
6. Albert:	(1.4) °No°.
7. DC1:	Beg your pardon?
8. Albert:	No.
9. DC1:	Well, WHAT IS the answer? (2.4) why did you lie about it? (33.4) WHY did you LIE?
10. Pros:	With respect- inconsistent answers don't necessarily imply lies and the witness hasn't yet accepted that either of them is a lie- I'd ask my friend to uh=
11. DC1:	=All right- well- I can take half an hour trying to get an answer from him (2.7) I think you told me that that didn't HAPPEN- what you claim there- [to solicitor] °didn't he say that didn't happen°- so if it didn't HAPPEN- is it a LIE THAT YOU'VE TOLD THERE?
12. Albert:	Yes.

[partly inaudible utterance of DC1 in aside to his assistant]

13. DC1: All right- well now why did you lie?
14. Albert: I don't know.
15. DC1: YOU LIED TO MAKE THINGS LOOK BAD FOR THE POLICE- DIDN'T YOU? (1.2) DIDN'T YOU?
16. Albert: (3.5) °Yes°.

In making sense of this extract, it is important not to rely on negative assumptions about the use and meaning of silence in interactions.[9] The widespread Anglo convention of interpreting silences as indicating that something is not working (e.g. Jefferson 1989) is not shared by Aboriginal people, who often use lengthy silences in either formal or informal interaction, and who find them neither uncomfortable nor remarkable (e.g. Eades 2007; Mushin & Gardner 2009; see also Basso 1970 and Scollon 1985 for North American indigenous societies). This contrasts with the dominant assumption in the legal system that silence in answer to a question is generally 'interpreted to the detriment of the silent person', such as implying that the person asked the question has something to hide (Kurzon 1995, p. 56).

In Turn 5 of this extract DC1 put the proposition that the reason that Albert had said that they were *grabbed* (by the police) was to 'MAKE THINGS LOOK WORSE FOR THE POLICE'. In his reply (Turn 6), Albert denied this proposition, and indeed one might think of a number of different reasons why a child might have said something different in the earlier interview (such as confusion, emotional reaction, tiredness, possible exaggeration, or difficulty in remembering all the details). It is also worth pointing out he did not say anything about being *grabbed* in his evidence-in-chief, and thus his evidence in court was consistent. This thirteen-year-old witness was given no credit for what may well have been his careful attention to avoiding exaggeration in court, following the magistrate's warnings about telling the truth in the court. It is also not at all clear whether Albert had used the word *grab* in his earlier report to mean physically take hold of, for example by taking his arm, or his shirt, or in the more colloquial sense of taking him aside, such as in 'I was working in my office when the boss came and grabbed me for an urgent meeting', where no physical contact is being reported. So we see here the impact of the ideology of decontextualised fragments. Defence counsel has taken the word *grab* out of the context of its original telling, and the thirteen-year-old witness has no way of explaining what he had meant when he used that word in his story ten months earlier.

But DC1 relied on the ideology of inconsistency to presuppose (in Turn 9) that Albert had lied when he used the word *grab* in the initial investigative interview, despite the prosecutor's attempt to object that 'inconsistent answers don't necessarily imply lies'. It is quite likely that Albert's answer in Turn 12 was gratuitous concurrence (discussed in Section 11.4.4 above), as he heard DC1's increased impatience, although of course we cannot know what was in the witness's mind.

From these repeated accusations — in Turns 9, 11, 13, and 15 — that Albert was 'lying', DC1 went back in Turn 15 to the proposition which the witness has already denied in Turn 6, and repeated the tag question 'DIDN'T YOU?', until the witness gave in after a 3.5 second silence and answered °*Yes*°, in a barely audible voice, in Turn 16. While of course we cannot know what was in the witness's mind, this extract has the hallmarks of classic gratuitous concurrence: saying *yes* to a question even if you don't agree with it, or even understand it. The witness was in a powerless situation, and was given no choice but to comply with the harassment of the lawyer. This is one of several occasions in the cross-examinations of the child witnesses in this case, where this defence counsel refused to accept the witness's answer and harangued the witness like this until he gave the answer defence counsel wanted. But the court appears to have ignored research about the likelihood of children changing their answer when asked the same question more than once in the same interview, as well as the Aboriginal tendency to use gratuitous concurrence. Albert's answers in this extract, which are highly likely to have involved gratuitous concurrence, were interpreted literally as agreements to the propositions questioned. And this literal interpretation became central in the way in which the legal system ended up deciding that the police had no case to answer, highlighting the central role in courtroom hearings of the ideology of repeated questioning, that is, that repeated questioning will enable the truth to emerge.

11.5.2 CLOSING ADDRESS, MAGISTRATE'S DECISION AND JUDICIAL REVIEW

After the witnesses had given evidence in both examination-in-chief and cross-examination, the lawyers made their closing addresses to the court. The other (second) defence counsel used the exchange presented in Extract 1 above to argue that Albert was a liar and therefore an untrustworthy witness:

Extract 2 DC2 Closing address (Eades 2008, p. 271)

> [Albert] told Mr Thorpe in cross-examination that the reason that he'd said the police had grabbed him and forced him into the car was to make- things- look- worse- for- the- police.[10]

But we have seen that Albert did not tell Mr Thorpe (DC1) that. He had initially refused to accept this suggestion, answering °*No*° in Turn 6, Extract 1. But DC1 had refused to accept this answer, and had continued to harass the witness until he finally said °*Yes*° in Turn 16, after a considerable pause. However, in DC2's closing address Albert's one-word °*yes*° answer was decontextualised and counted as uttering a damning twenty-five word statement. This is one of many instances in which DC2 switched authorship attribution, a discursive practice seemingly allowable because of the ideology of narrator authorship. That is, the propositions in lawyers' questions can be taken as originating with the witness, even if all he did was say °*yes*° when he was bullied and harassed into giving this answer. But we see nothing of this in DC2's summary, which blurred source distinctions. So DC2's recontextualisation of Albert's story misrepresented what Albert had said, relying on the ideologies of decontextualised fragments, repeated questioning, and narrator authorship and its related practice of switching authorship attribution.

The defence counsels' recontextualisation of the stories of all three witnesses was very effective. In his decision the magistrate dropped the charges against the police, finding that the boys 'all knew that they had the right to refuse to get in the police motor vehicle, but despite of [sic] this knowledge they proceeded and got in'. (One-third of his decision comprised criticism of the character and identity of the three boys.) He also referred specifically to the inconsistency over the use of the word *grabbed* between Albert's interview with the investigators and his evidence in court, completely ignoring the interactional context of this inconsistency. In a very unusual development, the families of the boys appealed against the magistrate's decision to drop the charges against the police officers. Thus, the case was reviewed by a judge, who fully supported the magistrate's decision. And, as with DC2 in his closing address, and the magistrate in his decision, the review judge also used Albert's early use of the word *grab* to refer to the police actions as evidence of his unreliability.

11.6 Why were these language ideologies privileged in this hearing?

A question frequently asked about this case is 'how did the lawyers get away with such bullying and harassment'? Surely there is more happening here than the normalised assumptions about how language works in the legal process, and the related normalised assumptions about how to interpret the evidence of witnesses and how to evaluate their credibility. Why were these language ideologies privileged in this hearing, to such an extent that experienced lawyers said that the cross-examination was the worst bullying and harassment they had ever seen in cross-examination? To answer this question, we need to examine two further issues that connect to the work being done by these everyday cross-examination language ideologies in this case, namely the function and practice of cross-examination (Section 11.6.1), and the role of this case in the ongoing struggle between Aboriginal people and the state (Section 11.6.2).

11.6.1 THE FUNCTION AND PRACTICE OF CROSS-EXAMINATION

A cornerstone of the legal system is the principle given in Article 11 of the Universal Declaration of Human Rights: 'Everyone charged with a penal offence has the right to be presumed innocent until proven guilty according to law in a public trial at which he has had all the guarantees necessary for his defence.' In the common law legal system, cross-examination plays a central role in protecting this basic human right. Thus, for example, a lawyer hired to present the defence of an accused person has the duty to be an advocate for that person, and to 'cross-examine competently, effectively and with the "maximum zeal permitted by law"' (Boyd & Hopkins 2010, pp. 155–156, citing Luban 1999, p. 140). Boyd and Hopkins further explain that although 'defence lawyers are bound by evidential, procedural and ethical rules which may facilitate discovery of the truth, their purpose is not to uncover the truth... unless the truth happens to coincide with their clients' instructions' (2010, p. 156). Further, when a defence lawyer is representing a client who has pleaded not guilty (as with the police officers in the Pinkenba case), the lawyer is legally obliged to challenge the truthfulness of the complainant/s (that is, the prosecution witness/es whose evidence substantiates the charge being tried, as is the situation of the three boys in this case).

In the Pinkenba case, we see two defence lawyers whose cross-examining 'zeal' on a number of occasions amounted to haranguing, harassing and even bullying abuse (see Eades 2008 for almost 100 excerpts). In the extremes to which a defence lawyer can go in defending their client's presumption of innocence, what protections exist for the complainant witnesses, who are called to substantiate the prosecution's case? Courtroom hearings within the common law system are adversarial, with the legal contest enacted as a dispute between two opposing parties. What mechanisms exist to bring a balance between the zeal of the defence on the one hand, and the role of the prosecution in protecting the community through bringing charges against persons accused of crime, on the other hand?

First, the prosecution can cross-examine witnesses for the defence, using the same linguistic strategies for challenging the truthfulness of these witnesses. But this case was not unusual in having no defence witnesses, and thus there could be no such cross-examining balance. Integral to the presumption of innocence in the common law system is the right of accused persons to remain silent in court (as in police interviews). This means that accused persons often choose not to give evidence themselves, or to call any witnesses in their defence. The onus is on the prosecution to prove the charge, and it is typical for prosecution witnesses to play a major role in the work of the prosecution. But, in such cases where there are no defence witnesses, the main mechanism to balance the zeal of the defence with the role of the prosecution takes the form of the rules or laws of evidence, which place restrictions on the ways in which evidence can be sought, given, and used in the deliberations about the guilt of the accused. The operation of these rules of evidence relies on the authority of the court (that is, the presiding judge or magistrate) and it is common for a lawyer on one side to object to a question from a lawyer on the other side, where the first lawyer believes that the second has contravened one of the rules of evidence. Unless the lawyer whose questioning is being objected to concedes to the objection, it is up to the presiding judge or magistrate to make a decision on the objection, usually after hearing the views of both lawyers.

We saw an example of the prosecutor objecting to a cross-examination question in Turn 10 of Extract 1. Referring to DC1's presupposition in Turn 9 that Albert had lied when he had told the investigators that the boys were *grabbed* by the police, the prosecutor objected with an incomplete utterance: 'With respect- inconsistent answers don't necessarily imply lies and the witness hasn't yet accepted that either of them is a lie- I'd ask my friend to uh'. Before the magistrate had the opportunity to respond to the objection, DC1 took the floor at the prosecutor's hesitation of 'uh', effectively conceding, while complaining in Turn 11 that he 'can take half an hour trying to get an answer from [Albert]'. DC1 then proceeded to ask Albert if his earlier statement had been 'a lie', using raised volume in a successful elicitation of Albert's apparent agreement (which may well have been an instance of gratuitous concurrence, as discussed above). The prosecutor raised few objections during the cross-examination of the boys, and as we saw in Extract 1, the objections he did raise were not raised strenuously, and nor did he engage in argument about them.[11]

The rules of evidence were explicitly referred to by DC1 in his closing address, while justifying his aggressive cross-examination. In this justification he indirectly relied on the assumption that repeated questioning enables the truth to emerge, saying:

Extract 3 DC1 closing address (Eades 2008, p. 274)

> ...there are times in court when there has to be- aggressive cross-examination- it's not very often that one has to resort to that- but if the cross-examination on my part was not aggressive... we wouldn't have obtained the truth of the situation...there's nothing wrong with aggressive cross-examination...

He then went on to co-opt the magistrate, pointing out that the magistrate had chosen not to exercise his legal right to stop questions, saying:

Extract 4 DC1 closing address (Eades 2008, p. 274)

> ...had I've been out of order your worship would have done something about it- your worship would have stopped me- you have the power under the Evidence Act- to stop questions if you feel I'm badgering a witness or- insulting or am scandalous or browbeating a witness- you have a duty and a power in relation to your running of the court to stop me.

Here defence counsel is referring to Section 21 of the Queensland *Evidence Act 1977* which gave the magistrate the power to stop any questions 'intended only to insult or annoy' or which are 'needlessly offensive in form'. This power is analogous to the power in Section 41 of the *Uniform Evidence Act* (which applies to Commonwealth and New South Wales jurisdictions), which was found to have been 'not always well-managed by judges who very often felt reluctant to intervene' (Wood 2004, p. 4, cited in Boyd & Hopkins 2010, p. 159).[12]

No doubt, there could be argument over whether any of the questions in the short excerpt given in Extract 1 constitutes a question 'intended only to insult or annoy' or 'needlessly offensive in form'. The fact that DC1 raised his voice on several occasions in this extract and repeated the tag question 'DIDN'T YOU?' would have been sufficient grounds for some magistrates and judges to say to the defence counsel something like 'You can't talk to the witness like that in this court' (as I have heard in other cases). Certainly, there were many examples throughout the cross-examination of the boys where the questioning could have constituted utterances 'intended only to insult or annoy' or 'needlessly offensive in form'. Some examples of metapragmatic directives addressed during questioning of these witnesses include:

Extract 5 (Eades 2008, p. 163)

> Come on you'll ANSWER me boy. (to thirteen-year-old David)
>
> Stop chewing your fingernails. (to thirteen-year-old Albert)
>
> I DON'T CARE HOW LONG YOU STAY THERE- YOU'LL ANSWER ME. (to fifteen-year-old Barry).[13]

But maybe it is not surprising that the prosecutor raised so few objections, and the magistrate did not use his power to stop any question, when we look at the situated power relationships within this courtroom. The defence counsel were the two most highly paid defence barristers in Queensland. While the magistrate had the ultimate decision-making power, he was definitely subordinate to each of the two defence counsel in terms of legal training, experience, income, and status. The prosecutor, who was from the Office of the Director of Public Prosecutions and had been a suburban police officer until about two years prior, had considerably much less courtroom experience than the defence counsel.

11.6.2 THE STRUGGLE BETWEEN ABORIGINAL PEOPLE AND THE STATE

Why was this case conducted with such an imbalance between defence and prosecution? In order to address this question, we need to turn to the role of the

Pinkenba case in the ongoing struggle between Aboriginal people and the state over police control of the movements of Aboriginal people. A consideration of this issue helps to understand the courtroom imbalance in this case, which privileged the language ideologies to such an extent that such extreme questioning tactics were used and allowed.

The police removal of the three Aboriginal boys from the shopping mall and their abandonment of them in a swampy industrial wasteland fourteen kilometres away was not an isolated incident. Indeed many Aboriginal people have reported similar incidents over a number of years (Eades 2008, p. 3). Within the city of Brisbane, where this incident occurred, Aboriginal people have been accustomed to police harassment, often accompanied by violence, for which no police officer has ever been convicted. In late 1993, some six months before the Pinkenba incident, a young Aboriginal dancer (Daniel Yock) died in a police van where he was detained for behaving in a disorderly manner near a park during the daytime. Such detention for making a public disturbance was widely argued to be unnecessary overpolicing. His death was followed by a riot outside police headquarters, and ten days later by a peaceful protest and city march by about 4000 demonstrators. Five months later, the investigation by the Criminal Justice Commission into his death found that there were insufficient grounds to charge any of the police officers involved. There was much anger and frustration in the Aboriginal community, with one of its leaders, Mary Graham, reporting that 'the general feeling [in the Brisbane Aboriginal community] is that the police have got away with it again...they are never going to find the justice authorities guilty of anything in this country' (Walker 1994).

Relations between Aborigines and police in Queensland have increasingly been seen since Yock's death in terms of war (e.g. Solomon 1993). Indeed, in his song *The Young Dancer is Dead* which laments Yock's death and asks 'how long will these killings go on?', Aboriginal singer songwriter Kev Carmody sings 'Our young dancer is dead, young <u>warrior</u> is dead' (emphasis added). This war between Aboriginal people and the police provided the immediate context for the Pinkenba incident, an incident which once again undeniably involved overpolicing in restricting the movements of Aboriginal people. It is not difficult, therefore, to see why the police union employed the most senior defence barristers to defend the six charged police officers in this case. And it is hard not to suggest that the state may have chosen a junior prosecutor out of some kind of loyalty to the charged officers, given the usually strong links between police and prosecution. When the committal hearing in the Pinkenba case opened, one year after the finding about Yock's death, it was clear that a new battle in the war between Aboriginal people and the police was about to begin.

For the defence to make their case that the actions of the police officers in taking the boys for a ride was 'not unlawful deprivation of liberty', they needed to show that the boys went willingly with the police, despite knowing that they did not have to. Yet, more than one-third of the cross-examination was not about the events on the night in question, but about the boys' criminal records. While the boys were not charged with an offence on that night, they all had criminal records for such offences as 'unlawful use of motor vehicle', 'break enter and steal' and 'destruction of property' (smashing street lights). Despite the fact that they had been dealt with by the law for these offences, and in this Pinkenba case were complainants, they were treated throughout their cross-examination as 'criminals'.[14] Thus, a key aspect of the cross-examination was the construction of the boys as 'lying criminals' who were a threat to public safety. Indeed the actions of the six police officers in taking them for a ride and abandoning them out of town was discussed in media interviews by police union officials in terms of the difficulties faced by these officers in 'dealing with juvenile offenders' (ABC 1996). So, to understand the cross-examination in this case requires a consideration of the wider social context of moral panic about Aboriginal people as criminals who need to be removed from the streets, and the related justification of police as having the right to go beyond the law.[15]

This moral panic is not a recent development, but has been a part of the colonial and neocolonial discourse since the beginnings of colonisation at the end of the eighteenth century. Cunneen (1994, 2001) highlights the central role of the police in the process of colonisation, starting with open warfare. The earliest police presence was in the form of a paramilitary force, fighting a 'bloody frontier war' against Aboriginal people, in which police duties were comparable to those of the United States army on the American frontier (Foley 1984, p. 161). From the end of the nineteenth century until the 1960s, police played a major role in moving Aboriginal people away from home and family for their 'protection', especially taking children away from parents and wider family to dormitories and foster homes. (Earlier referred to as the 'protective era', this is now known as the Stolen Generations.) Officially, colonisation formally ended in Queensland in 1984, when special laws governing Indigenous people on reserves were abolished. Until that time people could and did go to prison for drinking alcohol, or for leaving the reserve without permission (e.g. to go to another town to visit a relative). Again the police played a major role in these restrictions on the liberties of Aboriginal people. Despite formal equality for Aboriginal people since the later part of the twentieth century, police still play a major role in bringing about separations of Aboriginal young people from their families and communities. This occurs through the criminalisation process, which starts with selective policing and overpolicing. Research on police discretionary decisions shows that it is not that Aboriginal people are involved in more criminal activity than non-Aboriginal people, but that they are more often subject to police intervention (Cunneen 2001). For example, Cunneen (2001, p. 136) cites one report which found that the rate at which Aboriginal offenders are dealt with by an official police caution (or warning) is one-third of that of non-Aboriginal offenders. While the non-Aboriginal offenders are formally warned about possible consequences of such future offending behaviour, Aboriginal offenders are arrested and charged. The criminalisation process is not restricted to the actions of police officers. It is supported by legislation, which leads to people being arrested and detained for disturbing the peace, or swearing in public. And it is further supported by widespread moral panic, which is fuelled by some sectors of the media, including print media and radio 'shock-jocks' (Sercombe 1995; Trigger 1995; Eades 2008, pp. 60–63).

11.7 Beyond the courtroom to the print media

The role of the print media in fuelling this moral panic is easy to see in this case. Specifically, the recontextualisation of the part of Albert's story seen in the example above happened not only in the courtroom, and the magistrate's decision and the judicial review, but also in the print media. Just as the DCs in their closing addresses took propositions from cross-examination questions and recast them as propositions uttered by the boys, so too did newspaper reports. In ignoring what had actually been said by the boys, and what had been said by the lawyers, some newspaper reports assumed that the story which emerged during the interaction in cross-examination was the sole production of the boys (highlighting once again the ideology of narrator authorship). And as with the second defence counsel in his closing statement (Extract 2), some newspaper reports went further and switched authorship attribution. And once again, the misleading impression of verbatim accuracy was used in recontextualisation of evidence on issues central to the case. In Extract 1 we saw DC1's harassment to gain Albert's minimal answers of agreement to his insistence that Albert 'LIED TO MAKE THINGS LOOK BAD FOR THE POLICE'. On the day after Albert's evidence, the Brisbane newspaper (*The Courier Mail*, 22 February 1995) carried the headline '"I lied to embarrass police"' with the sub-headline 'Boy, 13, tells "dumping" trial'.[16] The statement 'I lied to embarrass police' was enclosed in quotation marks, which together with the verb 'tells' gives the clear, but completely wrong impression that these were the exact words used by the witness. As we have seen, the most that the witness ever said on this point was a very soft °*Yes*° after repeated harassment and DC1's rejection of his earlier answer of °*No*°. A few days after this newspaper headline, I discussed its misleading nature with one of the journalists involved. He told me that it is 'journalistic licence' for newspapers to use quotation marks for utterances attributed to speakers, but not actually uttered by them. He saw no problem with it, and refused to correct the misleading impression it had caused.

The story below the headline gave some transcript excerpts, which were edited in a misleading way. This is how the newspaper quoted the questions and answers on this point:

Extract 6 newspaper extract (see n. 16)

> 'You lied to make things look bad for the police?' Mr Thorpe asked.
>
> The boy replied: 'Yes.'
>
> 'You made these things up — made things up to make the police look bad?' Mr Thorpe repeated.
>
> The boy replied: 'Yes.'

The way that the second question was quoted in the newspaper gives the impression that it was a fairly close transcription, seeming to record the lawyer's false start (although after repeated listening to the tape-recording I am unable to find any utterance that matches this, and neither is it an accurate quoting of the official transcript). However, 'journalistic licence' was used to omit repeated tag questions, and there was no mention of the shouting, which we saw in the transcript given as Extract 1 above. Further, there was no mention that the boy denied this proposition (as we saw in Turns 6 and 8) until he was harassed into agreeing with it. In fact as we have seen in Extract 1 (of which Turns 15 and 16 are repeated below in Extract 7), a more accurate transcription of the first exchange quoted from the newspaper above would have found a way of indicating DC1's shouting, his repeated tag questions, the long delay before Albert's response, and the noticeable softness in this response.

Extract 7 DC1 to Albert (Eades 2008, p. 103)

15. DC1: YOU LIED TO MAKE THINGS LOOK BAD FOR THE POLICE- DIDN'T YOU? (1.2) Didn't you?

16. Albert: (3.5) °Yes°.

The second exchange in Extract 6, given in the newspaper as if it is verbatim, and as if it immediately followed the first exchange, is actually a summary of three questions and their answers, which occurred some minutes later. This six-turn exchange involved similar harassment as the first, as well as soft responses from Albert (but with less shouting by DC1). The newspaper summary of this six-turn exchange in the last two lines of Extract 6 has resulted in a transformation of Albert's answers, to support the presentation of him as a brazen teenager who 'lied to make things look bad for the police'. Here we see the operation of the ideology of decontextualised fragments, taking individual utterances out of their context, and removing crucial information such as that about volume and repetition. Such journalistic practices, supported by this language ideology, do the work of perpetuating moral panic, as does the practice of switching authorship attribution, which we saw in the newspaper headline, and which is supported by the ideology of narrator authorship. The media also have other linguistic strategies for fuelling moral panic, such as their choice of labels. For example, a newspaper headline on the day after the evidence of the first (youngest) witness read 'Police dumped us: teen thief'.[16] Referring to thirteen-year-old David as a 'teen thief' was consistent with defence counsel's construction of the boys not as victims of police abuse but as criminals legitimately removed by police.

It is interesting to reflect on the significance of the fact that the newspaper extract discussed above in Extract 6 was published on the day following Albert's evidence, and one day preceding the closing addresses (as exemplified in Extract 2). The newspaper did not wait for defence counsel to switch authorship attribution in its closing addresses, before it did just that in its headline '"I lied to embarrass police"'. The language ideologies of decontextualised fragments and narrator authorship are clearly at work in print media as well as courtroom cross-examination.

11.8 Conclusion

In many ways the Pinkenba case is extreme:[17] it reverses the usual positioning where police officers are prosecution witnesses against Aboriginal defendants. It is one of only a handful of cases in Australia where police officers have gone to court for alleged abuse of an Aboriginal person, and the only such case involving six police officers. This high stakes case in the ongoing struggle of Aboriginal people against police control resulted in a hearing characterised by the most extreme courtroom harassment and bullying witnessed by experienced lawyers. Elsewhere (Eades 2008, pp. 315–317), I have discussed the punitive effects of the cross-examination in this case. Repeated rebukes and reprimands, and menacing and aggressive questioning of the boys arguably comprised a form of punishment for their complaints, which had led to charges against police officers. And the naturalising effects of the cross-examination in this case seem unbelievable to many people: the courts legitimised the ongoing police practice of removing Aboriginal people from public spaces, even when they cannot find any grounds to charge them with an offence, and even though this removal contravenes legislated policing guidelines.

This chapter has shown the role of courtroom talk in the perpetuation of neocolonial control over Aboriginal Australians, not just through the language used, but also through language ideologies which facilitate these linguistic practices as well as their interpretation. Examining part of Albert's report about how the police got him and his friends into the police cars, we have seen the work done by the ideologies of decontexualised fragments, narrator authorship and repeated questioning. Albert's use of the word *grab* was interpreted literally and out of context. Then the ideology of inconsistency was used to present the interactionally constructed inconsistency as proof that the witness was a liar. The witness was then bullied into providing apparent agreement to the proposition that he had 'lied to make things look bad for the police'. The language ideologies at work through this process provided powerful interpretive devices leading to an important courtroom impact: the evidence of the boys was discounted and the charges against the police officers were dropped. The most significant wider consequences beyond the courtroom were:

(1) the constructed inconsistency in Albert's story, and the established 'fact' that he 'lied to make things look bad for the police', provided valuable 'evidence' to support the moral

panic that Aboriginal people cannot be trusted, especially in relation to claims of police abuse;

(2) this construction of Albert and the other two boys as unreliable witnesses, whose story of police abuse could not be believed, resulted in the legitimisation of the actions of police officers in removing Aboriginal people from the streets, driving them out of town and abandoning them there, without any charges or arrest; and

(3) the construction of the Aboriginal boys in this case as lying criminals was not confined to the courtroom: it was taken up by the print media, who play a major role in fuelling social panic about Aboriginal people as a danger on the streets.

This case highlights the fact that language ideologies are not just about language, and that they have consequences, not just in court, but in terms of actions and relationships beyond the courtroom. Sociolinguistic analysis can contribute to the understanding of how social inequality is practiced in and through the legal process, by examining widely held assumptions about language and communication, and the working of these assumptions in both the facilitation of problematic interactional practices and the evaluation of witnesses and their stories.

NOTES

1 I am grateful to Jeff Siegel, Barbara Johnstone, and two anonymous reviewers for valuable comments on earlier versions of this chapter.

2. The term 'Indigenous' in Australia encompasses both Aboriginal and Torres Strait Islander people. It is beyond the scope of this chapter and my expertise to consider Torres Strait Islander experiences in the legal process.

3. It is beyond the scope of this chapter to consider the wider applicability of the Australian findings presented here to other neocolonial situations (but see Eades 2008, pp. 336–337 for a brief consideration of this issue).

4. While the ideology of inconsistency was first discussed in Matoesian (2001), this definition reflects my understanding of the term.

5. The legal concept of 'fact', which is central to the court process, refers to something which is established legally, according to rules of evidence (which for example generally prevent a witness reporting what another person said). As Mertz (2007, p. 67) explains, the claim that something is a legal fact 'is not a strong assertion that [it] actually occurred. Rather, the claim is that this version of what occurred is to be accepted as true, based on the legal status of the case'.

6. The Australian committal hearing fulfils some of the functions of the United States Grand Jury trial. But it differs in being heard in an open court in front of a magistrate (analogous to a lower court judge), with no jury. As with trials, committal hearings must follow the rules of evidence (to be discussed in Section 11.6.1), and there is no obligation on the defence to provide any evidence.
7. Quotations from this hearing are based on my transcription of official tape-recordings.
8. See the appendix for transcription conventions.
9. However, on several occasions during this hearing DC1 overtly relied on such assumptions, for example when he said to Albert 'we have to take your silence as "no"' (Eades 2008, p. 111), and to the youngest witness David 'your silence probably answers [the question]' (p. 114).
10. In Eades (2006) I discuss the lexical struggle in this hearing over the meaning of the boys' use of the word *force*.
11. During a discussion with the prosecutor I asked why he was raising so few objections. He replied that he was concerned it would only make the defence counsel 'worse' (more aggressive), and that the boys 'were being given a hard enough time as it was'.
12. Boyd and Hopkins (2010, p. 159) report that in response to criticisms such as that of Justice Wood's cited here, the New South Wales parliament amended the *Criminal Procedures Act* in 2005 to expand the definition of improper questions in cross-examination and to 'impose a duty, rather than a discretion, on judicial officers to intervene and disallow improper questions, regardless of whether or not an objection was raised'. But, a small interview study carried out by Boyd and Hopkins with six lawyers with extensive experience in child sexual assault cases suggests that little has changed since the introduction of this provision.
13. The second and third of these two directives are given in the official court transcript with a question mark, supporting the legal fiction that everything that a lawyer says to a witness in court is a question (see Eades 2008, p. 224). The first example is within a longer utterance, which concludes with the lawyer saying to the magistrate 'Will your worship direct him to answer the question please?'.
14. This even involved the magistrate on three separate occasions mistakenly addressing one of the boys as 'defendant', despite the fact that the police officers were the defendants, and the boys were prosecution witnesses.
15. At that time Queensland had legislated guidelines about dealing with young troublemakers, and these guidelines took account particularly of the situation of Aboriginal children (consistent with recommendations from the Royal Commission into Aboriginal Deaths in Custody, and the United Nations Convention on the Rights of the Child). But these recommendations, legislated guidelines and international conventions were ignored that night in Pinkenba, when the boys were not even charged with an offence.
16. 'Police dumped us: Teen thief', *The Courier Mail*, 21 February 1995. The witness did not say the *police dumped us*, but this headline does not use quotation marks, so perhaps it is intended as a paraphrase. The only occasion on which the verb *dump* was used by one of the boys was in an answer by the oldest witness, on the day after this newspaper headline had appeared.
17 Despite the Pinkenba case being extreme, a reviewer has pointed out that the outcome does not seem so unusual when seen in the context of how courts in the United States 'rule in favour of the police'. Several sociolinguistic studies have highlighted the role of other language ideologies in such situations, e.g. Ainsworth (2008) in relation to the insistence of courts on a direct and literal assertion of suspects' Miranda rights, and Solan and Tiersma (2005) on the 'selective literalism' of courts' interpretation of the speech acts

involved in police searches. In Eades (2006) I discuss this issue in relation to the non-literal interpretation of the central speech act by police officers in the Pinkenba case: the uncontested speech act of the police officers saying to the boys 'Hop in the car' or 'Jump in the car' was interpreted by the defence as not being a command, and this was accepted by the court. See also Eades 2010, pp. 243–247.

Appendix

Transcription conventions

The following transcription conventions are used in chapters 7, 10 and 11.

DC1	first defence counsel
DC2	second defence counsel
DC	defence counsel
Pros	prosecutor
Mag	magistrate (lower court judge)
SMALL CAPS	raised volume
underline	emphasis
°before and after word°	very low volume
number in parentheses (2.0)	length of pause in seconds
hyphen -	pause within a turn of less than 0.5 seconds
equals sign =	latched utterances: no pause between end of one & start of next
square bracket [	start of overlapping talk and utterance which is overlapped

Glossary

appellant:

A person appealing against a decision of a court or tribunal.

bicultural person:

A person who has the ability to participate in two or more sociocultural groups. Many bicultural Aboriginal people can switch — consciously or unconsciously — between Aboriginal ways of interacting, and non-Aboriginal ways, depending on the context, the people involved, and the goal to be accomplished (see Section 1.5.2).

cross-examination:

Courtroom questioning of a witness by the lawyer for 'the other side' in the courtroom adversarial struggle. If the witness is giving evidence for the prosecution, they are cross-examined by the defence (and vice-versa).

culture:

Ways of thinking, believing and acting which are shared within a social group and passed on from generation to generation (see Section 1.2).

cultural conceptualisation:

Culturally based ways of seeing the world. For example, when many Aboriginal people talk about *family*, the meanings of this word are deeply rooted in Aboriginal experiences of family and kinship networks, relationships and expectations.

decontextualisation:

The process of taking a story (or part of it) out of its context. For example, in cross-examination a lawyer may take a part of what a person said in a police interview and ask questions about it. This involves decontextualising the person's story and recontextualising it (see Chapter 11). *See also* 'recontextualisation'.

determinism:

The view that everything that happens is determined by previously existing causes. It implies a limited or non-existent role for individual agency and choices (see Section 1.5.2).

dialect:
A variety of language which can be understood by speakers of other varieties of the same language, and which differs from them in systematic ways. These differences can be found in sounds, grammar, words and their meanings, and language use (see Chapter 5). *See also* 'language variety'.

entextualisation:
The process of making something into a text. For example when police interview a suspect, the conversation is entextualised in the written record of interview.

ethnography:
The study of how members of a social group live, and of their beliefs and values. The main approaches to ethnography start with careful observation and participation in daily life (rather than for example, with interviews).

ethnography of communication:
The study of ways of communicating within a particular social group.

ergative case system:
A grammatical pattern widespread in Australian Aboriginal languages, and many other languages around the world, but not found in English or in most European languages. In languages with an ergative case system, the subject of an intransitive sentence (such as *the woman* in *The woman smiled*) is treated in the same way as the object of a transitive sentence (such as *the cat* in *The woman saw the cat*).

essentialism:
The 'position that the attributes and behavior of socially defined groups can be determined and explained by reference to cultural and/or biological characteristics believed to be inherent to the group' (Bucholtz 2003, p. 400, and see Section 1.5.2). *See also* 'strategic essentialism'.

examination-in-chief:
Courtroom questioning of a witness by the lawyer who has called this person to give evidence. It is usually cooperative in nature and tone, as both lawyer and witness are 'on the same side'. (It is called 'direct examination' in some countries.)

gratuitous concurrence:
The conversational feature of saying *yes* in answer to a question (or *no* to a negative question), regardless of whether you agree with the proposition being questioned, and sometimes without even understanding the question.

interactional sociolinguistics:
An approach to the study of language use which examines the details of what people say, typically from close analysis of audio- or video-recorded data. Interactional sociolinguistic analysis highlights the contextual and cultural dimensions of language and interaction.

interlanguage English:
The language system of a person who speaks some English in addition to another or several other languages, but who has not finished learning English.

language ideologies:
Taken-for-granted assumptions about how language works, which are shaped by social, historical and cultural factors and experiences (see Section 11.3).

language variety:
A cover term to refer to a language or a dialect.

lexical perversion:
A term used by Eades (2006, 2008) to describe the way that cross-examining lawyers sometimes take a witness's description of what happened to them, and substitute their own words in place of the witness's words, in such a way that results in a misrepresentation or perversion of the witness's story.

lexico-semantics:
The study of the meaning (semantics) of words and phrases (lexical items).

linguistic anthropology:
'The study of language as a cultural resource and speaking as a cultural practice' (Duranti 1997, p. 2).

macro-structure:
Large scale social structures, such as institutions like the legal system (which are influenced by micro-practice, and also influence micro-practice, see Section 11.2).

metacommentary about a witness's evidence:
A commentary about the language involved in the evidence – such as the way that questions have restricted the answers. This contrasts with commentary about the evidence, for example about what was said, what it meant, and what was not said.

metapragmatic directive:
Something that one person says to someone else telling that person how he or she should use language (e.g. *speak up*, or *don't swear*).

micro-practice:
What people do in particular situations (which are influenced by macro-structure, and also influence macro-structure, see Section 11.2).

morpho-syntax:
The study of the structure of words (morphology) and sentences (syntax).

neocolonial:
The nature of the relationship between a former colonial power and the society it colonised, in which there is still domination, despite apparent equality.

non-traditionally oriented Aboriginal societies:
Societies in non-remote Australia, which have undergone many drastic changes since white invasion and settlement, and in which 'traditional' languages are no longer strong (see Section 1.3). *See also* 'traditionally oriented Aboriginal societies'.

norms:
Expectations or beliefs about how to act which are generally agreed upon (whether consciously or unconsciously) within a social group.

phonology:
The study of sound systems in languages.

pragmatics:
The study of language use in specific social contexts.

recontextualisation:
The process of retelling a story (or part of it) in a new context. *See also* 'decontextualisation'.

reification of languages:
The view that a language can exist as a thing, easily recognised and clearly separated from other languages or language varieties (see Section 1.2). ('Reification' means to turn an abstract concept into a concrete thing.)

socialisation:
The process by which someone learns how to be a member of a society or societies, whether implicitly and/or explicitly. Primary socialisation happens with the family and peers during childhood, and then through school. Secondary socialisations can happen, to varying degrees, with any social group a person spends time with, as a child or an adult.

sociocultural group:
A group of people who share social and cultural life and values.

sociolinguistics:
The study of the relationship between language and society.

strategic essentialism:
The position that it can be strategically helpful to sometimes talk or write with some essentialism, such as generalisations about a particular social group, or a focus on one aspect of a person's identity (see Section 1.5.2). *See also* 'essentialism'.

traditionally oriented Aboriginal societies:
Societies in remote Australia, where non-English related — or 'traditional' — languages often remain strong, as do a large number of social and cultural practices with strong continuities from pre-colonial times (see Section 1.3). See also 'non-traditionally oriented Aboriginal society'.

Readers who wish to explore sociolinguistics further are encouraged to consult Holmes (2008) and Swann et al. (2004).

Reference list

Cases Cited

Crawford v Venardos & Ors 1995, Unreported, Brisbane Magistrates' Court, 24 February.

McKinney v The Queen 1991, 171 *Commonwealth Law Reports* 468 (High Court of Australia).

Mooney v James 1949, *Victorian Law Reports* 22–32 (Victorian Supreme Court).

R v Aboriginal Dulcie Dumaia 1959, *Northern Territory Judgments* 694–699 (Northern Territory Supreme Court).

R v Aubrey 1995, Unreported, Queensland Court of Appeal, 28 April.

R v Condren 1987, 28 *Australian Criminal Reports* 261–299 (Queensland Court of Criminal Appeal).

R v Kenny Charlie 1995, Unreported, Northern Territory Supreme Court, 28 September.

R v Kina 1993, Unreported, Queensland Court of Appeal, 29 November.

R v Rankin 1998, Unreported, Northern Territory Supreme Court, 4 December.

References

ABC – *see* Australian Broadcasting Commission.

Abrahams, RD 1976, *Talking black*, Newbury House, Rowley, MA.

ABS – *see* Australian Bureau of Statistics.

Ahearn, LM 2012, *Living language: an introduction to linguistic anthropology*, Wiley-Blackwell, Chichester, UK.

AIATSIS – *see* Australian Institute of Aboriginal and Torres Strait Islander Studies.

Ainsworth, J 2008, '"You have the right to remain silent...but only if you ask for it just so": the role of linguistic ideology in American police interrogation law', *International Journal of Speech, Language and the Law*, vol. 15, no. 1, pp. 1–22.

ALRC – *see* Australian Law Reform Commission.

Altman, JC & Nieuwenhuysen, J 1979, *The economic status of Australian Aborigines*, Cambridge University Press, Cambridge.

Angermeyer, PS 2008, 'Creating monolingualism in the multilingual courtroom', *Sociolinguistic Studies*, vol. 2, no. 3, pp. 385–403.

Arthur, JM 1996, *Aboriginal English: a cultural study*, Oxford University Press, Melbourne.

Australian Broadcasting Commission 1993, *7.30 Report*, ABC TV, 30 November.

—— 1996, *Black and blue: Four Corners*, documentary, ABC TV, 8 March.

Australian Bureau of Statistics 2004, *Prisoners in Australia*, viewed 8 January 2013, <http://www.abs.gov.au/Ausstats/abs@.nsf/ lookupMF/8D5807D8074A7A5BCA256A6800811054>.

Australian Institute of Aboriginal and Torres Strait Islander Studies 2012, *Guidelines for ethical research in Australian Indigenous studies*, AIATSIS, Canberra.

Australian Law Reform Commission 1986, *Report no. 31: the recognition of Aboriginal customary laws*, Australian Government Publishing Service, Canberra.

—— 1992, *Report no. 57: Multiculturalism and the law*, Australian Government Publishing Service, Canberra.

Baker, S 1945, *The Australian language*, Angus & Robertson, Sydney.

Barwick, D 1974, 'The Aboriginal family in South-Eastern Australia', in *The family in Australia*, eds J Krupinski & A Stoller, Pergamon, Sydney, pp. 196–209.

—— 1988, 'Aborigines of Victoria', in Keen (ed.), pp. 27–32.

Basso, K 1970, '"To give up on words": silence in Apache culture', *Southwestern Journal of Anthropology*, vol. 26, no. 3, pp. 213–230.

Bauman, R & Briggs, C 1990, 'Poetics and performance as critical perspectives on language and social life', *Annual Review of Anthropology*, vol. 19, pp. 59–88.

Benor, SB 2010, 'Ethnolinguistic repertoire: shifting the analytic focus in language and ethnicity', *Journal of Sociolinguistics*, vol. 14, no. 2, pp. 159–183.

Berk-Seligson, S 1990, *The bilingual courtroom: court interpreters in the judicial process*, University of Chicago Press, Chicago.

—— 2009, *Coerced confessions*, Mouton de Gruyter, Berlin.

Berndt, RM & Berndt, CH 1964, *The world of the first Australians*, Ure Smith, Sydney.

Berry, R & Hudson, J 1997, *Making the jump: a resource book for teachers of Aboriginal students*, Catholic Education Office, Kimberley Region, Broome.

Black and white 2002, motion picture, Tartan Video, London.

Blake, BJ & Dixon, RMW 1979, 'Introduction', in *Handbook of Australian languages vol. 1*, eds RMW Dixon & BJ Blake, ANU Press, Canberra, pp. 1–26.

Blommaert, J 2005, *Discourse*, Cambridge University Press, Cambridge.

Bowe, H & Storey, K 1995, 'Linguistic analysis as evidence of speaker identification: demand and response', in Eades (ed.), pp. 187–200.

Boyd, R & Hopkins, A 2010, 'Cross-examination of child sexual assault complainants: concerns about the application of s41 of the Evidence Act', *Criminal Law Journal*, vol. 34, pp. 149–166.

Broken English 1993, video recording, City Pictures, New South Wales.

Brown, M & Wilson, P 1992, *Justice and nightmares: successes and failures of forensic sciences*, New South Wales University Press, Sydney.

Brown, P & Fraser, C 1979, 'Speech as a marker of situation', in *Social markers in speech*, eds KR Scherer & H Giles, Cambridge University Press, Cambridge, pp. 33–62.

Brumby, E & Vaszolyi, E (eds) 1977, *Language problems and Aboriginal education*, Mt Lawley College of Advanced Education, Mt Lawley WA.

Bucholtz, M 2003, 'Sociolinguistic nostalgia and the authentication of identity', *Journal of Sociolinguistics*, vol. 7, no. 3, pp. 398–416.

Ceci, SJ & Bruck, M 1993, 'Suggestibility of the child witness: a historical review and synthesis', *Psychological Bulletin*, vol. 113, pp. 403–439.

Chamberlain, R 1973, *The Stuart affair*, Rigby, Adelaide.

Chambers, J (ed.) 1983, *Black English: educational equity and the law*, Karoma, Ann Arbor, MI.

—— 1990, 'Forensic dialectology and the Bear Island claim', in *The language scientist as expert in the legal setting: issues in forensic linguistics*, eds R Rieber & W Stewart, The New York Academy of Sciences, New York, pp. 19–32.

Chomsky, N 1965, *Aspects of the theory of syntax*, MIT Press, Cambridge, MA.

Christie, M 1982, 'Teaching purposeful reading to Aboriginal children', *The Aboriginal Child at School*, vol. 10, no. 2, pp. 11–26.

Cicourel, AV 1981, 'Notes on the integration of micro- and macro-levels of analysis', in *Advances in social theory and methodology: toward an integration of micro- and macro-sociologies*, eds KD Knorr-Cetina & AV Cicourel, Routledge & Kegan Paul, Boston, pp. 51–80.

CJC – *see* Criminal Justice Commission.

Coldrey, J 1987, 'Aboriginals and the criminal courts', in Hazlehurst (ed.), pp. 81–92.

Collins, R 1988, 'The micro contribution to macro sociology', *Sociological Theory*, vol. 6, pp. 242–253.

Conley, JM & O'Barr, WM 1990, *Rules versus relationships: the ethnography of legal discourse*, University of Chicago Press, Chicago.

—— 2005, *Just words: law, language and power*, 2nd edn, University of Chicago Press, Chicago.

Conley, JM, O'Barr, WM & Lind, AE 1978, 'The power of language: presentational style in the courtroom', *Duke Law Journal*, pp. 1375–1399.

Cooke, M 1995a, 'Aboriginal evidence in the cross-cultural courtroom', in Eades (ed.), pp. 55–96.

—— 1995b, 'Interpreting in a cross-cultural cross-examination: an Aboriginal case study', *International Journal of the Sociology of Language*, vol. 113, pp. 99–111.

—— 1995c, 'Understood by all concerned? Anglo/Aboriginal legal translation', in *Translation and the law*, ed. M Morris, John Benjamins, Amsterdam, pp. 37–66.

—— 1996, 'A different story: narrative versus "question and answer" in Aboriginal evidence', *Forensic Linguistics*, vol. 3, no. 2, pp. 273–288.

—— 1998, 'Anglo/Yolngu communication in the criminal justice system', PhD thesis, University of New England, Armidale.

—— 2002, *Indigenous interpreting issues for the courts*, Australian Institute of Judicial Administration Incorporated, Carlton, Vic.

—— 2004, *Caught in the middle: Indigenous interpreters and customary law*, Law Reform Commission of Western Australia, Perth.

—— 2009, 'Anglo/Aboriginal communication in the criminal justice process: a collective responsibility', *Journal of Judicial Administration*, vol. 19, pp. 26–35.

Cotterill, J 2003, *Language and power in court: a linguistic analysis of the O. J. Simpson trial*, Palgrave Macmillan, Basingstoke.

—— 2004, 'Collocation, connotation, and courtroom semantics: lawyers' control of witness testimony through lexical negotiation', *Applied Linguistics*, vol. 25, no. 4, pp. 513–537.

Coulthard, M & Johnson, A 2007, *An introduction to forensic linguistics: language in evidence*, Routledge, London.

—— (eds) 2010, *Routledge handbook of forensic linguistics*, Routledge, London.

Coupland, N 2001, 'Introduction: sociolinguistics and social theory', in Coupland et al. (eds), pp. 1–26.

Coupland, N, Sarangi, S & Candlin, CN (eds) 2001, *Sociolinguistics and social theory*, Pearson Education Limited, London.

Criminal Justice Commission 1992, *Report on the investigation into the complaints of Kelvin Ronald Condren and others*, Criminal Justice Commission, Brisbane.

—— 1996, *Aboriginal witnesses in Queensland's criminal courts*, Criminal Justice Commission, Brisbane.

Cunneen, C 1994, 'Enforcing genocide? Aboriginal young people and the police', in *The police and young people in Australia*, eds R White & C Adler, Cambridge University Press, Cambridge, pp. 128–158.

—— 2001, *Conflict, politics and crime: Aboriginal communities and the police*, Allen & Unwin, Sydney.

Danet B, Hoffman K, Kermish N, Rahn J & Stayman D 1980, 'An ethnography of questioning in the courtroom', in *Language use and the uses of language*, eds R Shuy & A Shnukal, Georgetown University Press, Washington DC, pp. 222–234.

Dixon, RMW 1971, 'A method of semantic description', in *Semantics*, eds D Steinberg & L Jakobovits, Cambridge University Press, Cambridge, pp. 436–471.

—— 1977, *A grammar of Yidiny*, Cambridge University Press, Cambridge.

—— 1980, *The languages of Australia*, Cambridge University Press, Cambridge.

Dixon, T 1987, *The wizard of Alice*, Alella Books, Morwell, Vic.

Duranti, A 1997, *Linguistic anthropology*, Cambridge University Press, Cambridge.

Dutton, TE 1965, *The informal English of Palm Island Aboriginal children*, Unpublished MA thesis, University of Queensland, Brisbane.

Dwyer, J 1974, 'The school and the Aboriginal child', *The Aboriginal Child at School*, vol. 2, no. 1, pp. 3–19.

Eades, D 1983, 'English as an Aboriginal language in Southeast Queensland', PhD thesis, University of Queensland, Brisbane.

—— 1988a, 'Sociolinguistic evidence in court', *Australian Journal of Communication*, vol. 14, pp. 22–33.

—— 1988b, 'Applying sociolinguistics: the case for Condren', paper presented at the annual conference of the Australian Linguistics Society, University of New England, Armidale.

—— 1990, 'Language and the law: an Australian introduction', *Australian Journal of Linguistics*, vol. 10, pp. 89–100.

—— 1991a, 'Communicative strategies in Aboriginal English', in Romaine (ed.), pp. 84–93.

—— 1991b, 'A lesson from history: Aboriginal English and the law in 1959', paper presented at the annual conference of the Australian Linguistics Society, University of Queensland, Brisbane.

—— 1992, *Aboriginal English and the law: communicating with Aboriginal English speaking clients: a handbook for legal practitioners*, Queensland Law Society, Brisbane.

—— 1993, 'The case for Condren: Aboriginal English, pragmatics and the law', *Journal of Pragmatics*, vol. 20, no. 1, pp. 65–86.

—— 1994a, 'A case of communicative clash: Aboriginal English and the legal system', in Gibbons (ed.), pp. 234–264.

—— 1994b, 'Forensic linguistics in Australia: an overview', *Forensic Linguistics*, vol. 1, no. 2, pp. 113–132.

—— 1994c, 'Recognition of cultural differences in communication: the case of Robyn Kina', paper presented at the Fifth International Conference on Language and Social Psychology, University of Queensland, Brisbane.

—— (ed.) 1995, *Language in evidence: issues confronting Aboriginal and multicultural Australia*, University of New South Wales Press, Sydney.

—— 1996a, 'Legal recognition of cultural differences in communication: the case of Robyn Kina', *Language and Communication*, vol. 16, no. 3, pp. 215–227.

—— 1996b, 'Verbatim courtroom transcripts and discourse analysis', in *Recent developments in forensic linguistics*, ed. H Kniffka, Peter Lang, Frankfurt, pp. 241–254.

—— 1997, 'The acceptance of linguistic evidence about Indigenous Australians', *Australian Aboriginal Studies*, vol. 1, pp. 15–27.

—— 2000, '"I don't think it's an answer to the question": silencing Aboriginal witnesses in court', *Language in Society*, vol. 29, no. 2, pp. 161–196.

—— 2002, '"Evidence given in unequivocal terms": gaining consent of Aboriginal kids in court', in *Language in the legal process*, ed. J Cotterill, Palgrave, Basingstoke, pp. 162–179.

—— 2003a, 'The politics of misunderstanding in the legal process: Aboriginal English in Queensland', in *Misunderstanding in spoken discourse*, eds J House, G Kasper & S Ross, Longman, London, pp. 196–223.

—— 2003b, '"I don't think the lawyers were communicating with me": misunderstanding cultural differences in communicative style', *Emory Law Journal*, vol. 52, pp. 1109–1134.

—— 2004a, 'Understanding Aboriginal English in the legal system: a critical sociolinguistics approach', *Applied Linguistics*, vol. 25, no. 4, pp. 491–512.

—— 2004b, 'Beyond difference and domination?: intercultural communication in legal contexts', in *Intercultural discourse and communication: the essential readings*, eds C Paulston & S Kiesling, Basil Blackwell, Oxford, pp. 304–316.

—— 2006, 'Lexical struggle in court: Aboriginal Australians vs the state', *Journal of Sociolinguistics*, vol. 10, no. 2, pp. 153–181.

—— 2007, 'Understanding Aboriginal silence in legal contexts', in *Handbook of intercultural communication*, eds H Kotthoff & H Spencer-Oatey, Mouton de Gruyter, Berlin, pp. 285–301.

—— 2008, *Courtroom talk and neocolonial* control, Mouton de Gruyter, Berlin.

—— 2010, *Sociolinguistics and the legal process*, Multilingual Matters, Bristol.

—— 2011, 'Language ideologies in the discursive testing of witnesses' stories in court: examining prior inconsistent statements', paper presented at the First International Conference on Law, Language and Discourse, Hong Kong.

—— forthcoming, 'Aboriginal English', in *The languages and linguistics of Australia: A comprehensive guide* (*World of linguistics*), eds H Koch & R Nordlinger, de Gruyter Mouton, Berlin.

Eagleson, RD, Kaldor, S & Malcolm, IG 1982, *English and the Aboriginal child*, Curriculum Development Centre, Canberra.

Ehrlich, S 2001, *Representing rape: language and sexual consent*, Routledge, London.

—— 2007, 'Legal discourse and the cultural intelligibility of gendered meanings', *Journal of Sociolinguistics*, vol. 11, no. 4, pp. 452–477.

Elkin, A 1947, 'Aboriginal evidence and justice in north Australia', *Oceania*, vol. 17, pp. 173–210.

Ervin-Tripp, S 1976, 'Speech acts and social learning', in *Meaning in anthropology*, eds KH Basso & HA Selby, University of New Mexico Press, Albuquerque, pp. 123–53.

Fairclough, N 1989, *Language and power*, Longman, London.

Findlay M, Odgers, S & Yeo, S 2005, *Australian criminal justice*, 3rd edn, Oxford University Press, Oxford.

Fink, R 1957, 'The caste barrier — an obstacle to the assimilation of part-Aborigines in north-west New South Wales', *Oceania*, vol. 28, no. 2, pp. 100–110.

Fitzgerald, GE 1989, *Report of a commission of inquiry pursuant to orders in council*, Government Printer, Brisbane.

Flint, EH 1968, 'Aboriginal English: linguistic description as an aid to teaching', *English in Australia*, vol. 6, pp. 3–21.

Foley, M 1984, 'Aborigines and the police', in *Aborigines and the law: essays in memory of Elizabeth Eggleston*, eds P Hanks & B Keon-Cohen, Allen & Unwin, Sydney, pp. 160–190.

Fryer-Smith, S 2008, *Aboriginal cultural awareness benchbook for Western Australian courts*, 2nd edn, Australian Institute of Judicial Administration, Perth.

Gardner, R 2010, 'Question and answer sequences in Garrwa talk', *Australian Journal of Linguistics*, vol. 30, no. 4, pp. 423–446.

Gibbons, J (ed.) 1994, *Language and the law*, Longman, London.

—— 2003, *Forensic linguistics*, Blackwell, Oxford.

Goldflam, R 1995, 'Silence in court! Problems and prospects in Aboriginal legal interpreting', in Eades (ed.) pp. 28–54.

Goody, EN 1978, 'Towards a theory of questions', in *Questions and politeness: strategies in social interaction*, ed. E Goody, Cambridge University Press, Cambridge, pp. 17–43.

Gray P 2000, 'Do the walls have ears? Indigenous title and courts in Australia', *International Journal of Legal Information*, vol. 28, pp. 185–205.

—— 2007, 'Truth, justice and fact-finding', paper presented at the conference of the International Association of Forensic Linguists, Seattle.

Grayshon, MC 1977, *Towards a social grammar of language*, Mouton, The Hague.

Green, LJ 2002, *African American English: a linguistic introduction*, Cambridge University Press, Cambridge.

Gumperz, JJ 1982a, *Discourse strategies*, Cambridge University Press, Cambridge.

—— (ed.) 1982b, *Language and social identity*, Cambridge University Press, Cambridge.

—— & Gumperz, JC 1982, 'Introduction: language and the communication of social identity', in Gumperz (ed.), pp. 1–21.

Hale, S 2004, *The discourse of court interpreting: discourse practices of the law, the witness and the interpreter*, John Benjamins, Amsterdam.

Hall, R 1966, *Pidgin and creole languages*, Cornell University Press, Ithaca.

Hamilton, A 1981, *Nature and nurture: Aboriginal child-rearing in North-Central Arnhem Land*, Australian Institute of Aboriginal Studies, Canberra.

Harkins, J 1990, 'Shame and shyness in the Aboriginal classroom: a case for "practical semantics"', *Australian Journal of Linguistics*, vol. 10, pp. 293–306.

—— 1994, *Bridging two worlds: Aboriginal English and cross-cultural understanding*, University of Queensland Press, St Lucia.

Harris, J 1970, 'Gunkurrng, a mother-in-law language', in *Pacific Linguistic studies in honour of Arthur Capell*, eds SA Wurm & DC Laycock, Pacific Linguistics, Canberra, pp. 783–789.

—— 2007, 'Linguistic responses to contact', in Leitner & Malcolm (eds), pp. 131–152.

Harris, Sandra 1984, 'Questions as a mode of control in magistrates' courts', *International Journal of the Sociology of Language*, vol. 49, pp. 5–28.

Harris, Stephen 1977, *Milingimbi Aboriginal learning contexts*, University of New Mexico PhD dissertation, Albuquerque.

—— 1984, *Culture and learning: tradition and education in north-east Arnhem Land*, Australian Institute of Aboriginal Studies.

Haviland, JB 1979a, 'Guugu Yimidhirr brother-in-law language', *Language in Society*, vol. 8, pp. 365–393.

—— 1979b, 'How to talk to your brother-in-law in Guugu-Yimidhirr', in Shopen (ed.), pp. 161–240.

Hazlehurst, K (ed.) 1987, *Ivory scales: Black Australia and the law*, NSW University Press, Sydney.

Heerey, P 2000, 'Storytelling, postmodernism and the law', *The Australian Law Journal*, vol. 74, no. 10, pp. 681–691.

Heffer, C 2005, *The language of jury trial: a corpus-aided analysis of legal-lay discourse*, Palgrave Macmillan, Basingstoke.

Heller, M 2001, 'Undoing the macro/micro dichotomy: ideology and categorisation in a linguistic minority school', in Coupland, Sarangi & Candlin (eds), pp. 212–234.

Henderson, J & Nash, D (eds), 2002, *Language in native title*, Aboriginal Studies Press, Canberra.

Holmes, J 2008, *An introduction to sociolinguistics*, Longman, London.

House of Representatives Standing Committee on Aboriginal and Torres Strait Islander Affairs 2012, *Our land our languages: language learning in Indigenous communities*, Commonwealth of Australia, Canberra.

HRSCATSIA – see House of Representatives Standing Committee on Aboriginal and Torres Strait Islander Affairs.

Hudson, J 1992, 'Summary: fostering English language in Kimberley schools: an in-service course for teachers', in *Pidgins, creoles and non-standard dialects in education*, ed. J Siegel, Occasional Paper no. 12, Applied Linguistics Association of Australia, Melbourne.

Hymes, D 1974, *Foundations in sociolinguistics: an ethnographic approach*, Tavistock Publications, London.

Hymes, V 1975, 'The ethnography of linguistic intuitions at Warm Springs', *LACUS*, vol. 2, pp. 29–35.

Inglis, K 1961, *The Stuart case*, Melbourne University Press, Melbourne.

Jakubowicz, A, Goodall, H, Martin, J, Mitchell, T, Randall, L & Seneviratne, K 1994, *Racism, ethnicity and the media*, Allen & Unwin, Sydney.

Jefferson, G 1989, 'Preliminary notes on a possible metric which provides for a "Standard Maximum" silence of approximately one second in a conversation', in *Conversation: an interdisciplinary perspective*, eds D Roger & P Bull, Multilingual Matters, Clevedon, pp. 166–196.

Jensen, M-T 1995, 'Linguistic evidence accepted in the case of a non-native speaker of English', in Eades (ed.), pp. 127–146.

Jönsson, L & Linell, P 1991, 'Story generations: from dialogical interviews to written reports in police interrogations', *Text*, vol. 11, no. 3, pp. 419–440.

Kaldor, S & Malcolm, IG 1991 'Aboriginal English: an overview', in Romaine (ed.), pp. 67–83.

Keen, I 1994, *Knowledge and secrecy in an Aboriginal religion*, Oxford University Press, Oxford.

—— (ed.) 1988, *Being black: Aboriginal cultures in 'settled' Australia*, Australian Institute of Aboriginal Studies, Canberra.

Keenan, EL & Ochs, E 1979, 'Becoming a competent speaker of Malagasy', in Shopen (ed.), pp. 113–160.

Keesing, R 1974, 'Theories of culture', *Annual Review of Anthropology*, vol. 3, pp. 73–97.

Kirby, M 1980, 'TGH Strehlow and Aboriginal customary laws', *Adelaide Law Review*, vol. 7, pp. 172–199.

Koch, H 1985, 'Nonstandard English in an Aboriginal land claim', in *Cross-cultural encounters: communication and miscommunication*, ed. J Pride, River Seine Publications, Melbourne, pp. 176–195.

—— 1991, 'Language and communication in Aboriginal land claim hearings', in Romaine (ed.), pp. 94–103.

—— 2000, 'Central Australian Aboriginal English: in comparison with the morphosyntactic categories of Kaytetye', *Asian Englishes*, vol. 3, no. 2, pp. 32–58.

—— 2011, 'The influence of Arandic languages on Central Australian Aboriginal English', in *Creoles, their substrates and language typology*, ed. C Lefebvre, John Benjamins, Amsterdam, pp. 437–460.

Komter, M 2002, 'The suspect's own words: the treatment of written statements in Dutch courtrooms', *Forensic Linguistics*, vol. 9, no. 2, pp. 168–192.

—— 2006, 'From talk to text: the interactional construction of a police record', *Research on Language in Social Interaction*, vol. 39, no. 3, pp. 201–228.

Kroskrity, PV 2004, 'Language ideologies', in *A companion to linguistic anthropology*, ed. A Duranti, Blackwell, Oxford, pp. 496–517.

Kurzon, D 1995, 'The right of silence: a socio-pragmatic model of interpretation', *Journal of Pragmatics*, vol. 23, pp. 55–69.

Labov, W 1972, *Language in the inner city: studies in the Black English vernacular*, University of Pennsylvania Press, Philadelphia.

—— 1988, 'The judicial testing of linguistic theory', in *Linguistics in context: connecting observation and understanding*, ed. D Tannen, Ablex, Norwood, NJ, pp. 159–182.

Langton, M 1981, 'Urbanizing Aborigines: the social scientists' great deception', *Social Alternatives*, vol. 2, no. 2, pp. 16–22.

—— 1988, 'Medicine Square', in Keen (ed.), pp. 201–226.

—— 2012, 'The quiet revolution: Indigenous people and the resources boom', ABC Radio National Boyer Lectures.

Lavery, D 1992, 'Review of *Aboriginal English and the law*', *Aboriginal Law Bulletin*, vol. 2, no. 59, pp. 13.

Leitner, G & Malcolm, IG (eds) 2007, *The habitat of Australia's Aboriginal languages: past, present, and future*, Mouton de Gruyter, Berlin.

Lester, Y 1974, *Aborigines and the courts and interpreting in court*, Institute for Aboriginal Development, Alice Springs.

Levinson, SC 1979, 'Activity types', *Linguistics*, vol. 17, pp. 365–399.

Liberman, K 1980, 'Ambiguity and gratuitous concurrence in intercultural communication', *Human Studies*, vol. 3, pp. 65–85.

—— 1981 'Understanding Aborigines in Australian courts of law', *Human Organization*, vol. 40, pp. 247–255.

—— 1982a 'Some linguistic features of congenial fellowship among the Pitjantjatjara', *International Journal of the Sociology of Language*, vol. 36, pp. 35–52.

—— 1982b 'Intercultural communication in Central Australia', *Working Papers in Sociolinguistics*, no. 104, pp. 1–10.

—— 1985, *Understanding interaction in Central Australia: an ethnomethodological study of Australian Aboriginal people*, Routledge & Kegan Paul, Boston.

Loftus, E 1979, *Eyewitness testimony*, Harvard University Press, Cambridge, Mass.

Luban, D 1999, 'Twenty theses on adversarial ethics', in *Beyond the adversarial system*, eds M Lavarch & H Stacy, Federation Press, Sydney, pp. 134–154.

Luchjenbroers, J 1997, '"In your own words...": questions and answers in a Supreme Court trial', *Journal of Pragmatics*, vol. 27, pp. 477–503.

Malcolm, IG 1982, 'Communicative dysfunction in the Aboriginal classroom', in *Aboriginal education: issues and innovations*, ed. J Sherwood, Creative Research, Perth, pp. 153–172.

—— 1992, 'English in the education of speakers of Aboriginal English', in *Pidgins, creoles and non-standard dialects in education*, ed. J Siegel, Occasional Paper no. 12, Applied Linguistics Association of Australia, Melbourne, pp. 15–41.

—— 2000, 'English and inclusivity in education for Indigenous students', *Australian Review of Applied Linguistics*, vol. 22, no. 2, pp. 51–66.

—— 2008a, 'Australian creoles and Aboriginal English: phonetics and phonology', in *Varieties of English 3: the Pacific and Australasia*, eds K Burridge & B Kortmann, Mouton de Gruyter, Berlin, pp. 124–141.

—— 2008b, 'Australian creoles and Aboriginal English: morphology and syntax', in *Varieties of English 3: the Pacific and Australasia*, eds K Burridge & B Kortmann, Mouton de Gruyter, Berlin, pp. 415–443.

—— & Grote, E 2007, 'Aboriginal English: reconstructed variety for cultural maintenance', in Leitner & Malcolm (eds), pp. 153–180.

——, Haig, Y, Königsberg, P, Rochecouste, J, Collard, G, Hill, A & Cahill, R 1999, *Two-way English*, Education Department of Western Australia, Perth.

—— & Koscielecki, MM 1997, *Aboriginality and English*, report to the Australian Research Council, Edith Cowan University, Centre for Applied Language Research, Mt Lawley, WA.

—— & Rochecouste, J 2000, 'Event and story schemas in Australian Aboriginal English', *English World-Wide*, vol. 21, no. 2, pp. 261–289.

—— & Sharifian, F 2002, 'Aspects of Aboriginal English oral discourse: an application of cultural schema theory', *Discourse Studies*, vol. 4, no. 2, pp. 169–181.

Maryns, K 2006, *The asylum speaker: language in the Belgian asylum procedure*, St Jerome Press, Manchester.

Masters, C 1992, *Inside story*, Angus & Robertson, Sydney.

Matoesian, G 1993, *Reproducing rape: domination through talk in the courtroom*, University of Chicago Press, Chicago.

—— 2001, *Law and the language of identity: discourse in the William Kennedy Smith rape trial,* Oxford University Press, Oxford.

Mauet, T 2000, *Trial Techniques*, 5th edn, Aspen Publishers, Gaithersburg.

McClellan, P 2006, 'Who is telling the truth? Psychology, common sense and the law', *The Australian Law Journal*, vol. 80, no. 10, pp. 655–666.

McCorquordale, J 1987, 'Judicial racism in Australia? Aborigines in civil and criminal cases', in Hazlehurst (ed.), pp. 30–59.

McKillop, B 2002, 'What can we learn from the French criminal justice system', *The Australian Law Journal*, vol. 76, no. 1, pp. 49–72.

McRae, H, Nettheim, G & Beacroft, L 1997, *Indigenous legal issues*, 3rd edn, Law Book Company, Sydney.

Mertz, E 2007, *The language of law school: learning to think like a lawyer*, Oxford University Press, Oxford.

Mesthrie, R, Swann, J, Deumert, A & Leap, WL 2009, *Introduction to sociolinguistics*, 2nd edn, Edinburgh University Press, Edinburgh.

Mildren, D 1997, 'Redressing the imbalance against Aboriginals in the criminal justice system', *Criminal Law Journal*, vol. 21, no. 1, pp. 7–22.

—— 1999, 'Redressing the imbalance: Aboriginal people in the criminal justice system', *Forensic Linguistics*, vol. 6, no. 1, pp. 137–160.

Morrow, P 1996, 'Yup'ik Eskimo agents and American legal agencies: perspectives on compliance and resistance', *Journal of the Royal Anthropological Institute*, vol. 2, pp. 405–423.

Moses, K & Wigglesworth, G 2008, 'The silence of the frogs: dysfunctional discourse in the "English-only" Aboriginal classroom', in Simpson & Wigglesworth (eds), pp. 129–153.

Moses, K & Yallop, C 2008, 'Questions about questions', in Simpson & Wigglesworth (eds), pp. 30–55.

Mushin, I & Gardner, R 2009, 'Silence is talk: conversational silence in Australian Aboriginal talk-in-interaction', *Journal of Pragmatics*, vol. 41, pp. 2033–2052.

Neate, G 2003, 'Land, law and language: some issues in the resolution of Indigenous land claims in Australia', paper presented at the conference of the International Association of Forensic Linguists, Sydney, viewed 8 January 2013, <http://www.nntt.gov.au/News-and-Communications/Publications/Speeches-and-papers>.

Nero, SJ (ed.) 2006, *Dialects, Englishes, creoles and education*, Lawrence Erlbaum Associates, Mahwah, NJ.

Ngarritjan-Kessaris, T 1997, 'School meetings and Indigenous parents', in *Indigenous education: historical, moral and practical tales*, eds S Harris & M Malin, Northern Territory University Press, Darwin, pp. 81–90.

Norrick, NR 1998, 'Retelling stories in spontaneous conversation', *Discourse Processes*, vol. 25, no. 1, pp. 75–97.

Parkin, A 1999, *Memory: a guide for professionals*, John Wiley & Sons, Chichester.

Philips, S 1976, 'Some sources of cultural variability in the regulation of talk', *Language in Society*, vol. 5, pp. 81–95.

Piller, I 2011, *Intercultural communication: a critical introduction*, Edinburgh University Press, Edinburgh.

Potas, I, Smart, J, Brignell, G, Thomas, B & Lawrie, R 2003, *Circle sentencing in New South Wales: a review and evaluation*, Judicial Commission of New South Wales, Sydney.

Queensland Department of Justice, 1997, *Juvenile justice: a legal practitioner's guide*, 2nd edn, Department of Justice, Brisbane.

—— 2000, *Aboriginal English in the courts: a handbook*, Department of Justice, Brisbane.

Rampton, B 2001, 'Language crossing, cross-talk and cross-disciplinarity in sociolinguistics', in Coupland et al. (eds), pp. 261–296.

Rampton, B, Maybin, J & Tusting, K (eds) 2007, *Linguistic ethnography: links, problems and possibilities*, special issue of *Journal of Sociolinguistics*, vol. 11, no. 5, pp. 575–695.

RCIADC — *see* Royal Commission into Aboriginal Deaths in Custody.

Reay, M & Sitlington, G 1948, 'Class and status in a mixed-blood community (Moree, New South Wales)', *Oceania*, vol. 18, no. 3, pp. 179–207.

Reeders, E 2008, 'The collaborative construction of knowledge in a traditional context', in Simpson & Wigglesworth (eds), pp. 103–128.

Ritter, D & Garnett, M 1999, *Building the perfect beast: native title lawyers and the practise of native title lawyering*, vol. 1, no. 30, AIATSIS Native Title Research Unit, Canberra.

Rock, F 2001, 'The genesis of a witness statement', *Forensic Linguistics*, vol. 8, no. 2, pp. 44–72.

Romaine, S (ed.) 1991, *Language in Australia*, Cambridge University Press, Cambridge.

Rowley, CD 1971, *Outcasts in White Australia*, Australian National University Press, Canberra.

Royal Commission into Aboriginal Deaths in Custody 1988, *National report*, Australian Government Publishing Service, Canberra.

Sansom, B 1980, *The camp at Wallaby Cross: Aboriginal fringe dwellers in Darwin*, Australian Institute of Aboriginal Studies, Canberra.

Sarangi, S 2001, 'A comparative perspective on social-theoretical accounts of the language-action interrelationship', in Coupland et al. (eds), pp. 29–60.

Sato, C 1991, 'Sociolinguistic variation and language attitudes in Hawaii', in *English around the world*, ed. J Cheshire, Cambridge University Press, Cambridge, pp. 647–663.

Schiffrin, D 2006, *In other words: variation in reference and narrative*, Cambridge University Press, Cambridge.

Schmidt, A 1990, *The loss of Australia's Aboriginal language heritage*, Aboriginal Studies Press, Canberra.

Schwab, J 1988, 'Ambiguity, style and kinship in Adelaide Aboriginal identity', in Keen (ed.), pp. 77–96.

Scollon, R 1979, 'Variable data and linguistic convergence: texts and contexts in Chipewyan', *Language in Society*, vol. 8, pp. 223–242.

—— 1985, 'The machine stops: silence in the metaphor of malfunction', in *Perspectives on silence*, eds D Tannen & M Saville-Troike, Ablex, Norwood, NJ, pp. 21–30.

SCRGSP – *see* Steering Committee for the Review of Government Service Provision.

Sercombe, H 1995, 'The face of the criminal is Aboriginal: Representations of Aboriginal young people in the *West Australian* newspaper', in *Cultures of crime and violence: the Australian experience*, eds J Bessant, K Carrington & S Cook, La Trobe University Press, Melbourne, pp. 76–94.

Sharifian, F 2001, 'Schema-based processing in Australian speakers of Aboriginal English', *Language and Intercultural Communication*, vol. 1, no. 2, pp. 120–134.

—— 2005, 'Cultural conceptualisations in English words: a study of Aboriginal children in Perth', *Language and Education*, vol. 19, no. 1, pp. 74–88.

—— 2007, 'Aboriginal language habitat and cultural continuity', in Leitner & Malcolm (eds), pp. 181–196.

—— & the Department of Education Western Australia 2012, *'Understanding stories my way': Aboriginal-English speaking students' (mis)understanding of school literacy materials in Australian English*, Western Australia Department of Education, Leederville, WA.

——, Rochecouste, J & Malcolm, IG 2004, '"But it was all a bit confusing...": comprehending Aboriginal English texts', *Language, Culture and Communication*, vol. 17, no. 3, pp. 203–228.

——, Rochecouste, J, Malcolm, IG, Konigsberg, P & Collard, G 2004, *Improving understanding of Aboriginal literacy: factors in text comprehension*, Western Australia Department of Education and Training, Perth.

Sharpe, MC 1977, 'Alice Springs Aboriginal English', in *Language problems and Aboriginal education*, eds E Brumby & E Vaszolyi, Mt Lawley College of Advanced Education, Mt Lawley, WA, pp. 45–50.

—— 1979 'Alice Springs Aboriginal children's English', in *Australian linguistic studies*, ed. S Wurm, Pacific Linguistic Studies C54, Canberra, pp. 733–747.

Shnukal, A 1988, *Broken: an introduction to the creole language of Torres Strait*, Pacific Linguistics C107, Canberra.

Shopen, T (ed.) 1979, *Languages and their speakers*, Winthrop, Cambridge, MA.

Shuy, R 1986, 'Language and the law', *Annual Review of Applied Linguistics*, vol. 7, pp. 50–63.

—— 2005, *Creating language crimes: how law enforcement uses (and misuses) language*, Oxford University Press, Oxford.

Sidnell, J 2010, *Conversation Analysis: an introduction*, Wiley-Blackwell, Malden, MA.

Siegel, J 2010, *Second dialect acquisition*, Cambridge University Press, Cambridge.

Simpson, J & Wigglesworth, G (eds) 2008, *Children's language and multilingualism: Indigenous language use at home and school*, Continuum, London.

Solan, LM & Tiersma, PM 2005, *Speaking of crime: the language of criminal justice*, University of Chicago Press, Chicago.

Solomon, D 1993, 'A case of US and THEM', *The Courier Mail*, 18 December.

Steering Committee for the Review of Government Service Provision 2011, *Overcoming Indigenous disadvantage: key indicators 2011*, Productivity Commission, Melbourne.

Strehlow, TGH 1936, 'Notes on native evidence and its value', *Oceania*, vol. 6, pp. 323–335.

—— 1947, *Aranda traditions*, Melbourne University Press, Melbourne.

Stroud, N 2006, 'Accommodating language difference: A collaborative approach to justice in the Koori Court of Victoria', in *Selected papers from the 2005 Conference of the Australian Linguistic Society*, ed. K Allan, viewed 8 January 2013, <http://www.als.asn.au/proceedings.html>.

Sutton, PJ 1978, *Wik: Aboriginal society, territory and language at Cape Keerweer, Cape York Peninsula, Australia*, University of Queensland PhD thesis, Brisbane.

—— & Walsh, M 1979, *Revised linguistic fieldwork manual for Australia*, Australian Institute of Aboriginal Studies, Canberra.

Swann, J, Deumert, A, Lillis, T & Mesthrie, R 2004, *A dictionary of sociolinguistics*, Edinburgh University Press, Edinburgh.

Syder, F & Pawley, A 1974, 'The reduction principle in conversation', unpublished manuscript, Department of Linguistics, University of Hawai'i, pp. 27.

Tiersma, P 1999, *Legal language*, University of Chicago Press, Chicago.

—— 2006, *Communicating with juries: how to draft more understandable jury instructions*, National Centre for State Courts, Williamsburg, VA.

Trigger, DS 1995, '"Everyone's agreed, the *West* is all you need": Ideology, media and Aboriginality in Western Australia', *Media Information Australia*, vol. 75, pp. 102–122.

Trinch, S 2003, *Latinas' narratives of domestic abuse: discrepant versions of violence*, John Benjamins, Amsterdam.

Troy, J 1993, 'Language contact in early colonial New South Wales 1788 to 1791', in Walsh & Yallop (eds), pp. 33–50.

Trudgill, P 1983, *Sociolinguistics*, Penguin, Harmondsworth.

Von Sturmer, J 1981, 'Talking with Aborigines', *Australian Institute of Aboriginal Studies Newsletter*, vol. 15, pp. 13–30.

WADET – *see* Western Australia Department of Education.

Walker, J 1994, 'Aborigines stand firm on Yock accusation', *The Australian*, 7 April.

Walsh, M 1994, 'Interactional styles in the courtroom: an example from northern Australia', in Gibbons (ed.), pp. 217–233.

—— 1999, 'Interpreting for the transcript: problems in recording Aboriginal land claim proceedings in northern Australia', *Forensic Linguistics*, vol. 6, no. 1, pp. 161–195.

—— 2008 '"Which way?" Difficult options for vulnerable witnesses in Australian Aboriginal land claim and native title cases', *Journal of English Linguistics*, vol. 36, no. 3, pp. 239–265.

—— & Yallop, C (eds) 1993, *Language and culture in Aboriginal Australia*, Aboriginal Studies Press, Canberra.

Western Australia Department of Education 2012, *Tracks to two-way learning*, Western Australia Department of Education & Department of Training and Workforce Development, Perth.

Williams, M 1981, Unpublished Master's Qualifying Report, Griffith University.

Wolfram, W, Adger, CT & Christian, D 1999, *Dialects in schools and communities*, Lawrence Erlbaum Associates, Mahwah, NJ.

Wood, J 2004, 'Child witnesses: the New South Wales experience', paper presented at the Australian Institute of Judicial Administration conference on Child witnesses – Best practice for courts, Sydney.

Woodbury, H 1984, 'The strategic use of questions in court', *Semiotica*, vol. 48, no. 3/4, pp. 197–228.

Woolard, KA 1998, 'Introduction: language ideology as a field of inquiry', in *Language ideologies: practice and theory*, eds B Schieffelin, KA Woolard & PV Kroskrity, Oxford University Press, Oxford, pp. 3–47.

Woolard, KA. & Schieffelin, BB 1994, 'Language ideology', *Annual Review of Anthropology*, vol. 23, pp. 55–82.

Yallop, C 1993, 'The structure of Australian Aboriginal languages', in Walsh & Yallop (eds), pp. 15–32.

Index

Note: *italics* indicate text box, 'n' indicates an endnote, and **bold** indicates entry in Glossary.

www.ingramcontent.com/pod-product-compliance
Lightning Source LLC
LaVergne TN
LVHW010054110826
845155LV00028B/339